Allergy &
Gluten Free
Cookbook

Lisa A. Lundy, B.S., DTM

Love.Life.™

State College

Important Note to Readers: The author of this book is not a medical physician or medical practitioner in any capacity or form. Readers should seek personal medical evaluations and advice from qualified, licensed health care professionals. The author and publisher of this book recommends that you consult with your primary health care provider before implementing dietary changes. Since food allergies can be fatal, and restricted diets can lead to vitamin and mineral deficiencies, it is extremely important that you receive proper individualized advice from your physician before you make changes to your diet. The author and publisher of this book disclaim any liability directly or indirectly arising from the use of this book, any suggestions contained in this book, and from any products mentioned in it. Products mentioned in this book may change formulation and may not be free of allergens in the future. Readers must be vigilant and monitor product labels at all times.

Additionally, the author and publisher make no representation or warranty with respect to the accuracy of information contained on any websites referenced in this book. The author and publisher have received no financial support from any products or websites mentioned herein. The author and publisher disclaim any liability for products mentioned in this book.

This book is dedicated to

My three amazing children

Luke, Noah and Anne

For inspiring recipes, inventing some recipes,

And being reliable testers among other things!

To those who inspired me to finally complete this book!

To the memory of my friend and mentor Bette Hagman,

A.K.A. *The Gluten Free Gourmet.*

CONTENTS

IMPORTANT INFORMATION FOR SUCCESS WITH MY RECIPES

In the early days of gluten-free baking, meaning over 21 years ago back when the grocery stores did not stock xanthan gum or gluten-free flours, measuring gluten-free flour was done by sifting the flour two times, which was a technique pioneered by my friend and mentor Bette Hagman. This was done because Bette was converting standard recipes to be gluten-free. As a mother with three very young children and a lot of other responsibilities, I found that to be both tedious and time consuming so I opted to use a different method for measuring flour to save time. It is important that you understand this because if you use a level cup of gluten-free flour for my recipes they simply will not turn out.

Converting a standard recipe to be gluten-free, assuming you can use eggs and dairy is fairly straight forward. Converting a typical recipe to be free of gluten and dairy and eggs is a horse of a different color and is much more difficult. You can't just use substitutions and expect it to work out because frequently it does not work out and you have to adjust the recipe, try it again, and keep doing that until you get it right. Many of the recipes in this cookbook are original recipes meaning that I just invented the recipe from nothing.

After my first allergy and gluten-free cookbook came out, I was contacted by numerous customers over the years with questions about why a recipe that they made from my cookbook did not turn out well. What I did with these customers was problem solve and use a process of elimination to figure out where they went wrong. So, the following is what you need to do to be successful with my recipes. These are not optional for success.

1. **Use a heaping cup for measuring flour:** What this means is that the flour is heaped on top of the measuring cup until it falls off. If you don't do this then your recipes will be off by anywhere from ¼ cup to ¾ cup of flour depending on the amount of flour used in the recipe. This is extremely important.

2. **An oven thermometer is REQUIRED:** Use an oven thermometer in your oven for success. Most ovens are off by between 25 and 50 degrees or more. You will have to adjust the temperature of your oven based on the thermometer reading.
3. **Withhold some liquid until** you are sure that it is necessary: It is always prudent to withhold some liquid until you are absolutely sure it is necessary because of the difference in measuring and flour brands and quality.
4. **Do NOT USE a Convection Oven:** Convection ovens operate differently than conventional ovens. My recipes will not turn out well with the convection feature. I wish that was not true, but unfortunately it is true. Do NOT use a convection oven for these recipes.
5. **Dry powdered Ener-G egg replacement** is used in these recipes because some other egg substitutes are allergenic for some. Results may vary with different types of egg replacers. While you can use other egg substitutions, I simply can't say that the recipes will work out with other egg substitutions because the recipe testers used the recipes as written.

INTRODUCTION

Welcome to my second allergy and gluten-free cookbook and thank you for your purchase! Special thanks to my returning customers. Be sure to read the Important Information for Success with My Recipes so that you are successful because it is based on working with previous customers who had failures and pinpointing what they were doing wrong. That page matters immensely so please don't skip over it! My recipes have been tested by multiple testers over the years. While my first allergy and gluten-free cookbook was extremely successful, it is no longer in print for a few reasons one of them being that one or more ingredients used in a majority of the recipes are no longer being manufactured, which renders the recipes useless. To offset the issue of my first cookbook not being in print, I have included the best recipes from that cookbook in this one. Because of product reformulations that have happened in the past decade, I am no longer listing name brands of products in this cookbook for the most part, which is for safety and liability reasons.

I am very excited about the recipes in this cookbook. The addition of a roux sauce allowed me to make a mock cream sauce, which is very helpful for making recipes that typically have dairy or a cream sauce. The bargain baking mix recipe provides an economical alternative to commercially made baking mixes. I am also very happy about the new chocolate and white cake recipes, the brownie bite recipe, the chocolate ganache frosting and so many soups and main dish recipes. And to be very honest, I am thrilled with the salad dressings, sauces and dip recipes some of which were a challenge to create to get the right taste, texture and consistency.

In the vein of being authentic and real, one of my valued traits, I have to say that I have no choice at this time but to print this cookbook using print-on-demand (POD) printing, which is the most expensive way to print a book because you lose the economies of scale available when you print hundreds or in the case of my first book 2,500 copies per run. In addition, because I have to use POD as a way to print this book, I have to add 55% of the book costs to cover royalty fees and other charges – all of which makes this book more expensive than I would like. I am optimistic that one day in the future I will be able to print this book in a traditional fashion and get the price down. For now, it is what it is.

Many of you reading this now are struggling with depression, anxiety, sadness, loneliness, anger, resentment and a host of other negative emotions related to the pandemic and impact of the pandemic as well as other life issues. I have deep compassion for this because two years ago I got to start my life over with basically nothing not by choice, unrelated to the pandemic, and much to my shock and awe. I would say more about that but it is not prudent or safe for me to do that. And now you hopefully understand why I have to use POD printing for this book.

Designed for your personal empowerment and to help you get on the road to being well loved, happy and healthy I have a book's worth of blog posts, over 29 podcasts, and over 120 YouTube videos – all free to help you, which you can find on my website at: www.LisaALundy. com. The podcasts are carried by 6 major podcast platforms. I compiled my blog posts into a book in December 2020 at the request of a regular reader who was taking notes from my blog posts and felt having the blog posts in a book format would be very helpful. But you don't have to purchase the book because you can read 98% of the book for free on my website.

The blog posts well as the YouTube videos and podcasts have been reviewed by and approved by multiple therapists as grounded, research based and therapy approved techniques and approaches to living a happy and healthy life. It is my hope that these materials can help you get life turned around and moving in a more positive way. Life is hard. There is no doubt about that. How can I help you live your best life? How can I support you in your journey? Please let me know.

Love,

Lisa

APPETIZERS & SNACKS

Bread Sticks

Any roll recipe in this cookbook can be used to make bread sticks. Bread sticks are a festive appetizer. You can spice up your roll batter with garlic, onions, rosemary, thyme and other herbs. Or you can make plain bread sticks and serve a nice olive oil for dipping. The easiest way to make bread sticks is if you can invest in a bread stick pan which will save you a great deal of time and energy. If you don't have a bread stick pan, you can use aluminum foil to create a bread stick form. Imagine folding up your aluminum foil into peaks and valleys. The roll batter will then be piped into the valleys of your aluminum foil. You can also just pipe roll batter onto a greased baking sheet and pipe the batter into strips as this will give you a similar effect although both alternatives will give you a flat bottom instead of a round bottom. I did this for a short time to make not only bread sticks, but also to make hot dog rolls. A bread stick pan is a great little invention.

Fresh Vegetables & Dip

The fancy name for fresh vegetables is crudités (pronounced kroo-da-tey), which simply means pieces of raw vegetables served as an hors d'oeuvre usually with a dip. Many restaurants will offer crudités on the menu as an appetizer with a dip. There are several dip recipes are a wonderful match for fresh vegetables in this book. Arrange the fresh vegetables on a platter and you are set to go.

Fresh Fruits and Smashing Fruit Dip

One amazing appetizer is a fresh fruit platter with a delicious dip served with it. The recipe in this book for the Smashing Fruit Dip is easy to make and very popular.

Garlic Rounds

This appetizer is another idea born from a restaurant. For garlic rounds, simply slice up any rolls that you have made and lightly drizzle with your favorite oil. Then sprinkle lightly with garlic salt and onion salt. Use a dash of paprika and a bit of crushed up parsley to give your garlic rounds that restaurant look. Broil under the broiler until nice and toasty.

Potato Skins

Most of us don't make potato skins at home, however if you are having guests or a party, they make a nice finger food. Potato Skins can be made as half a potato, or one-third or one quarter of a potato. Determine how many actual potato skins you would like per person, and what size. Then bake that number of potatoes. Cut the potatoes into the desired size. Place on a baking sheet and top with non-dairy cheese, bacon bits, or any other toppings that you like. Broil under the broiler until piping hot, or until the non-dairy cheese melts. We serve our potato skins with Tofutti non-dairy sour cream.

Chicken Wings

This cookbook contains recipes for barbecue sauce that can be used on chicken wings. Cook your chicken wings completely and drain off any excess fat or liquid. Then apply your barbecue sauce and heat until piping hot. Chicken wings are excellent with the Mock Ranch Dip or dressing recipe in this cookbook. This is a wonderful party food or appetizer.

Nachos

Easy and a crowd pleaser, I have included a recipe in this cookbook to make it fool proof.

Stuffed Celery

Celery can be stuffed with non-dairy cream cheese or a ground butter (ground sunflower seeds that look like peanut butter for those of use who have to skip tree nuts and peanuts). You can even add some taco seasoning to the Tofutti non-dairy cream cheese for a special kick. A recipe for taco seasoning is included in this cookbook for those who are allergic to commercially made taco seasoning mixes.

Mini Pizzas

Any of the pizza recipes in this cookbook can be made as mini pizzas, which can be served whole as an appetizer, or can be served as slices for an appetizer. You can also make large pizzas and cut them into slices and serve that as an appetizer. We also occasionally cut rolls in half and use them as a pizza crust base for mini pizzas. If you are using rolls cut in half for mini pizzas, toast the rolls well before applying sauce and toppings.

Mini Slider Sandwiches

I had these at a luncheon that were made with gluten, dairy and thought – wow – these would be cool to make without the allergens! Delicious! To give credit where credit is due, I was told that this recipe came from a 1970 Republican Woman's Cookbook. If that is true, then this recipe has been circulating for 50 years!

Preheat Oven to 350°
> **Acceptable Mini rolls or bread rounds*(see directions)**
> **Acceptable ham slices**
> **Acceptable nondairy cheese slices**

> **Topping:**
> **½ pound acceptable nondairy margarine, melted**
> **2 tablespoons mustard**
> **1 tablespoon Worcestershire sauce**
> **2 tablespoons Poppy seeds**
> **¼ to 1/3 cup brown sugar or more**
> **1 small onion, minced (or minced onion flakes)**

Assemble sandwiches in a suitable pan. Mix the melted butter and topping ingredients together and pour over top of the sandwiches. Bake in a 350° oven for 20 minutes. You can freeze these but I wouldn't be expecting any leftovers. These are absolutely delicious!

Addressing the issue of the bread: The challenge for this recipe is finding mini gluten-free and allergen free rolls. In making this recipe I made gluten free rolls but just made them very small using a standard muffin tin and not filling the muffin tin too high. Another time I made this recipe I made a French loaf of gluten-free and allergy free bread using a French loaf pan and then I cut the bread into slices, which made perfect round sandwiches and worked extremely well. You could also simply cut commercially made acceptable bread into small sandwich size pieces and use that.

South of the Border Baked Fiesta Dip

This was a favorite recipe of mine from my old dairy days. The original recipe was filled with dairy and baked in a hollowed-out loaf of bread. We like this dip warm with fresh vegetables, on top of a baked potato, or with some crisp crackers.

Preheat oven to 350°.

12 ounces non-dairy sour cream
8 ounces non-dairy cream cheese
6 ounces acceptable salsa

Place all ingredients in a glass baking casserole and mix ingredients together until creamy. This will seem too runny and you will think that you have made a mistake. Place the casserole dish in the oven uncovered and bake for 1 to 1½ hours, stirring every 20 minutes or so. The dip will thicken up and have a delightful southwestern taste!

Mexican Fiesta Dip

I got the idea for this dip while attending a party that served the typical dairy and gluten food items. If you cannot tolerate soy, you could simply either skip the non-dairy sour cream or use pureed white beans with a little added oil or water to thin them and use that in place of the non-dairy sour cream. This recipe is wonderful with either a chip or fresh veggies.

9 ounces of salsa
1 – 16 ounce container of non-dairy sour cream
1 – 16 ounce can of refried beans
14 ounces of guacamole
½ teaspoon of paprika
¼ teaspoon of chili powder
Optional: green onions or fresh, chopped tomatoes

Spread the refried beans in the bottom of a 9" x 7" baking pan (or similar sized pan) to make one smooth, even layer using a fork to mash the beans down. A 9" x 13" baking pan is too large for this recipe as it is written. In a small mixing bowl mix the non-dairy sour cream, paprika and chili powder and mix well. Next spread the guacamole over the bean layer. To accomplish this, I dot the guacamole in spots and then spread together. Spread the sour cream mixture over the guacamole layer in the baking pan. Then add the salsa, spreading this over the guacamole so that the sour cream layer is covered. For garnish or added pizzazz, you may top with fresh cut green onions or chopped tomatoes or your favorite non-dairy cheese shreds. This appetizer is best served with either fresh vegetables or some type of dipping chip. Makes about 24 – ¼ cup servings or 12 – ½ cup servings.

Black Bean Dip

This recipe is great for corn chips or raw vegetables. You can also use it with fajitas. You can use pinto beans or refried beans instead of black beans. The recipe for "Refried Beans a la Natural" will yield beans that are perfect for this dip.

> **2 cups black or pinto beans, rinsed and mashed well (or refried beans)**
> **2 cups salsa**
> **1/3 or ½ cup non-dairy cheddar cheese shreds**

Mix all ingredients together. This can be served hot or cold. If serving hot, heat over medium low heat until the cheese is melted and the dip is hot. This makes about 4 cups of dip.

Roasted Red Pepper Dip

I came up with this dip when we had to reduce our use of soy (again). It is really a red pepper hummus. I don't like store-bought hummus. This dip is so good that one adult at a party I attended asked if she could eat it with a spoon! It is equally as good with raw vegetables as with chips and crackers.

> **2 cups or 1-25 ounce can of garbanzo beans, rinsed and drained**
> **2 roasted red peppers**
> **1 tablespoon lemon juice**
> **4 tablespoons pure water**
> **2 cloves of minced garlic**
> **1 tablespoon of oil**
> **1 teaspoon Celtic salt**

Roasting your own red peppers is much less expensive than purchasing roasted red peppers. To do this quite simply, remove red pepper top and seeds and place on a baking sheet under the oven broiler. Watch carefully as you broil the red peppers until they are roasted. If they get black, as some pieces are sure to do, you can peel the black off of the pepper. Place all ingredients in a food processor or blender and puree. This makes 2 to 2-1/4 cups. It will keep well in the refrigerator for several days. We enjoy it with raw vegetables as well as chips and crackers.

Green Bean Fingers

A restaurant chain inspired this recipe! The tempura batter can be used to coat any vegetable.

1 cup garfava flour
1/3 cup tapioca flour
1 teaspoon salt
1 teaspoon baking powder
1 tablespoon Ener-G Egg Replacer
1 tablespoon oil
1 cup water
10 ounces of green beans (or other raw vegetable)
oil for frying

Mix all the dry ingredients together in a medium-mixing bowl. Add the liquid ingredients and stir well. Coat green beans in batter and lightly fry. Serve as an appetizer or side dish. Serves 3 to 4.

Pepperoni Bread

We got the idea for this recipe from a dish that our friend, Alberta, brought to our house for a New Year's Eve party! Her dish contained gluten, dairy and other allergens, but provided the seed for a great idea! This dish was an instant hit and just took a few tries to get the mechanics of making the bread.

Preheat Oven to 375°
- 1 batch garfava or other roll dough (recipe in this book)
- 1 small onion, sliced
- 2 teaspoons acceptable oil
- ¼ teaspoon dried basil
- ¼ teaspoon dried oregano
- 1 cup grated non-dairy cheese
- 1 cup sliced acceptable lunchmeat, pepperoni or other cooked meat
- 4-6 Tablespoons of spaghetti sauce or tomato sauce flavored with herbs

Sautee onions in the oil in a frying pan over medium heat until soft and lightly browned. Spread ½ of roll dough in an oblong shape on a greased baking sheet. Top with sauce, non-dairy cheese, meat, and herbs. Take remaining dough and cover the oblong shape – using a spatula to spread the dough to cover. Seal edges well with spatula. Bake in a 375° oven for 25 minutes or until done. Makes one 16-inch loaf.

Mrs. Smith's Sausage Balls

This recipe was from Kim Smith's mother, Molly, and her sister, Deb. Kim was one of my roommates in college and is a dear friend! I cherish the memories of time spent at her home with her family in while we were in college and after. These freeze well and are great for a snack, a party, or just as an entrée with vegetables and a salad or soup.

Preheat oven to 350°
- **1 pound ground sausage**
- **8 ounces non-dairy cheddar "cheese"**
- **3 cups Herbed Bargain Baking Mix (recipe in this book)**
- **¾ cup water* (1 tablespoon more at a time, only if needed)**

In a large mixing bowl combine sausage, non-dairy cheddar shreds and 3 cups Herbed Bargain Baking Mix (recipe in this cookbook). Mix very well. Add ¾ cup pure water and incorporate into sausage mixture. The amount of water needed will depend on the quality and fat content of the sausage you are using. You may need up to 1 cup, but add the **water with great reserve**. Too much water will make the sausage balls much harder to form. The type on non-dairy cheese you use will also impact the amount of water needed. Basically, you only add water to help the balls stick together. Bake in a 350° oven for 21 to 24 minutes or until a meat thermometer comes out done. This recipe will be very, very bland if you do not use the Herbed Bargain Baking Mix. This makes about 45 to 75 meatballs depending upon the size meatball made.

Spinach and Artichoke Dip

The idea for this dish came from a major chain restaurant. The chain restaurant dip contains both gluten and dairy. We were elated to figure out how to make a celiac and allergy friendly version of this popular dip! Serve with raw veggies, chips, or any type of cracker or bread.

½ cup gluten-free flour (brown rice*)
¼ cup plus 1 tablespoon non-dairy margarine
2 cups non-dairy milk substitute
1 teaspoon Celtic salt
½ teaspoon onion powder
½ teaspoon garlic powder
1 clove minced garlic
½ to ¾ cup finely chopped spinach or other greens (not bitter or spicey)
¼ to ½ cup artichoke hearts, chopped

In a large frying pan, over medium heat – cook the non-dairy margarine and flour until it is a paste. Then cook a bit longer, but not much. Gradually, add the rice milk about 1/3 cup at a time – then stir the roux. Once it becomes kind of creamy and smooth – add more milk. Continue this process until all of the rice milk has been added. Add the garlic and onion powder and salt. Add the chopped spinach or other greens and artichokes. Stir until the sauce is a desired thickness. This makes about 2 cups of dip.

Nacho Grande

You really don't need a recipe for Nacho's unless you do! So here you go. For vegan Nacho's use refried beans in place of the ground beef.

Preheat Oven to 450°

40 +/- organic corn chips
1-1/4 cup cooked ground beef
1 cup non-dairy cheese shreds
Taco Seasoning (Recipe in this book if needed)
Optional: Hot Peppers, Sweet Peppers, Onions
Garnishes:
>**Salsa**
>**Non-dairy sour cream**
>**Guacamole**
>**Black Bean Dip (recipe in this book)**
>**Refried Beans**

On a large baking sheet, place the first layer of corn chips (about 25 corn chips) and layer ground beef and non-dairy cheese over the layer of corn chips. Sprinkle a bit of taco seasoning over this layer to taste. Place a second smaller layer of corn chips on top of the first and layer the ground beef and cheese as before topping with the taco seasoning. Place in the oven until the cheese gets melted watching closely as it can burn very easily.

Sesame Spinach Spread

I got this idea from a restaurant and then experimented until I had a close end result. This is great for crackers, chips and raw vegetables!

1 cup non-dairy sour cream
1 cup chopped green onions
1 teaspoon garlic salt
¼ teaspoon pepper
1 teaspoon roasted sesame seeds
10 ounces of chopped spinach (if using frozen, drain
    extremely well)
8 ounces of water chestnuts

As noted, if you are using frozen spinach all of the water needs to be drained out of it. Mix all ingredients well. Makes about 1-1/2 cups of spread. Serve with crackers, raw vegetables or chips.

Spinach Dip

This tastes just like the spinach dip that I used to make for parties. It is excellent with fresh vegetables or crackers.

1½ teaspoons onion powder
1 teaspoon sugar
1 teaspoon salt
3 tablespoons dried onion flakes
1 can diced water chestnuts (if you can tolerate)
12 ounces non-diary sour cream
10 ounces frozen spinach, defrosted and drained well
1 clove of garlic, minced through a garlic press
3 to 5 stalks of green onions, sliced

Place spinach in a colander or mesh drainer and press well to remove additional liquid. Place all ingredients in a mixing bowl and mix well. This looks and tastes just like the real thing, so feel free to take it to parties

All Purpose Party Mix

This is a recipe that we love! You can spice it up by using other spices if you like hot and spicy or other spices that you like.

Preheat oven to 250°

7 tablespoons acceptable margarine or oil

3 tablespoons GFCF Worcestershire sauce

¾ teaspoon onion powder

¾ teaspoon garlic salt

5 cups acceptable cereal

3 cups of a different type of acceptable cereal

1¾ cups of acceptable pretzels

½ package (3½ ounces) brown rice snaps - <u>broken into pieces</u> (about 1 cup or so)

Bake for 1 hour, stirring every 15 minutes!! This mix can be made to be "stronger" in flavor by increasing the spices and Worcestershire sauce. The fat can also be decreased or increased depending upon dietary needs (our kids need more fat). Also, for a spicy version, you can add chili powder to the mix (starting with about ½ teaspoon and adding more if desired).

Dijon Style Party Mix

Snack mixes or party mixes are something that you can really have fun with. This uses honey and Dijon mustard for flavoring.

Preheat oven to 250°

3 tablespoons Dijon mustard
⅓ cup oil
2 tablespoons honey
8 cups dry cereal
1 cup roasted sunflower seeds or other cereal or seeds
1½ cups gluten-free pretzels or other snack (like corn chips broken up)

Place cereal in a greased 9" x 13" baking pan and set aside. In a small pan, cook oil, honey and mustard over medium heat until foamy. Pour over cereal in baking pan and stir well to coat. Bake 1 hour, stirring every 15 minutes. After baking, allow cereal to cool. Then add 1 cup of roasted sunflower seeds or other acceptable seeds or cereal, and 1½ cups pretzels or other snack item like broken up corn chips.

Honeyed Snack Mix

A sweet version of the regular party mix.

Preheat oven to 250°

6 cups acceptable cereal
2 cups gluten-free pretzels
1 cup sunflower seeds OR 1 cup other crunchy cereal or seed
⅓ cup oil
⅓ cup honey
1 teaspoon garlic powder
½ teaspoon onion powder
¼ teaspoon dried ginger
2 tablespoons soy sauce substitute

Place the oil, honey and all of the spices and soy sauce substitute into a saucepan over medium heat. Grease a 9" x 13" baking pan. Place the cereal, pretzels and sunflower seeds in the baking pan. Bring the honey and oil mixture to a light boil. The mixture will get all light and foamy. Remove from heat and pour over the cereal mixture in the baking pan. Stir well to coat all of the ingredients. Bake for 1 hour and 30 minutes, stirring every 15 minutes. If I was making this for adults only I would kick up the spices a bit by adding more ginger, onion and garlic.

Deep Fried Zucchini

This is a flexible recipe that can be used to coat and deep fry any vegetable so you can make onion rings, cauliflower or whatever you like.

1 cup corn flour or other flour
⅓ cup sorghum flour or other flour
1 teaspoon salt
1 teaspoon baking powder
2 teaspoons sugar
1 tablespoon Ener-G Egg Replacer™
1 tablespoon sunflower oil or other oil
¾ cup pure water
2 large onions

high temperature sunflower or other oil for frying

Heat the sunflower oil to about 370°. Use a thermometer and try to get the temperature stabilized. I use a small saucepan on the stove top and have it set at medium heat. There is organic sunflower oil available that is specifically for high heat applications (up to 460°)

Mix dry ingredients and then add the 1 tablespoon oil. Add water until the batter is somewhere between creamy and runny. It should drip off a spoon in flat triangular drips. If time allows, refrigerate the batter for an hour or so.

Slice the onions into pieces about ⅜ inches thick and separate into individual rings. If the onion has a "slimy" skin between the rings, remove it. Dip a few rings into the batter so that they are evenly coated and carefully drop into the hot oil. The rings may stay at the bottom at first. I let them cook for about 15 seconds before I nudge them off the bottom, and then let them float. Cook until they just begin to turn brown, somewhere between 1 and 2 minutes. Remove from the oil and drain on a paper towel or wire rack.

Good Morning Granola

I'll be perfectly frank with you, I invented this recipe to use up expired cereal! What started as a lark, turned out very well! The use of sunflower seeds and flax meal add nutrition and fiber. We've used a variety of dried fruits in this granola. This recipe fits with our fourth rotation day completely since we use dried strawberries and raspberries.

Preheat oven to 225°
> **1 cup sunflower seeds or other seed**
> **6 cups acceptable dry cereal**
> **2 cups of a second type of other acceptable dry cereal**
> **½ cup flax meal**
> **⅛ teaspoon ground cinnamon**
> **½ cup sunflower or other acceptable oil**
> **½ cup maple syrup or other liquid sweetener**
> **2 cups dried fruit of your choice, bite size pieces**

Grease a 9" x 13" baking pan. Measure the sunflower seeds, and cereals into a very large mixing bowl. On top of the dry ingredients place the flax meal. Do not mix. Place oil and maple syrup in a small saucepan and bring to a boil until it is nice and foamy. Boil for 2 minutes and remove from heat. Pour over cereal and flax mixture. Stir well to coat. Add cinnamon to taste. Pour into your greased baking pan and bake for 1½ to 2 hours, stirring every 30 minutes or so. Once the mixture has cooled completely, add 2 cups of dried fruit of your choice. There are now a wide variety of dried fruits commercially available that lend themselves well to dry granola recipes like this one.

Trail Mix or GORP

This is a great tasting and nutritious snack recipe for busy people on the go. It is also a fantastic topping for non-dairy yogurt. When I was growing up this was the favorite snack for hikers. I believe that the acronym GORP stood back then for "good old raisins and peanuts". This is an allergen-free version of that old favorite!

2 cups raw sunflower seeds (unsalted)
1 cup raw pumpkin seeds
1 cup raisins
1 cup dried cranberries
½ cup to 1 cup acceptable chocolate chips
1 cup acceptable pretzel pieces, broken into bite-sized pieces

While you can use salted sunflower or pumpkin seeds, we find that unsalted, raw seeds give you the best flavor. My children prefer less raisins and dried cranberries than I do, which I why I have provided a range. If you use 1 cup each of the raisins and dried cranberries, this recipe will make 6 to 6-1/2 cups. Store in an airtight container. Over time the pretzels will become a bit stale, so if you are not going to eat it up quickly – cut the recipe in half.

Granola Bars

We found delightful organic granola bars in the grocery store, however they contained ingredients that my children could not have. So, we set about to duplicate the granola bars. One horrible flop later, we were right on the money.

2 cups rice cereal or other acceptable gluten-free cereal
1 cup of a different type of gluten-free cereal (different for texture)
½ cup crunchy seeds (like soy nuts, squash seeds, etc.)
1 cup raw pumpkin seeds or other gluten-free seeds
1/3 cup flax seeds
3/8 cup white rice flour or other gluten-free flour
¼ teaspoon salt
Dash of Cinnamon
¾ cup brown rice syrup
1/3 cup liquid sweetener
¼ teaspoon molasses

Lightly grease a 9" x 13" baking pan and set aside. Combine the dry ingredients in a large mixing bowl and set aside. Mix the brown rice syrup, Lyle's Syrup®, and molasses in a medium saucepan and bring to a light boil over medium high heat. Boil lightly for 2 to 3 minutes. Pour the liquid over your dry ingredients and mix well until thoroughly incorporated. Pour the mixture into your prepared baking pan. Using the back of a greased spatula, evenly spread the mixture into the pan and pat evenly. Cut into bars and wrap individually in plastic wrap or waxed paper. Store in an air-tight container.

Sweet n' Spice Toast

My son, Luke Garrett – age 10, came up with this snack recipe all on his own. Pretty tasty we think!

1 Tablespoon of oil or melted margarine
Small amount of oil for sautéing
1 hamburger or dinner roll
Onion powder
Garlic powder
Optional: your favorite jam or preserve

Slice your hamburger or dinner roll in thin slices and coat with oil or melted margarine. Sprinkle roll with garlic and onion powder lightly. Place roll in frying pan and fry over medium heat and fry until light brown. Excellent served with preserves or jam.

SOUPS

Lisa's Creamy Dry Soup Base

I created this recipe so that we could have chicken divan and other recipes that call for a cream of celery-type soup. You can use it to make soup with, or to make a white cream sauce. It is flavorful. This is modified because the dry milk substitute powder that I originally used in this recipe is no longer being made.

¼ cup tapioca starch
½ cup potato starch (or rice flour or other acceptable flour substitute)
4 tablespoons corn starch
1 tablespoon salt
½ teaspoon white pepper
1 teaspoon garlic powder
½ teaspoon sweet basil
1 teaspoon onion salt
½ teaspoon crushed rosemary
½ teaspoon thyme
1 tablespoon chopped dried onion
½ teaspoon dried mustard
½ teaspoon oregano
1 tablespoon parsley
1 tablespoon sugar
Dash of turmeric
Dash of paprika

Optional:
Dash of cayenne pepper

Mix above and store in an airtight container. To use, mix about 4 tablespoons of dry soup base (or more) with about 8 ounces of water. It can also be used in your own recipes that call for a condensed cream soup. This will thicken as it cooks.

Potato Leek Soup

I saw potato leek soup on a restaurant menu and that gave me the idea for a new slow cooker soup! It proved to be a good way to use up our fall leeks and potatoes from our CSA cooperative!

15 cups pure drinking water
2 cups sliced leeks
6 cups of diced potatoes
1 tablespoon dried parsley
½ cup chopped celery
1 clove minced garlic
1 tablespoon Celtic salt
Pepper to taste
Optional: 2 - 3 cups potato flakes as a thickener

Combine all ingredients in either a large stock pot or a slow cooker and cook on high until the potatoes are cooked through. Cool soup and then puree in a blender about 3-4 cups at a time. Puree the soup in batches pouring into a large mixing bowl until all of the soup is pureed. Then return the soup to the slow cooker for another 20 minutes or more for the flavors to simmer. As an optional ingredient, you may add 2 to 3 cups of instant potato flakes to thicken the soup. This is done for creating a thicker soup and is quite optional. My children happen to like soups that have a thicker consistency. Makes about 11 cups of soup.

Italian Wedding Soup

I got the idea for Italian Wedding Soup one day when I was eating at a restaurant! Needing more "fast" foods, I decided to try my first attempt at Italian Wedding Soup in the slow cooker! At the mid-point of cooking, I thought it was a failure, but in the end it turned out fantastic! The big surprise was that my children just love this soup! It is one of their most requested soups! This makes a large volume of soup so you can serve a large group or have some to freeze. If there are just one or two of you, I would cut this recipe in half.

8 cups of chicken broth
2 teaspoons salt or to taste
pepper to taste
1-1/2 cups gluten-free Anellini
¾ pound to 1 pound ground beef to make 2-1/2 to 3 cups tiny
    meatballs
1 tablespoon oil for browning the meat
6 cups water
1 cup chopped celery
1 cup chopped carrot
1/3 cup onion, finely chopped
3 tablespoons spinach, kale or other green – very, finely diced
    into paper fine pieces

Place all ingredients except for beef or meat in large slow cooker and place on high or place in a very large stockpot on a stove and cook on medium high. With the ground beef or other meat, add salt and pepper to taste and then make tiny meatballs as small as you can comfortably make them. My meatballs were about the size of a small to medium size grape. Place the meatballs in a frying pan with 1 tablespoon of oil and cook on medium heat to brown. Drain the meatballs and add to the stock pot or slow cooker. To save time, you may skip making the beef into meatballs and simply brown the beef and add it to the soup. I did this to save time one day and my taste testers thought it was equally as good as having the meatballs. Cook until the soup is creamy and the vegetables are cooked through.

Note on the gluten-free pasta: I used a brand of gluten-free pasta by the name of Schar, and the type of pasta shape I used is called Anellini, which is very tiny round circle shapes with holes in the center – a very delicate pasta. What happened since I had put the pasta in the slow cooker at the beginning was that the pasta mostly disintegrated, which is why I initially thought my soup was a failure. However, the pasta did not all disintegrate, and it gave the soup a perfect consistency and texture, in my humble opinion. I would not change a thing. Makes about 21 cups of soup.

Vegetarian Version
Increase onion to one whole medium onion. Increase celery to 1-1/2 cups and increase greens to 6 tablespoons. Use vegetable broth instead of chicken broth.

Note on freezing: While this soup freezes quite well, you will need to have it completely defrosted before warming it up otherwise the meatballs will break up if you try to warm it up from a frozen state in a hurry.

White Vegetable Soup

After making such wonderful vegetable soup, I thought of the people who are allergic to tomatoes! Yes, there are people who are allergic to tomatoes! This soup was inspired for those who want a vegetable soup sans tomatoes.

12 cups of pure water
1-1/4 chopped onion
1-1/2 cups Anelli gluten-free, dairy-free pasta or other type of small pasta
1-1/2 cups chopped red pepper
5-6 Tablespoons chopped greens: spinach, kale or other
1-1/2 cups chopped carrots
1-1/2 cups chopped celery
2 cups cauliflower
1 cup diced potato or turnip
2 cups broccoli
1 teaspoon dried basil
½ teaspoon dried thyme
½ teaspoon dried dill
1 tablespoon Celtic salt or to taste
Pepper to taste
Optional: other spices

This soup is easy to do in a slow cooker! Place all ingredients in a very large slow cooker and place on high for 4-6 hours until the pasta has mostly dissolved and the vegetables are relatively soft and the flavors have melded. I would add additional spices, however my children liked it just as is. Makes about 14 cups of soup.

Garden Lentil Soup

14 cups pure water
1-1/2 cups diced celery
1-1/2 cups diced carrots
1-1/2 cups diced onion (1 large)
1-1/2 cups orange or yellow split lentils
2 cloves minced garlic
1 medium diced potato
3 tablespoons finely chopped spinach (frozen or fresh)
2-6 ounce cans of tomato paste
1 tablespoon sugar
1 tablespoon salt
Pepper to taste
Extra water as the soup thickens and cooks down

This recipe calls for split lentils, which will cook much faster than regular lentils. If you use regular lentils you should cook them first. Mix the tomato paste with 3 or so cups of water and then add to a very large stockpot or slow cooker. Add remaining water and other ingredients. If cooking in a slow cooker - cook on high until the vegetables are soft and the lentils are cooked (4 or more hours). On the stove, simmer until the vegetables are soft and the lentils are cooked stirring often. This soup thickens as it cooks and as it stands. If you don't add additional water, it will be too thick. I added two cups of water while cooking the soup as it cooked down and later added more water when it came out of the fridge as a leftover. Makes 14 to 15 cups of soup.

Grandma Jean's Superstar Soup

My Mom, Jean Gottas, made this delicious Butternut squash soup that my two sons loved! I took out the milk and butter and increased the proportions to make this a family sized recipe that makes some to freeze! You can use any type of squash for this soup by simply increasing the amount of spices. I made this soup for a large 50-person community potluck social and it was so popular that people came and asked if they could take some home!

> **6 cups cooked squash**
> **6 large potatoes cut into quarters**
> **32 ounces of chicken broth or water (if you use water, increase the spices)**
> **1 large onion, chopped (or dried onion powder to taste – 2 teaspoons or more)**
> **1 tablespoon of acceptable oil**
> **1 tablespoon plus 2 teaspoons of paprika**
> **2 cloves garlic, minced (or dried garlic powder to taste about 2 teaspoons or more)**
> **1 tablespoon of dried chives**
> **1-1/2 tablespoon of salt**
> **10 to 12 cups of potato water (water from cooking the potatoes)**

In a large saucepan boil the potatoes until cooked through about 20 minutes. Set aside to cool. In a second very large stockpot, place the onion in 1 tablespoon of oil and sauté until the onion is cooked through and soft. Add the garlic and lightly fry making sure not to scorch. If you are in a hurry or you don't have an onion as has happened repeatedly to me, you can substitute dried onion powder and garlic powder for the onion and garlic. If you use water, which I often do to save money, increase the spices to make up for the loss of flavor. Using water in place of broth is a good budget stretcher, but it does decrease flavor so you will have to bump up the spices to get the same great taste. Add the chicken broth or water and squash, paprika, salt and dried chives and cook for 10-20 minutes.

Allow the potatoes to cool. Then puree about 2 to 3 cups of the potatoes with some of the cooking water in a blender until creamy. Place the pureed potatoes in a separate large mixing bowl. Repeat this process until all of the potatoes are pureed. Then puree the squash mixture in small batches until all of the squash is pureed also placing the squash puree in a large mixing bowl or the same one you have the potato puree in. When the squash stockpot is empty place all of the pureed mixture back in the stockpot and mix well. Cook over a medium low heat, stirring often until the flavors mix and meld. Add additional spices as desired – meaning more paprika, chives, salt or garlic and onion powder. Add water to thin this soup out to your desired consistency. It tends to thicken as it stands, which means that you will have to add water to it because it thickens up over time. This soup freezes well. Makes 24 to 26 cups of soup depending upon the consistency of the soup.

Swiss Chard Soup

I made up this recipe to use up the excess Swiss chard that we received from our CSA share in the summer. It was so good that my two sons even asked for seconds! This is a great way to use up greens, and you could use any green not just Swiss Chard. It has an unusual color with the greens and the tomato. If you are allergic to tomato, simply eliminate the tomato and substitute a chicken broth or other flavored broth and increase the spices.

1 medium onion, chopped
1 Tablespoon of acceptable oil
8 ounces of broth
15 ounces of tomato sauce
24 ounces of water
Large bunch of Swiss Chard (or spinach or other greens)
½ teaspoon of dried basil
¼ teaspoon of garlic powder
Dash of crushed Rosemary
Dash of sugar
Salt and Pepper to taste

Sauté the onion in the oil in a large stockpot until the onions are caramelized and soft. Add the water, tomato sauce and Swiss chard. Cook over medium heat until the Swiss chard is cooked and soft. Add all remaining ingredients. Allow the soup to cool and then puree in a blender. I left small pieces of the greens in the soup the first time I made it, which my children did not go for, so I would puree this soup well if serving to children. Makes about 5 to 6 cups of soup.

Garden Vegetable Soup

This is a fast way to have a delicious and nutritious soup that warms the soul. The great thing about this recipe is that you can use the vegetables that you have on hand! It is a flexible and forgiving soup.

½ to 2/3 of a medium onion, chopped
4-5 cups cauliflower broken into bite size pieces
2 cups broccoli pieces
1 cup peas
1 clove garlic, minced
1 cup chopped carrots
1 cup chopped celery
1 cup chopped red pepper
1 hand full of fresh spinach torn into tiny pieces or 1-2
    Tablespoons of Frozen spinach
5 cups of water
2-15 ounce cans of tomato sauce
1-6 ounce can of tomato paste
2 tablespoons of sugar
½ teaspoon of oregano
1 teaspoon of basil
½ teaspoon of thyme
1 tablespoon of salt
Pepper to taste

Place all ingredients in the slow cooker on high for 4 hours or until all the vegetables are cooked to desired softness. You can also cook this all day on low or make it quickly on the stove top using a higher temperature. Use whatever vegetables you like or whatever you have an abundance of for this tasty treat. This soup makes 13-14 cups.

French Onion Soup

I took on making a recipe for French Onion Soup when I had an abundance of onions from our CSA coop. This was surprisingly easy to make and tasted great. We obviously skip the cheese, but you can use a slice of non-dairy cheese and pop it under the broiler. Gluten-free croutons or a slice of toast will add to the image of regular French Onion Soup!

> **8 cups of onions slices (about 8 – 9 medium onions)**
> **2 tablespoons acceptable oil**
> **1 tablespoon of sugar**
> **8 cups of broth***
> **3 cloves of minced garlic**
> **¼ teaspoon of dried thyme**
> **1-1/2 teaspoons of salt or to taste**
> **½ cup of acceptable white wine (free of additives, preservatives, etc.)**

Sauté the onions in the oil over medium high heat in a large stockpot – stirring frequently. Keep stirring to caramelize the onions. Add the sugar towards the end of the cooking. After all of the onions are good and soft and caramelized, add the broth. Note on the broth: Beef broth will give the soup a naturally darker color than chicken or vegetable broth. Beef is the most often used broth for this type of soup. Add the wine, salt, garlic and thyme and then simmer over medium low heat for 1 to 2 hours. This soup will cook down over time. To get the full effect of French Onion Soup, place soup in a broiler safe bowl. Then place a piece of toasted gluten-free bread – we use the top or bottom of a homemade gluten-free roll – on top of the soup and top with acceptable non-dairy cheese shreds. Place under the broiler until the non-dairy cheese shreds melt and the soup is hot and bubbly! Makes about 7 cups of soup.

Shepherd's Pie Soup

I came up with this soup idea one evening when we had Shepherd's Pie. I speculated out loud that wouldn't it be great to have a soup that tasted just like Shepherd's Pie! Many months later I finally got around to trying it out. I had never heard of Shepherd's Pie Soup before making this recipe myself. We really love it!

4 cups of beef broth
7 cups of pure water
1 cup fresh or frozen peas
1-1/4 cups chopped carrots
1 medium onion, diced
3 cups of instant organic potato flakes or 1-1/2 to 2 cups of mashed potatoes
2 tablespoons of Worcestershire sauce
2 teaspoons of Celtic salt or to taste
1 cup diced celery
15 ounces of tomato sauce
1 pound ground beef, browned
1 tablespoon oil
2 cups finely diced potatoes
Pepper to taste

Optional: Additional mashed potatoes as a garnish, about ¼ cup to one cup of soup or you can use instant potato flakes in place of mashed potatoes

This soup is easily made on the stovetop or in a slow cooker. Brown ground beef in the oil until cooked through. Combine all ingredients in a large stockpot or slow cooker or a large stock pot on the stove top and cook until the vegetables are soft. I make 3 cups of mashed potatoes separate from the soup and serve ¼ cup of mashed potatoes on top of the soup as a garnish! The use of instant potato flakes is a real time saver for this recipe. Taste testers liked this soup in a variety of consistencies – some liked it thicker and some liked it without much or any thickener. For that reason, I place a bowl of potato flakes on the table when serving this soup so each person can add the instant potato flakes to his or her own taste. This recipe makes about 15 cups of soup and freezes well.

Tortilla Soup

The idea for this soup came from a store bought container of soup that was just a tad bit too spicy for the kids and just a tad bit too pricey for me! This is a naturally vegan soup. If you wanted a heartier soup for the meat-lover in your family, you could always add ground beef, turkey or chicken.

4 cups vegetable broth
1 large can of pinto beans (about 25 ounces)
8 cups of pure water
6 ounces of tomato paste
1 medium onion, diced
1 clove garlic, minced
1 tablespoon of salt or to taste
1 cup corn
1 cup carrots, diced
¼ cup red pepper, chopped
1 teaspoon celery seed
¼ teaspoon cayenne pepper
2 teaspoons dried parsley
2 cups cooked brown rice
Pepper to taste
Garnish: Corn chips or other chips to break into the soup

Place all ingredients into a large stockpot or slow cooker and cook until the vegetables are tender and cooked through to the desired tenderness. Broken pieces of corn chips or other chips will give this dish a restaurant style look and appeal. This recipe makes about 15 cups of soup. This soup freezes fairly well.

Diane's Chicken & Rice Soup

I made this soup for a dear friend when she was not feeling so well.
It is a simple yet hearty soup that freezes well.

16 to 18 cups chicken broth
1 cup celery, chopped
1-1/2 cups carrots, chopped
1 small onion, diced
1 clove garlic, minced
2-1/2 cups cooked brown rice
2 cups cooked chicken
salt and pepper to taste

Place all ingredients into a large stockpot and cook until the vegetables are cooked and tender. Salt and pepper to suit your taste. This recipe makes about 18 cups of soup.

Simple Simon's Vegetable Soup

This is the ultimate in simple soups because it uses ingredients that you are likely to have either in the fridge or in the freezer. My children love it. I add a few more spices to my bowl and for adults, you may want to increase the spices or add a few more of your own.

8 cups of pure water
30 ounces of tomato sauce with spices*
1-1/2 cups chopped carrots
1 cup chopped onion
1 cup chopped celery
1 clove of garlic, minced
1 cup of peas
2 cups of diced potatoes
Optional: 3 tablespoons or more of fresh or frozen greens like spinach, kale, bok choi
Celtic salt to taste
Pepper to taste

*I used tomato sauce from my freezer, which had basil, oregano, thyme and parsley. Many commercially made tomato sauces will contain such spices. If you use plain tomato sauce, add about ½ teaspoon to 1 teaspoon of basil, oregano, thyme and parsley to your soup. Place all ingredients in either a large stockpot on the stove or in a slow cooker and cook until all the vegetables are soft and the flavors are melded. This makes about 11 cups of soup.

Winter Warm Up Soup

I invented this soup recipe to use up our CSA winter root vegetables. I was actually taken aback that my children loved the soup! This soup has a unique taste and will not be loved by everyone. It's the best way that I have come up with to use up those winter root vegetables that are abundant with organic cooperatives.

    4 cups or 32 ounces of chicken or vegetable broth
    6 cups of pure water
    1-1/4 cups of chopped onion or 1 large onion chopped
    4 cups parsnips, peeled and chopped
    2 cups carrots, peeled and chopped
    4 cups potatoes, diced (we leave the skins on)
    2/3 cup shredded or grated celeriac
    1-1/2 cups turnips, diced
    4 teaspoons Celtic salt
    2-1/2 teaspoons dill
    2 teaspoons basil
    1 teaspoon thyme
    dash of marjoram

Combine all ingredients in a large stockpot and cook over medium heat until the vegetables are cooked through and the flavors well melded. Let the soup cool and then puree. Puree the soup and return to the pot. This makes about 11 cups of soup. If you simmer it for a longer time, you may want to add more water. This does thicken up as it stands, so add water to your desired consistency. This freezes well. When my husband makes it, he does not puree this soup. Personally, I don't like it very much if it is not pureed so you can experiment with this as you please.

Black Bean & Sausage Soup

This recipe came about to help me use up our organic sausage in the freezer to make room for the fresh pork that was coming soon. You could certainly make it without the sausage or substitute a different type of meat. Personally, I would kick the spices up a bit for my tastes. This is the spice level that will be more widely acceptable if you are serving a family.

14 to 16 ounces of cooked sausage, sliced or dices*(see note about cooking sausage)
8 cups chicken broth
9 cups pure water
1-1/2 cups diced carrots
1-1/4 cups diced celery
1-1/4 cups diced onion
2 cups cooked black beans (or one 25 oz. can drained and rinsed)
1 clove garlic, minced
1 teaspoon ginger
1 teaspoon thyme
¼ teaspoon cinnamon
black pepper to taste
¼ teaspoon chili powder
dash cayenne pepper
1 teaspoon Celtic salt

I recommend that you always pre-cook sausage because it is fatty and this removed excess fat from your final dish. Cooking directions for fresh organic sausage: Place sausage in a large volume of water with1 tablespoon of lemon juice. Cook over medium heat for 1 to 1-1/2 hours. Drain and rinse sausage. If you are using ground sausage, cook completely and then drain well by patting with paper towels to remove excess grease or your soup will end up greasy. Place all ingredients in a large stockpot and cook over medium heat until the vegetables are the desired tenderness and the flavors have melded together or about 1 hour. This recipe makes about 23 cups of soup. You can freeze this soup.

Mellow Yellow Soup

I purchased some organic yellow split peas on a whim! This recipe was invented simply to use up those organic split peas. This soup will freeze well and will appeal to a variety of tastes. My surprise was that my children liked this soup well enough to ask for it again!

6 cups broth or water
2 cups diced carrots
1 medium onion, chopped
1 red pepper, chopped
2 cups split yellow or green peas, rinsed and drained
4 cups water
2 teaspoons salt
Pepper to taste
2 cups cauliflower broken into small pieces
1-1/2 to 2 teaspoons dried rosemary

This recipe can be made on the stove or in a slow cooker as with all soups. Combine all ingredients and cook until the vegetables and split peas are cooked through. Allow soup to cool and then blend in a blender to puree the soup. This recipe makes about 14 cups of soup.

Creamy Broccoli Soup

Two of my children had a restaurant soup, which was in my opinion not very good at all! However, they really liked it. Having no idea what the soup had in it save for broccoli, I went to work to re-create the soup that they desired! I would not - underscore not – put this in a category of great soups just so you know!

10 cups of water or broth
8 to 9 cups of fresh or frozen broccoli pieces
2 teaspoons salt or to taste
1 cup diced onion
1-1/2 cup gluten-free Anellini noodles
Black pepper to taste

Place all ingredients in a large stockpot or slow cooker and cook until the broccoli is cooked through and the Anellini noodles have dissolved and thickened the soup. This is by nature a very thick soup. Too thick for my tastes. It does, however, made as indicated match a chain restaurant soup quite well. You may want to add water to this if you are not making it to duplicate a chain restaurant! This recipe makes about 8 to 9 cups of soup!

Country Cottage Potato Soup

One of my sons had the occasion to try a delicious chain restaurant soup that contained loads of dairy. He, of course, loved it and wanted to make it at home without the dairy. Make sure you remove the fat from the sausage or the soup will be greasy, which is so yuck in my humble opinion.

8 cups chicken broth
4 cups pure water
1 small chopped onion
1 pound ground sausage
4 large potatoes
1 teaspoon Celtic salt
2 to 4 ounces non-dairy cheddar cheese shreds
½ cup chopped spinach
Pepper to taste
½ cup or more of potato flakes (as a thickener)

In a large frying pan brown the sausage and onion until the sausage is thoroughly cooked. Place the cooked sausage on a plate covered with paper towels (or in a colander lined with paper towels). Blot out excess oil. Repeat the process until the fat is removed. This step is important otherwise you will end up with greasy soup! Place the chicken broth, water, potatoes, salt and pepper in a large stockpot and cook until the potatoes are cooked through. Remove 4 cups of the potatoes and broth and puree. Add the pureed potatoes and broth back to the stockpot. Then add the sausage, spinach, non-dairy cheddar cheese shreds. Add the potato flakes as the last step to thicken this soup. This makes about 15 cups of soup.

Loaded Baked Potato Soup

I had a restaurant soup similar to this that was to die for! Of course, I had no idea what was in it other than potatoes, bacon, and dairy. So I bought some preservative free bacon that day and just as soon as I could I started experimenting! My children had not tasted the soup, so they had no idea what taste I was shooting for. We all love this soup. I am not representing it as a healthy soup, but rather a comfort food.

> 10 medium potatoes, washed well and cut into quarters (skins on for fiber)
>
> Water to cover the potatoes in a large stock pot plus a little extra
>
> 4 cups chicken broth (or other broth)
>
> ¾ cup finely chopped carrot
>
> ½ cup finely chopped celery
>
> 4 ounces of preservative-free, nitrate-free bacon, cooked and broken into pieces
>
> 1 tablespoon dried parsley
>
> 8 ounces of acceptable non-dairy cheddar cheese shreds
>
> 1 tablespoon salt or to taste
>
> Pepper to taste
>
> 1 medium onion, diced (about ½ cup)
>
> 1 to 2 cups of instant potato flakes depending upon desired consistency of soup
>
> 2 Tablespoons oil
>
> 6 to 10 cups of potato water (water that the potatoes were cooked in)

Cook the preservative-free, nitrate and nitrite free bacon, crumble and set aside. Cook the potatoes in a large stockpot covered in water plus a little extra. When the potatoes are cooked through, reserve 6 to 8 cups of the cooking water. If you have a stick blender, see directions below. This recipe is significantly easier if you have a stick blender. When the potatoes are cool, place 2 or so cups of the cooked potatoes in a blender with some of the reserved potato cooking water and blend to a creamy consistency. Place the blended potatoes in either a second, clean stockpot or into a large mixing bowl (if you don't have a second large stock pot). Repeat this process until all of the potatoes have been pureed. Place the pureed potatoes into a large stockpot if you have not already done so. Add the chicken stock and remaining ingredients including the cooked bacon and simmer over medium low to medium until the vegetables are cooked through, about 1 hour. Stir every so often as you do not want the soup to burn on the bottom of the pan, so make sure your heat is not too high. This recipe makes about 14 to 15 cups of soup!

Made as is, this recipe will have a very thick, bisque like consistency, which my children love! Personally, I would like it with additional water added – not quite so thick. This does thicken from being refrigerated, so you will have to add water when leftovers come out of the fridge. I have served this to regular people who loved it even though it was sans dairy!

Stick Blender directions: Saute onions, carrots and celery in a large stockpot in oil. Cook potatoes separately reserving the cooking water. Add the cooked potatoes to the sautéed onions, carrots and celery mashing lightly. Add potato water, salt, parsley and cook for 20-30 minutes over medium heat. Then use the stick blender until pureed to your desire. Add crumbled bacon. Add potato flakes as desired and non-dairy cheese stirring constantly because it can burn easily.

Better Black Bean Soup

I invented this soup to use up some dried black beans from our CSA. You can definitely use canned beans if you don't have the time to cook dried beans. I did not discard the bean cooking water in this recipe, so it is packed with all those good nutrients. The result was a soup loaded with nutritionally dense, low fat soup, which tastes great!

3 cups dried black beans, rinsed and drained (or 4 cups canned black beans)
10 cups pure water
1 large onion, diced (about 1 cup)
1 clove garlic, minced
28 ounces whole, peeled tomatoes
28 ounces tomato puree
1 ¼ cup chopped carrots
¾ cup chopped celery
1 cup fresh or frozen corn
½ teaspoon cinnamon
1 Tablespoon Taco seasoning (recipe in this book)
2 teaspoons salt
1 tablespoon sugar or other acceptable sweetener (if desired)
1 teaspoon orange zest – the zest of one small orange
¼ cup orange juice (the juice from one orange)

Pick out any stones from the dried beans and place in a large stockpot covered with water. Let beans soak for about 10 minutes and then stir very well to remove any dirt. Rinse and drain the beans. Place the beans back in the stockpot and cover with 10 cups of pure water. Add the chopped onion and cook until the beans are completely soft and cooked through (about 1 ½ hours) on low to medium low heat. Once the beans are completely cooked, blend them and the cooking water in a blender in two batches. Leave about 1 cup of beans whole. Return the pureed black beans to a larger stockpot and then add the remaining ingredients. Simmer on low heat until the vegetables are cooked. Makes about 17 cups of soup. This soup freezes well.

Original Black Bean Soup

This soup has a great flavor and is a food that some young children will eat. At least some of mine did!

> **4 cups chicken or vegetable broth**
> **2 cups black beans, cooked or canned (if canned, rinse and drain)**
> **½ cup diced celery**
> **½ cup diced carrots**
> **¾ cup diced onion**
> **¼ cup vinegar**
> **1 teaspoon orange zest**
> **½ teaspoon ground cinnamon**
> **½ teaspoon cayenne pepper**
> **2 teaspoons minced garlic**
> **2 teaspoons sugar**

Bring ingredients to a boil and then reduce heat to a medium simmer. Simmer for at least one hour. Then purée either all or some of the soup in a blender. My children prefer a smooth and creamy soup so I purée all of the soup. For adults you could purée ½ to ¾ of the soup leaving the balance, giving the soup more texture. This soup can be served with rice for a complete protein. If you like a thinner soup you may add additional broth or pure drinking water. You may garnish the top of the soup with a sprinkle of green onion slices or a dollop of Tofutti non-dairy sour cream.

Hot & Sour Soup

This is one of my all-time favorites! Many Hot & Sour soup recipes call for ingredients that you simply don't have on hand and some that are hard to come by. The ingredients for my version of Hot & Sour Soup are stocked in most standard grocery stores.

2 tablespoons sesame oil (or other acceptable oil)
1 cup julienned cooked pork
One 8 ounce can sliced bamboo shoots
2 cups julienned carrot strips
½ cup sliced mushrooms
1 can water chestnuts, drained
8 cups chicken broth
One 16 ounce package firm tofu, drained and sliced into
    strips
⅓ cup Bragg™ Liquid Aminos
3 tablespoons sugar or to taste
¼ cup vinegar
½ cup green onions or leeks sliced thin
3 tablespoons chili and garlic sauce (or any combination of
    garlic and hot sauce)

6 tablespoons corn starch dissolved in
3 cups cold water (or other thickener)

This recipe makes a very large quantity of soup, which suits us just fine. If you live alone or are making it for the first time and are not sure how you will like it, feel free to cut the recipe in half. This soup does not freeze well unless you omit the tofu and water chestnuts. Trust me, the tofu and water chestnuts will not be pleasant after freezing! Without them, it survives freezing fairly well. To make the soup, sauté the cooked pork and raw carrots in the oil until hot and sizzling. Then add the chicken broth. Add all remaining ingredients saving cornstarch dissolved in water for last. Add the cornstarch and simmer for 30 minutes. Makes one large stockpot of soup, or approximately 17-20 cups of soup.

Look for the Chili and Garlic Sauce in the oriental section of the grocery store. If you can't find it, you may substitute hot sauce or chili oil, however my caution here is that you will be missing the garlic flavor. So if you substitute any hot sauce or chili oil, then please and be sure to add a good hit of minced garlic or your soup will come up short on flavor.

Savory Split Pea Soup

This is a delicious soup that is best made in a slow cooker where it is low maintenance.

1-organic ham hock
1 pound organic split peas
10 cups pure water or chicken broth*
1 medium diced onion
1 cup diced carrots
½ cup diced celery
½ teaspoon salt or to taste
Pepper to taste
Dash of marjoram
Dash of ground thyme
Meat from cooked ham hock

Combine all ingredients in a slow cooker and cook for 4-6 hours on high. Remove ham hock from the slow cooker and take all of the meat off of the bone cutting it into bite sized pieces or soup sized pieces. Set the meat aside. Using a stick blender, puree the soup in the slow cooker until creamy. If you are using a blender instead of a stick blender be very careful and be sure that the lid is cracked slightly to allow the hot air to escape or you will have a mess on your hands. This makes about 12-14 cups of soup.

Chicken Noodle Soup

This is my recipe for homemade chicken noodle soup. If you don't have noodles you can use cooked rice, but be careful not to add too much rice because rice will expand in the soup over time.

8 cups chicken stock (canned or homemade, see below)
1½ cups carrots, chopped
1 cup celery, chopped
2 cups onion, chopped
1 clove garlic, minced
½ cup peas (canned, frozen or fresh)
2 teaspoons salt
¼ teaspoon celery seed (whole)
½ teaspoon seasoning salt (see page 338)
½ teaspoon rosemary
1 teaspoon basil
1 teaspoon oregano
2 teaspoons parsley flakes
2 to 3 cups cooked, gluten-free noodles of your choice
To taste: pepper
2 or more cups cooked chicken, cut into small pieces

Simmer all of the above ingredients in a large pot. As the soup cooks, the liquid will cook down. Add more water as needed. Simmer for 1 hour (or more) to blend the flavors.

Tomato Basil Soup

My sons tasted some Tomato Basil soup at our local co-op store and begged me to make some. We had no idea what the ingredients were except for tomatoes and basil. We kept adding ingredients until it tasted and looked like the soup that they had tried and loved so much!

> **One 15 ounce can tomato sauce**
> **One 28 ounce can crushed tomatoes**
> **2 cups non-dairy milk substitute**
> **1 large onion, finely diced**
> **2 cloves garlic, minced**
> **2½ teaspoons dried basil**
> **1 tablespoon acceptable oil**

Sauté chopped onion in oil over medium to medium high heat until soft and cooked through. Add dried basil and minced garlic and stir constantly for 1 to 2 minutes over medium low heat. Add remaining ingredients and cook over medium heat for 30 minutes to 1 hour. Purée soup in a blender and return to the saucepan. My children prefer a creamy consistency. If you like chunks of tomato in the soup then don't purée it. This recipe makes a large quantity good for family gatherings or parties. For a smaller number of guests, this recipe may be cut in half.

Potato Chowder

This is a family recipe converted. While it is very different from the original recipe it has lots of flavor and none of the allergens that we avoid.

1 onion, chopped
1 clove garlic, minced or crushed
3 to 4 medium potatoes, chopped
2 stalks celery, sliced
1 medium red pepper, seeded, halved and sliced
4 tablespoons acceptable oil
5 cups stock or water
To taste: salt and pepper
2 cups non-dairy milk substitute
One 15 ounce can corn (with juice)
Pinch of dried sage

Place the oil in a large skillet over medium-high heat. Add the onion, celery, red pepper and sauté for 2 to 3 minutes. Add the potatoes, cover the pan and reduce the heat. Because you are cooking potatoes, they will need a lower heat for a longer amount of time. Add the garlic and cook the potatoes and vegetables for approximately 10 minutes on low heat (not your lowest setting, however). Add the stock or water, salt and pepper, and simmer for 15 minutes, stirring occasionally. Add the milk substitute, corn and sage, and cook for 10 more minutes. Different milk substitutes have different flavors. If the milk substitute you are using has a stronger flavor, this will change the flavor of the soup, and you may have to add more spices to compensate, or try adding more onion, garlic and red pepper.

Lisa Lundy's 5 Bean Soup

You can use canned or dried beans for this hearty and nutritious soup. The orange zest is what makes the soup so special!

One 19 ounce can red kidney beans
One 15 ounce can white kidney beans
One 15 ounce can black beans
One 14 ounce can pinto beans
One 15 ounce can Navy beans or white northern beans
One 28 ounce can tomato sauce
One 6 ounce can tomato paste
1 tablespoon olive oil
1 medium red pepper, chopped (optional)
1 large onion, chopped
2 medium carrots, chopped
2 cloves garlic, minced
¾ cup white or brown rice
4 cups water (and more later)
1 tablespoon salt
1 teaspoon ground cinnamon
1 teaspoon ground cumin
½ teaspoon cayenne pepper
⅓ cup vinegar
Zest from 1 orange (the peel of 1 orange grated)-this will completely change the taste!

Sauté the pepper, onion, and carrots, in the olive oil for about 5 minutes adding the garlic at the end of the cooking so as not to burn it. Meanwhile, drain and rinse all of the canned beans. In a large pot, combine the vegetables and canned beans. Add all of the remaining ingredients. Simmer for 1 hour. As the soup cooks down, you will need to add more water.

Please note, for the proper taste, the grated orange peel (Zest from one orange) is a required ingredient! Trust me. After the soup has simmered for about an hour, purée it in a blender or use a stick blender. Since there is more soup than will fit in any blender, purée it in "batches". We leave a small amount of the soup not puréed so that it has more texture to it.

This soup will be thick and you will need to thin it to a consistency that suits you. Some people like it thicker than others. Also, it thickens sitting in the refrigerator so you will need to add water prior to reheating.

Makes a large amount, so freeze some! If you would like to use dried beans instead of canned, they work well for this soup and are even more nutritious. When we use dried beans, we use the quick soak method. Rinse your beans and place in a large stock pan filled with pure drinking water. Cover and boil for 10 minutes. Remove from heat and let sit for 1 hour. This process produces about the same result as soaking the beans in water for 24 hours. Drain beans and add to the large pot with the sautéed vegetables. Follow the recipe from there.

Creamy Cauliflower or Broccoli Soup

This soup is excellent and reminds me of the creamy cauliflower soup my mother made for my cousin's bridal shower which was of course, delicious and contained dairy. I do not feel deprived with this creamy soup.

6 cups pure drinking water
1 head cauliflower or broccoli
2 tablespoons oil
1 teaspoon salt (more or less to taste)
To taste: pepper

Place the water in a medium to large stockpot over medium to high heat. Wash and cut cauliflower or broccolli florets into medium to small pieces and place in the stockpot. Bring to a boil and reduce to medium heat. Cook for 10 minutes. Check to make sure that the cauliflower or broccoli is knife tender. Remove from heat. Remove 2 cups of the water from the stockpot and dispose of this excess cooking water. Pour the cauliflower or broccoli and remaining cooking liquid into a second saucepan or mixing bowl. Then place ½ of the cauliflower or broccoli and ½ of the cooking liquid in a blender and purée until creamy (or use a stick blender in the pan). Pour this creamy cauliflower or broccoli back into your original stockpot. Take the remaining cauliflower or broccoli and cooking liquid and place this in the blender. Add 2 tablespoons of acceptable oil in the blender with 1 teaspoon of salt and a few grinds of pepper. Purée until smooth and pour back into your original stockpot with the existing soup. Stir well and taste. This recipe is sensitive to salt since it has very little other flavoring. If you need more salt, and only then, add more to taste. If you are one of the very few Americans who needs to gain weight, you can add more oil to this recipe to add fat and calories. However, we like it with just the minimal amount of oil.

Soup Stock

If you never made chicken broth or stock from scratch, this is the recipe for you.

1 large chicken breast (with the bone)
1 large onion
2 stalks celery
2 medium carrots
1 teaspoon dried rosemary
½ teaspoon salt
3-4 cloves of fresh garlic whole
1 tablespoon dried parsley

Use a large stockpot filled with at least 10 to 12 cups of purified water. The vegetables should be cleaned and cut into large chunks or about 2-3 inch pieces. Place all ingredients in the large stockpot and simmer on medium heat until the chicken is fully cooked. Remove the chicken from the pot, let it cool, and cut it into pieces for the soup. Remove the vegetables from the soup stock and strain the remaining liquid through a cheese cloth or fine linen towel. Straining is important as it will clarify your soup stock and also because it removes fat and subtle impurities. You can add water to make 8 cups for the recipe above.

ROLLS, MUFFINS, BAGELS, PANCAKES, WAFFLES & PIZZA CRUST

Bargain Baking Mix

We do bargain gluten-free and allergy baking! This recipe was designed to rival a large, name-brand gluten-free baking mix that became available at a premium price. This can be used as a basis for "impossible dinner pies", and the sausage balls featured in the appetizer chapter of this book.

> 3 cups gluten-free flour (1-1/2 cups brown rice and 1-1/2 cups tapioca or other gf flour of your choice)
> ¼ cups sugar
> 1 tablespoon baking powder
> 1 tablespoon xanthan gum
> ½ teapoon salt
> **Herbed Bargain Baking Mix**
> Add the following to the bargain baking mix above:
> 1 teaspoon garlic powder
> 1 teaspoon onion powder
> 1 teaspoon dried rosemary
> 1 teaspoon dried oregano
> 1 teaspoon dried basil

This is easy to make ahead and store in a plastic bag until needed. I typically make 3 batches of this at a time. This recipe is used in the Sausage Balls appetizer, in a pancake recipe and in the Impossible Lasagna pie recipe. This makes 3 cups of dry baking mix.

Fabulous Flatiron Flatbreads

We started making my classic Versatile Roll recipe into flatbreads by spreading the batter paper thin on a pizza stone or on a baking sheet. I realized that I had an old waffle ice cream cone maker in the basement, which we decided to try for making flatbreads. It was an immediate hit. With a few minor changes, we have what I feel is infinitely healthier, tastier and more flexible than traditional bread or rolls. Good for those who are watching their weight as the flatbreads have less calories than a gluten-free roll.

  1 ½ cups garfava flour
  1 ½ cups tapioca flour
  3 teaspoons xanthan gum
  4 teaspoons Ener-G® egg replacer
  3 teaspoons baking powder
  1/3 cup oil
  1 cup liquid non-dairy milk substitute
  ½ cup club soda or water

Mix the dry ingredients in a large mixing bowl. After the dry ingredients are well mixed, add the oil, milk substitute, and club soda. Mix well. In this recipe, it does not matter as much what the consistency of the batter is because you are making flatbreads. Place 2 tablespoons of batter in the center of a pre-heated flatbread iron OR a waffle ice cream cone iron. Cook for 90 seconds. This recipe will make 22 flatbreads that are approximately five inches in diameter.

Garfava Roll, Danish, & Pizza Crust Mix (also good for bagels & breadsticks)

Preheat oven to 350°.

1½ cups garfava flour (or chickpea)

1½ cups tapioca flour

3 teaspoons xanthan gum

3 teaspoons baking powder

1 teaspoon salt

4 teaspoons Egg Replacer™ (OR 2 eggs if you can tolerate eggs)

⅔ cup oil

1 cup non-dairy milk substitute of any type

1+ cup sparkling water or club soda until the *batter is creamy*

Mix dry ingredients in a bowl. Add liquid ingredients and mix well. Batter will be light and kind of fluffy. If necessary, add more club soda or water.

To make rolls:

We like to add dry, minced onion flakes and garlic powder/salt to our batter for a different taste. You can add any or no herbs to yours. Try a taste test by dividing the batter in half and add herbs, onion flakes, etc. to half the batter and leave half of the batter plain. Grease muffin tins. This will make about 18 rolls (+/-) depending upon how full you fill the muffin tins. Place the batter into a plastic ziplock bag. Cut off one corner of the bag (about ½" or less of an opening). Pipe the batter into the muffin tins filling about ½ or ⅔ for smaller rolls, and more for larger rolls. Bake about 18 to 24 minutes or until lightly golden but not too brown. The baking time depends upon the size of your rolls and the accuracy of your oven. These will freeze well, and are good on day two as well. You can use English muffin rings or hamburger bun pans to make larger rolls. Smooth out the tops of the rolls with either a spatula or wet fingers.

To make pizza crust:
This recipe will make two pizza crusts and the size will depend upon whether you like thin or thick crust. Place ½ of the batter on a greased cookie sheet or baking sheet. Using either your wet fingers or a greased or wet spatula spread the batter out to the thickness you think that you desire. You will have to experiment a bit on this the first or second time. Bake the crust for about 10 or more minutes until it starts to look fairly baked. Then top with your favorite sauce, and toppings. Return to the oven and bake another 10 minutes more or until done.

To make Danish
Place the batter into a ziplock bag with a corner cut off. Pipe the batter onto a greased cookie sheet. Pipe the batter into circles; start in the center and wind around the center circle until you have made the desired size circle. This will make about 18 or more medium size Danish. Make a small indentation in the center and fill with about ¼ teaspoon of your favorite jam or jelly. Bake 18 or so minutes until the bottom starts to just turn light golden color. Let cool, then drizzle with a confectioners' glaze. These freeze well and are delicious.

Basic Gluten-Free, Dairy-Free Tortilla

2 cups tapioca flour (or starch)
1/2 cup quinoa flour*
1/2 cup amaranth flour*
1 teaspoon baking powder
1 teaspoon salt
1 teaspoon Ener-G™ Egg Replacer
1 teaspoon xanthan gum
1/4 cup sesame oil (or other acceptable oil)
1 cup warm water (or enough to make the dough the right consistency)

*You may use other gluten-free flours in place of the quinoa and/ or amaranth flours. In a large mixing bowl, combine all of the dry ingredients and 1/2 cup of the water. Mix well with your hands. Add more water to the dough until it forms a solid ball but is not too sticky. If needed, you may add additional flour. Divide the dough into 7 or 8 balls. Place one of the dough balls on a piece of waxed paper that is covered with tapioca flour and roll out until nice and thin. Repeat this process, adding more flour between the tortillas until all 7 or 8 have been rolled out.

Heat a frying pan or griddle to medium heat. Add oil to the pan and cook the tortillas individually for about 30 seconds each side. Continue this process until all tortillas have been cooked. If your pan is too hot, you will scorch your tortillas. This recipe makes between 7 and 8 tortillas. They freeze well and would probably keep in the refrigerator for a few days or more.

For filling the Quesadillas use non-dairy cheeses (rice and soy), leftover chicken lunchmeat, and whatever else appeals to you! Broil them under the broiler until the "cheese" is melted or just load up with your favorite fillings.

To Make Flatbreads: Add 2/3 cup water in addition to the above ingredients and use the flatiron or ice cream cone maker.

Everything Sorghum Rolls

The idea for this recipe came from the fact that my kids were tired of our old sandwich roll that was made with sorghum flour. These rolls were a big hit on the first try. Since my children do not relish the taste of sorghum, I have to use flavoring agents to mask the taste and smell of sorghum.

Preheat oven to 350°
   1-1/2 cups sorghum flour
   ½ cup millet flour
   ½ cup tapioca flour
   1 tablespoon xanthan gum
   1 tablespoon baking powder
   1 tablespoon Ener-G® Egg Replacer
   5 tablespoons Everything spices
   2/3 cup oil
   12 ounces club soda or water

Mix all of the dry ingredients together in a large mixing bowl. Add the oil and club soda and mix well. If your batter is too stiff to be piped through a plastic freezer bag, add water 1 tablespoon at a time. Pipe dough into a greased baking pan, either a muffin tin, English muffin round, hot dog pan or hamburger bun pan. Bake in a 350° oven for 23 to 25 minutes or until lightly browned.

New Wonder Rolls

This recipe was invented to meet the demand for a basic white gluten-free, casein-free roll. While these rolls taste great, they are simply not a nutrient dense baked good. I used multiple flours in this roll, which do not follow our rotation diet. They are, for that reason, a treat that we do not eat all that often.

Preheat oven to 350°
   ½ **cup garfava flour**
   ½ **cup brown rice flour**
   ½ **cup millet flour**
   1 **cup tapioca flour**
   ½ **cup potato starch**
   1 **tablespoon xanthan gum**
   1 **tablespoon baking powder**
   1 **tablespoon Ener-G Egg Replacer**®
   2/3 **cup of acceptable oil**
   1 **can (12 ounces) of club soda or water**

Preheat oven to 350°. These rolls can be baked in either hamburger or hotdog bun pans or in a regular muffin baking pan or even in English muffin rings. Grease your baking pans and set aside. In a large mixing bowl, combine all of your dry ingredients and mix well. Add oil and club soda or water and mix again. You may need to add 1 to 3 tablespoons of water depending upon how you measured your flour. This batter will be fairly firm and thick. Place into a freezer plastic bag with one corner cut off (a triangle cut off of one corner which will serve as an opening to pipe out the dough). Pipe the batter into the prepared baking pans. Use a spatula dipped in water to smooth out the dough to make nicely formed rolls. Bake for 25 minutes or until lightly browned. These rolls will not brown a lot. These rolls freeze well. Makes 6 hamburger buns or 7 hotdog buns.

Fabulous Five Pizza Crust

I made this pizza crust for one of our Super Bowl Parties! It was a raving success. In this recipe, I again broke our rotation diet to create this recipe. You may substitute other flours for the ones I have provided.

Preheat oven to 400°

1-1/2 cups Garfava flour
1-1/2 cups tapioca flour
½ cup brown rice flour
½ cup millet flour
½ cup potato flour
1-1/2 tablespoons baking powder
1-1/2 tablespoons xanthan gum
1 tablespoon Ener-G Egg Replacer®
1 teaspoon onion powder
1 teaspoon garlic powder
1 tablespoon dried basil
1 tablespoon dried oregano
1 teaspoon dried thyme
1 tablespoon dried parsley
½ teaspoon Celtic salt
1 cup olive oil or other acceptable oil
1 cup non-dairy milk substitute
1-1/2 cans (about 18 ounces) of club soda or water
¼ cup water

Preheat oven to 400° and grease cookie or pizza baking sheets. This recipe will make approximately 5 – ten inch pizzas, which you can make as round pies or rectangular pizzas. Mix all dry ingredients in a large mixing bowl and mix well. Add the liquid ingredients and stir to mix well. Place dough on greased baking sheets and form into pizza circles or rectangles with a wet spatula. Place the pizza in the oven for about 12 – 15 minutes or until the crust starts to brown. Remove from oven and top. Return to the oven and broil for 3 – 4 minutes or until done. See main dish meals chapter for a variety of different types of pizza you can make that will meet your allergy and celiac needs.

All-Star Pizza Crust

We do our best to continue our rotation diet. I invented this recipe to have pizza on a sorghum flour day. I added the rice and millet not to keep with our rotation diet but to make it more "palatable" to the typical gluten-free palate.

Preheat oven to 400°
   1 cup rice flour
   1 cup millet flour
   1-1/2 cups tapioca flour
   1 cup sorghum flour
   1 tablespoon xanthan gum
   ¼ teaspoon Celtic salt
   1 teaspoon basil
   2 teaspoons oregano
   1 teaspoon thyme
   1 teaspoon rosemary
   1 clove garlic
   1 package pizza yeast
   1 teaspoon sugar or other sweetener
   ½ cup oil
   1 cup to 1-1/4 cup water
   ½ cup water heated to 120° (mix sugar and yeast with this water)

Measure dry ingredients in a large mixing bowl except for yeast and sugar. In a separate measuring cup or bowl, mix heated water with the sugar and yeast to proof. Allow yeast to sit for about five minutes to proof. While the yeast is proofing, add the water and oil to the large mixing bowl with the flours, but do not mix yet. Add the yeast and then mix the batter well. Place the batter on greased baking sheets. This will make about 5 – personal size pizzas (about 10 inch) or 2- larger sheet pizzas. Shape into your pizza size with a wet spatula. Baking will be determined by the size of the pizza as well as the thickness of the crust. Bake in a 400° oven for about 10 minutes or until the crust starts to brown and looks reasonably cooked. Top pizza and return to the oven for 5 to 10 minutes or until bubbly and cooked.

Deep Dish Basil Pizza Crust

I purchased some deep-dish pizza crust pans at a local cooking store, which provided the motivation and inspiration for deep dish pizza. Now, you don't have to go and purchase special pans. You could easily use a 7" or 8" cake pan for the deep-dish pizza pan! This recipe was enthusiastically received in our household by everyone!

Preheat oven to 400°
- 1 cup garfava flour
- 1 cup sorghum flour
- 1 cup tapioca flour
- ½ cup millet flour
- 1 tablespoon baking powder
- 1 tablespoon xanthan gum
- 1 tablespoon Ener-G® Egg Replacer
- pinch of salt, if desired
- 2 teaspoons of dried basil
- ½ teaspoon of oregano
- 1 clove garlic, minced
- 1 teaspoon thyme
- ½ cup oil
- 1 cup Dari-Free or non-dairy milk substitute (liquid)
- 6 ounces club soda or water

Preheat oven to 400°. Mix dry ingredients together in a large mixing bowl. Add liquid ingredients and stir to incorporate. Spread dough into greased deep dish pizza pans or round cake pans. This makes four deep dish pizza crusts in the 6" to 7" size. Bake in the oven for 20 to 24 minutes or until the crust is well baked and lightly browned. Top with your favorite toppings and return to the oven for 5 minutes or until hot.

Pita Style Tortilla Bread

This is more like a hybrid of pita bread and a tortilla. It was delicious and preferred over commercially made tortillas. We use this as a sandwich wrap and for sautéed vegetables!

2/3 cups amaranth flour
1 cup quinoa flour
1 1/3 cups tapioca flour
1 teaspoon xanthan gum
1 tablespoon agave syrup
1 packet active dry yeast
½ cup warm water (120-130°F)
1 teaspoon sugar
2 tablespoons olive oil or other acceptable oil
1 teaspoon salt
An additional 1/3 to ½ cup water

Preheat oven to 400°. Mix flours, salt and xanthan gum in a large mixing bowl and set aside. Heat water to 120-130° using a thermometer to check the actual temperature. Add sugar and yeast packet to warm water and stir well. Let yeast rise for about 5 minutes, then add to the dry ingredients. Add oil and agave syrup to dry ingredients and mix well. Knead for about 5 minutes. Place in an oiled bowl and let rise for 30 to 60 minutes depending upon if you are using regular or fast acting yeast. Punch down and divide into 8 balls of dough about 2-1/2" in diameter. Let dough sit for 20 minutes on greased cookie sheets, 4 per sheet Cover with greased waxed paper.

Flatten the balls into circles, which will be roughly 6" in diameter while they are on the greased cookie sheet. Bake for 15 minutes or until golden brown. Turn over after 15 minutes and bake for an additional 3 or so minutes. Makes about 8 tortillas.

Chocolate Chocolate Chip Scones

I picked out a mini-scone pan for my birthday as a gift from my Mother. This was the first recipe I made from scratch to use this new pan. Luckily, it was a hit.

Preheat oven to 350°
  1 cup gluten-free flour
  ¾ cup millet or other gluten-free flour
  3 tablespoons sugar
  3 tablespoons gfcf chocolate chips
  1 tablespoon baking powder
  ½ cup non-dairy margarine
  3 tablespoons cocoa powder
  ¾ teaspoon xanthan gum
  ½ cup non-dairy milk

Preheat oven to 350°. Grease scone pan and set aside. Place dry ingredients in a large mixing bowl and mix well. Add margarine and cut into flour until well incorporated. Add non-dairy milk and mix. Add chocolate chips and stir just to mix. Pat mixture, which is very dry, into a mini-scone pan – patting down the mixture pretty well - and bake in a 350° oven for 18 to 20 minutes. Makes 16 mini-scones. Drizzle with confectioner's icing if desired.

Blueberry-Orange Scones

I have to say that I do not have a personal history with scones. My interest in scones was only spawned by my purchase of a mini-scone pan, which was in reality a birthday gift from my Mother. My non-family taste testers gave this the highest marks.

Preheat oven to 350°
> 2-1/4 cups gluten-free flour (1 cup garfava and 1-1/4 cups tapioca)
> ¼ cup sugar
> 1 tablespoon baking powder
> ½ cup acceptable margarine
> ¾ teaspoon xanthan gum
> ¾ cup blueberries
> juice of one orange plus enough OJ to make ½ cup
> zest of one orange
> ¼ cup non-dairy milk

Preheat oven to 350°. Grease mini-scone pan and set aside. Place dry ingredients in a large mixing bowl and stir well. Cut margarine into the flour mixture in tiny pieces. Mix the margarine into the flour well until it is a coarse mixture. Add orange juice, orange zest, non-dairy milk and blueberries and mix well, but do not over mix. Bake in a 350° for 23 to 26 minutes or until done.

Sweet Breakfast Focaccia

This recipe as well as the other Focaccia recipes included in this book were inspired by a visit to my Mom's house where she had a gluten Focaccia bread that contained herbs. I was looking for a new breakfast food, so I thought it might work to spread jam over the top and skip the herbs. It was an immediate it and it even froze well.

Preheat the oven to 350°

2 cups Garfava flour or other acceptable gf flour
2-1/2 cups tapioca flour or other acceptable gf flour
1 tablespoon plus one teaspoon xanthan gum
1 tablespoon plus one teaspoon of baking powder
1 tablespoon of Ener-G Egg replacer
1/2 cup brown sugar
1-1/2 cups non-dairy milk substitute
2/3 cup oil
1-1/2 cups club soda or water (some extra water if needed)
½ to 2/3 cup of natural jam or preserves (or more), stirred until creamy
Confectioner's sugar glaze

Preheat oven to 350°. Grease and set aside a sheet cake size pan (insert measurements of pan 17-1/2" x 11". Place all dry ingredients in a large mixing bowl and stir to mix. Add liquid ingredients and mix well. Place batter on greased baking pan and use a wet spatula to spread the batter to fill the pan evenly. Stir the jam or preserves well until creamy and then spread jam or preserves over the top of the batter. Bake for 20-24 minutes or until lightly browned. Drizzle a confectioner's sugar glaze over the top when cooled.

Herb Focaccia Bread

I got the idea for this recipe when we were visiting my Mom and she had a gluten herb focaccia bread. I made this when we got home by simply modifying one of our versatile recipes for rolls. It was an instant hit!

Preheat oven to 350°

> **4 cups gluten-free flour (1-1/2 cups garfava, 1-1/2 cups tapioca, 1 cup millet)**
> **1 tablespoon xanthan gum**
> **1 tablespoon baking powder**
> **1 tablespoon Ener-G Egg Replacer® dry powder**
> **2 tablespoons minced onion**
> **2 teaspoons thyme**
> **2 teaspoons sage**
> **2 teaspoons oregano**
> **1 teaspoon rosemary**
> **Optional: 1 clove garlic, minced**
> **¾ cup acceptable oil**
> **1 cup non-dairy milk substitute**
> **10 ounces of club soda or water**

Preheat oven to 350°. Grease a large jellyroll pan measuring 17-1/2" x 11" and set aside. You may substitute other flours for this recipe. In a large mixing bowl, combine all of the dry ingredients and mix well to blend. Add the oil, non-dairy milk substitute and club soda. If you are using a clove of garlic, add it to the mixing bowl. Stir well to mix all ingredients. Add a touch more club soda or water only if needed. Spread the batter into your prepared baking pan. Bake for 20-24 minutes.

Half-Grain Blueberry Flax Waffles

I invented this recipe when my children got tired of the waffles we were using on our 'Chicken/Amaranth' food rotation day. Amaranth and quinoa flours are quite simply not my favorite flours. None of us like the taste of amaranth or quinoa, which is why I used blueberries, and cinnamon in this recipe – to kind of mask the taste of the amaranth and quinoa flours.

> 1-1/2 cups quinoa flour
> 1 cup amaranth flour
> 1 cup tapioca flour
> 2/3 cup ground flax seed meal (ground flax seeds)
> 1 tablespoon baking powder
> 1 tablespoon xanthan gum
> 1 cup pure maple syrup
> dash of cinnamon
> 2 cups blueberries
> 1/3 cup oil
> 1-1/2 cups to 1-3/4 cups of water (use only as much as
>   needed)

In a large mixing bowl, combine the dry ingredients including the cinnamon. Add the oil, maple syrup, blueberries and water and combine well. This batter will be reasonably thick (very thick compared to pancake batter). Preheat and grease your waffle iron. Place batter into a plastic freezer food storage bag and cut a ½ inch diagonal off of the corner of your freezer food bag. This will serve as a piping bag for you to pipe the batter onto your waffle iron. Cooking time and yield will depend on the depth and size of your waffle iron. For a deep waffle iron of average size, this recipe will make between 11 to 14 waffles, which will cook for 3 to 4 minutes.

Homestyle Pancakes

If you have the Bargain Baking Mix already made up – this is a fast recipe to make. You can add optional flavoring ingredients like chocolate chips, blueberries, etc.

1 cup Bargain Baking Mix (recipe in this book)
1 cup rice milk or other non-dairy milk substitute
1-1/2 teaspoons Ener-G Egg Replacer
2 tablespoons acceptable oil

Mix dry ingredients in a medium sized mixing bowl. Add liquid ingredients and mix well. Cook pancakes on a greased skillet on medium heat. Makes about 10 small pancakes. You can add optional flavoring ingredients like chocolate chips, blueberries, etc.

Gourmet Stuffing

At a festive gathering I sampled a gourmet stuffing. This is a different stuffing that has a more adult flavor. It is not far off of the traditional stuffing we make, but kids might want you to skip the dried and fresh fruit.

7 cups bread cubes, slightly toasted
¼ cup plus 1 tablespoon dried cranberries
¼ cup plus 1 tablespoon raisins
½ cup chopped apple (about ½ of a large apple)
3 cups broth (use 1 cup at a time)
3 teaspoons of dried sage
3 teaspoons of dried thyme
2 teaspoons of salt
1 clove of garlic, minced

Grease a medium sized baking dish and set aside. Add bread cubes and all dry ingredients and spices. Add 1 to 2 cups of the broth depending upon how dried out your bread cubes are. The drier they are the more liquid you will need. Bake in a 350-375 degree oven for 40 minutes, stirring at 20 minutes. Remove from oven and determine the level of moistness you desire. If needed, add the remaining broth and return to the oven for 20 more minutes.

Fast and Easy Stuffing

I created this recipe to use up some gluten-free, dairy-free cereal, which had expired. The kids loved it. And it freezes well.

6 cups bread crumbs or crushed cereal
2 tablespoons acceptable oil
1 medium onion, diced
1 clove garlic
1 teaspoon sage (or to taste)
1½ teaspoons thyme (or to taste)
1 teaspoon salt
5 to 6 cups broth of choice (or more)

Place bread crumbs or crushed cereal in a large mixing bowl and set aside. Sauté onion in the oil of your choice. When onion is very soft and cooked through, add 1 clove garlic minced or put through a garlic press. Sauté 1 minute longer, then remove from heat. Add sautéed onion and garlic to bread crumbs or crushed cereal and mix well. Add sage, thyme, and salt and mix well. Then add 5 cups of the broth of your choice. Some people like their stuffing dry, and some people like their stuffing moist. If you have both types in your household, then divide the stuffing in half and add more broth to one bowl to get it to the right consistency for those members. If you like very moist stuffing, you will continue to add either broth or water to reach the texture/consistency that you prefer. This is now ready to serve as a tasty side dish.

Old Fashioned Stuffing

We call this old-fashioned stuffing because we make it just like my Mom used to make. You will either need bread or rolls to cut into pieces and toast or you will need acceptable commercial bread cubes. This recipe makes enough to feed a crowd. If you are having a small gathering, this will freeze well. We make this size batch of stuffing and then freeze it in meal size portions. My children love this! We will use the roll recipes in this cookbook and make a double batch of rolls for this stuffing recipe.

> 16 cups toasted or dried bread cubes
> 3 tablespoons acceptable oil
> 3 large stalks celery, minced
> 1 medium to large onion, diced
> 1 clove garlic, minced
> 2 teaspoons salt (or to taste)
> Pepper to taste
> 4 to 6 teaspoons thyme or to taste
> 4 to 6 teaspoons ground sage or to taste
> Up to 8 cups turkey broth (or other broth of your choice)

Place bread cubes in either a large mixing bowl or the bottom of a very tall roasting pan and set aside. Sauté onion and celery in oil. When the onion and celery are soft, add minced garlic and sauté one more minute. Add onion mixture to bread cubes. Sprinkle salt, sage, thyme over bread cubes and mix well. Pepper to taste. Add 4 cups of the broth of your choice and mix well. Place bread cubes in a large greased baking pan or two smaller baking dishes and bake in a 375° for 30 minutes. Remove from oven and check moistness. Add additional broth to reach your desired level of moistness. We like very moist stuffing since we typically don't use gravy, so we will use all 8 cups of broth. This freezes well.

Wild Rice Stuffing

This is a fast way to make stuffing compared to the traditional recipes that I use. This makes about 4 cups of stuffing.

4 cups wild rice, cooked
2 tablespoons acceptable oil
1 large onion, finely chopped
3 stalks celery, finely chopped
½ teaspoon sage
½ teaspoon thyme
1 teaspoon salt
1½ cups broth

Sauté the onions and celery in the oil until soft. Add the rice, broth, and herbs and mix gently. This can be used to stuff a bird or as a side dish. If you like heavily flavored foods, you can increase the sage and thyme to your tastes. You can add raisins or dried cranberries or other ingredients to make it more gourmet.

Chocolate Chip Muffins

I invented this recipe to quell some boredom in our house on breakfast foods. These are tasty and freeze well.

Preheat oven to 350°
- 3 cups of gluten-free flour (1 cup sorghum, ½ cup amaranth, ½ cup millet, 1 cup tapioca)
- 1 tablespoon baking powder
- 1 tablespoon Ener-G egg replacer
- 1 tablespoon xanthan gum
- ½ cup acceptable cocoa powder
- dash of cinnamon
- ½ cup acceptable chocolate chips
- ¾ cup pure maple syrup
- ½ cup acceptable oil
- 2/3 cup non-dairy milk substitute
- 1 cup applesauce
- Optional: sugar or confectioner's icing

Preheat oven to 350°. Place muffin papers in a muffin tin and set aside. Place the dry ingredients in a large mixing bowl. Add the liquid ingredients and gently mix well to incorporate. Do not overmix. This is a fairly thick batter. Bake muffins for 23-25 minutes or until done. Makes 20-23 muffins. You may top these muffins with either regular granular sugar, which is done before baking or confectioner's icing, which you would do after baking.

Cherry Muffins

I was in the mood for a new muffin and looking at ways to add a boost of nutrition. It didn't hurt that what I had on hand was frozen organic cherries from our local CSA share.

Preheat oven to 375°
   2 cups gluten free flour (1 cup garfava and 1 cup tapioca)
   1-1/2 teaspoons baking powder
   1 teaspoon baking soda
   1 cup sugar
   ½ teaspoon Celtic salt
   1 tablespoon Ener-G egg replacer
   ¾ cup orange juice
   ¼ cup oil
   2 cups coarsely chopped fresh or frozen cherries
   1-1/2 teaspoons xanthan gum
   Extra sugar for top of muffin (1-2 tablespoons)

Preheat oven to 375°. Line muffin tins with muffin papers and set aside. In a large mixing bowl, mix all dry ingredients together. Add liquid ingredients and cherries and mix enough to incorporate. Bake at 375° for 25 to 30 minutes.

Sweet Potato Donuts or Muffins

These are good for breakfast or a treat on the run. With sorghum flour and flax meal, you have got some whole grain goodness. Add sweet potatoes and you've got a sweet treat with some nutritional value. We make them in mini-donut pans and mini-muffin pans for that gourmet look.

Preheat oven to 350°.

2 ½ cups sorghum flour
½ cup ground flax meal
1 tablespoon xanthan gum
1 tablespoon Ener-G Egg Replacer™
1 tablespoon baking powder
Dash of ground cloves

¾ cup oil
One 15 ounce can sweet potato purée (or pumpkin or squash)
1 cup maple syrup (or other sweetener)
1 to 3 tablespoons water (only if needed)
½ to ¾ cup gluten-free, dairy-free chocolate chips

Mini muffin baking pans or mini-donut pans are recommended. If you don't have these pans, you can use a regular muffin baking pan. Grease baking pans and set aside. Mix dry ingredients in a large bowl and stir well. Add oil, sweet potato or other purée, and maple syrup. Stir to incorporate well, but do not over mix. Add chocolate chips. Clip corner of a gallon size plastic bag and place ⅓ of the batter in the plastic bag. Using the plastic bag for piping, and fill donut pan or muffin tins ¾ full or more. Bake for 20 to 22 minutes for mini donuts or mini-muffins, and 26 to 30 minutes for regular size muffins. Do not over bake. These freeze well.

Chocolate Chip Zucchini Bread

I had some delicious zucchini bread at Lake Mokoma. I came right home and decided to try my hand at zucchini bread. The first attempt tasted good, but was over baked for sure. Each subsequent time, it got better and better. You will need to use a cake tester to determine if the bread is done on the inside, so be forewarned.

Preheat oven to 350°
   1 ½ cups millet or sorghum flour (or rice)
   2 cups garfava flour
   1 cup tapioca flour
   2 cups sugar
   2 ½ cups grated zucchini
   ½ teaspoon salt
   1 teaspoon cinnamon
   dash of cloves
   1 teaspoon baking soda
   3 teaspoons baking powder
   2 teaspoons xanthan gum
   ½ cup chocolate chips
   1 cup acceptable oil
   1 tablespoon Ener-G® Egg Replacer mixed with 1/3 cup
      water
   ¾ cup pure water
   dash of pure vanilla extract

Grease and flour two loaf pans. Place the dry ingredients except for the sugar in a large mixing bowl and set aside. In a second mixing bowl, mix the sugar, egg replacer (mixed with the water), oil, and vanilla and stir until completely combined. Add the grated zucchini, chocolate chips and mix. Add the liquid mixture to the dry ingredients and stir until combined. Do not over mix. Place batter into the two loaf pans. Bake at 350° for 40 minutes, then lower the temperature to 325° and bake for another 15 minutes. Use a cake tester to check to see if the bread is done. For regular sized muffins bake for 30 to 35 minutes.

Better Than Ever Chocolate Chip Zucchini Bread

This recipe was inspired by the previous Chocolate Chip Zucchini Bread. It is lower in fat and calories due to the use of Stevia in the Raw and applesauce.

Preheat oven to 350°
  1 ½ cups millet or sorghum flour (or rice)
  2 cups garfava flour
  1 cup tapioca flour
  1 cup sugar
  1 cup Stevia in the Raw or other baking sugar substitute
  2 ½ cups grated zucchini
  ½ teaspoon salt
  1 teaspoon cinnamon
  dash of cloves
  1 teaspoon baking soda
  1-1/2 Tablespoons baking powder
  4 teaspoons xanthan gum
  ½ cup chocolate chips
  ½ cup applesauce
  ½ cup acceptable oil
  1 tablespoon Ener-G® Egg Replacer
  1 cup pure water plus 3 Tablespoons of water
  dash of pure vanilla extract

Grease and flour two loaf pans. Place the dry ingredients except for the sugar in a large mixing bowl and set aside. In a second mixing bowl, mix the sugar, Stevia in the Raw (or other Sugar substitute), oil, applesauce and vanilla and stir until completely combined. Add the grated zucchini and chocolate chips and mix. Add the liquid mixture to the dry ingredients and stir until combined. Do not over mix. Place batter into the two loaf pans. Bake at 350° for 40 minutes, then lower the temperature to 325° and bake for another 15 minutes. Use a cake tester to check to see if the bread is done. For regular sized muffins bake for 30 to 35 minutes.

Blueberry Buckle

This is another recipe from my childhood! Blueberry Buckle is a sweet coffeecake type food. I debated including it in the dessert section. However, we eat it more as a special breakfast food! It is pretty high in sugar, which is why this is a real treat in our house!

Preheat oven to 325°
- **2 tablespoons pure water**
- **2 teaspoons Ener-G Egg Replacer®**
- **½ cup sugar**
- **½ cup acceptable shortening**
- **2 cups gluten-free flour (1 cup garfava flour; ½ cup rice flour; ½ cup tapioca)**
- **1-1/2 teaspoon xanthan gum**
- **2-1/2 teaspoon baking powder**
- **¼ teaspoon salt**
- **½ cup non-dairy milk substitute**
- **2 cups blueberries**

Topping:
- **½ cup sugar**
- **½ cup gluten-free flour (1/4 cup tapioca; ¼ cup rice flour)**
- **½ teaspoon cinnamon**
- **¼ cup non-dairy margarine or margarine substitute**

Preheat oven to 325°. Grease a 9" square glass baking dish and set aside. Place the 2 tablespoons of water and the egg replacer in a large mixing bowl and whisk with a fork to incorporate. Add the ½ cup sugar and ½ cup acceptable shortening and mix well. In a separate small to medium bowl, combine the 2 cups gf flour, xanthan gum, baking powder, and salt and stir well. Add ¼ cup of the non-dairy milk to the sugar/margarine mixture and stir well. Alternate the flour with the milk stirring well after each addition until no milk or flour is left. You will have a very thick batter that is almost like cookie dough. Spread the batter into your prepared pan.

Cover the batter with the blueberries. Mix the topping together and spread over the blueberries. Bake for 45 to 50 minutes in a 325° oven. Increase the oven temperature if you are not using a glass pan (to about 350°). Cut into squares and serve warm. This serves 8 to 10 depending upon the size piece cut.

Nan's Cinnamon Fluff

This is my grandmother's recipe for a coffee cake converted to be free of gluten and milk of course. The recipe was originally published in The Cosgrove Family Cookbook, a collection of recipes collected by Mary Cosgrove, my Dad's first cousin.

Preheat oven to 350°

   1 cup sugar
   2 ½ cups gf flour (1 cup garfava; 1 cup brown rice; ½ cup tapioca)
   3 teaspoons baking powder
   1 ½ teaspoon xanthan gum
   1 cup non-dairy milk
   3 tablespoons lard or non-dairy margarine substitute
   ¼ cup brown sugar
   1 teaspoon cinnamon

   Topping:
   1 teaspoons cinnamon
   1 additional tablespoon non-dairy margarine
   ¼ cup additional brown sugar

Grease and flour an 8" or 9" square baking pan. Mix the flour, baking powder, xanthan gum, cinnamon and brown sugar in a small mixing bowl and set aside. In a medium mixing bowl combine the 1 cup sugar, and the non-dairy margarine substitute, cutting the sugar and margarine together. Add the non-dairy milk. Add the dry ingredients to the liquid ingredients and gently mix to incorporate. Do not overmix. Place batter in prepared baking pan. Mix the topping ingredients together and sprinkle over the top of the coffee cake batter. Bake at 350° for about 30 to 35 minutes or so.

Garfava & Tapioca Pancakes

1 cup garfava flour
1 cup tapioca flour
1 teaspoon salt
1 ½ teaspoons xanthan gum
2 tablespoons Egg Replacer™

2 cups water
¼ cup olive oil or other acceptable oil
¼ cup cane sugar syrup or honey

2 teaspoons baking powder

Combine all dry ingredients together *except* baking powder. Add liquid ingredients and mix well. Add the baking powder and stir. Drop batter into a large, oiled skillet and cook on medium to medium-high heat until lightly brown. Turn pancakes over and brown on the other side. This batter yields "puffy" pancakes, so spread the batter out thinly to ensure that they cook all the way through by the time they are browned.

Chocolate Chip Pancakes
Use the above pancake recipe and add either chocolate chips or carob chips to the batter.

Blueberry Pancakes
Use the above pancake recipe and add blueberries to the batter. Dry blueberries off before adding them to the batter or the water will make the batter too runny. If that happens, just add a bit more flour to thicken it up.

Luscious Lemon Poppy Seed Muffins

This recipe was oh, so hard to perfect! I tried converting recipes and no matter what I did, they were just unacceptable to us. After many failed attempts, we were finally successful! This is another recipe that works well if you want to take food to a party that will be popular.

Preheat oven to 350°.

   1½ cups rice flour
   1½ cups tapioca flour
   2 teaspoons xanthan gum
   1½ cups sugar
   1½ tablespoons baking powder
   ¼ teaspoon salt
   1½ tablespoons poppy seeds
   1 tablespoon lemon peel (optional)
   1 stick unsalted margarine (or acceptable margarine
       substitute) room temperature

   ½ cup water mixed with
   4 teaspoons Egg Replacer™ (or 2 eggs if you can use them)
   1 tablespoon lemon extract
   1½ to 1¾ cups non-dairy milk substitute or club soda or
       water

Mix dry ingredients in a large mixing bowl. Cut margarine or margarine substitute into the dry ingredients. Add liquid ingredients and mix well. Bake for 20 to 24 minutes for mini-muffins and about 25 to 30 minutes for regular sized muffins or until done. We have used this primarily for mini-muffins, which I highly recommend. It makes 48 mini-muffins and 2 small mini-loaves. It would make approximately 24 regular sized muffins with some extra batter. The batter should be nice and creamy-not too stiff, and not too runny. The muffins freeze well.

Pumpkin Chocolate Chip Muffins

These are a delightful treat for parties! I have taken these muffins to many gatherings and they are devoured by both children and adults. They are sweet enough to be a dessert, but they can also be used for breakfast! It is one way to get pumpkin into your children. Mini-muffin tins work very well for this recipe.

Preheat oven to 350°.
In a large bowl combine:
> ½ **cup garfava flour**
> 1 **cup tapioca flour**
> ¾ **cup sugar**
> 2 **teaspoons ground cinnamon**
> **Dash of ground cloves**
> **Dash of ground ginger**
> ½ **teaspoon baking soda**
> 1 **tablespoon baking powder**
> 1½ **teaspoons xanthan gum**
> 4 **teaspoons Egg Replacer™ (or 2 eggs)**

In a separate bowl, combine:
> ¾ **cup acceptable mini-chocolate chips**
> **One 15 ounce can of pumpkin**
> 1 **stick acceptable margarine (½ cup), melted OR ½ cup oil**
> **NOTE: Additional water as needed see instructions**

Use either greased muffin tins or paper baking cups. Note: several years ago, in my opinion, the canned pumpkin seemed to increase the water content to the pumpkin, which caused this recipe result to change. To compensate I have removed water from this recipe and listed additional water as needed. This is a thick batter. Pour liquid ingredients over dry ingredients and mix until just moistened. Fill muffin tins 2/3 full. Bake for 20 to 25 minutes for regular size muffins or 12 to 16 minutes for mini muffins---until puffed and springy to touch in the center. Makes 12 regular or 48 mini muffins. These muffins freeze well.

Half-Grain Bagels

The reason that I have coined the term "half-grain" here is because while both the amaranth and quinoa flours are whole grain, the tapioca flour would not qualify as a whole grain. I have used the tapioca flour to cut the taste of the amaranth and quinoa to make them more appealing for children. If you use a whole grain flour in place of the tapioca, you will have whole grain bagels.

Preheat oven to 375°.

    1 cup amaranth flour
    1 cup quinoa flour
    1½ cups tapioca flour
    ½ teaspoon salt
    ½ cup sugar
    3 teaspoons Egg Replacer™ dry powder
    1½ teaspoons gelatin
    3 teaspoons xanthan gum
    ⅓ cup oil
    ¾ cup water, more only if needed

    1 package active dry yeast
    ½ cup warm water
    1 teaspoon sugar

Grease a baking sheet. In a mixing bowl, combine flours, salt, sugar, dry powdered Egg Replacer™, gelatin, and xanthan gum. If you are not familiar with proofing yeast, please read about proofing yeast in the Technical Know-How Section as it is important to proof the yeast the correct way. In a separate measuring cup, mix yeast with warm water and 1 teaspoon sugar. When the yeast has been proofed, add the yeast mixture, oil, and some of the water to the flour mixture. Mix well. You may need to add more water, however add it carefully. The dough for the bagels should not be too soft. The dough should be very, very firm and thick. If you add too much water by mistake, simply add more flour. If the dough is too soft, the bagels will fall apart.

Greasing your hands with oil, form the dough into balls. Poke a hole in the ball to form a bagel. Place on a greased baking sheet. This recipe makes about 8 to 9 small to medium sized bagels or 5 to 6 large sized bagels. Cover the bagels with a greased sheet of waxed paper and place in a warm spot to rise for 30 minutes if you are using rapid rise yeast, and 60 minutes for regular yeast. Make sure the bagels are in a warm spot, but not one that is too hot. After the bagels have had time to rise, place them 3 or 4 at a time in a pot of boiling water to which 1 to 2 teaspoons of sugar has been added. Boil for only 1 minute, turning the bagels at 30 seconds. Drain on paper towels. Then bake on a greased baking sheet for 20 minutes or until done.

Blueberry Half-Grain Bagels
Use the recipe above, but delete the ¾ cup of water and add 1 to 2½ cups of blueberries according to taste. Do not add any water until after you add the blueberries. If they are drained well, you can add water, a few tablespoons at a time until the dough is firm and thick. If you use store-bought, frozen blueberries, and they are not drained, you may not need to add any water. The dough for these bagels should not be too soft or moist – it should be very firm and thick. If you add too much water by mistake, simply add more flour. If the dough is too soft, the bagels will fall apart. In addition, you may choose to add another 2 to 4 tablespoons of sugar. These blueberry bagels are simply delightful!

Cinnamon Raisin Half-Grain Bagels
Use the above recipe and add 2 teaspoons of ground cinnamon and ½ to ¾ cup raisins depending upon how much you like raisins. You may add an extra tablespoon or two of sugar if you like.

Everything Half-Grain Bagels
Use the above recipe except cut the sugar to 2 tablespoons. Add ingredients that you can tolerate. We add sesame seeds, sunflower seeds, dried minced onion, a clove or two of pressed garlic, and poppy seeds to the batter. Once you form the bagels, cover the outside of the bagel in a mixture of the same ingredients that you added to the batter pressing the mixture into the dough.

Rice & Millet Rolls, Danish & Waffles

Preheat oven to 350°.

   1¼ cup rice flour
   1 cup tapioca flour
   ¾ cup millet flour
   3 teaspoons xanthan gum
   4 teaspoons baking powder
   1 teaspoon salt
   4 heaping teaspoons Egg Replacer™ (OR 2 eggs if you can
      tolerate eggs)
   ⅔ cup oil
   1 cup rice milk or other milk substitute of any type
   1+ cup sparkling water or club soda until the *batter is creamy*

Mix dry ingredients in a bowl. Add liquid ingredients and mix well. Batter will be light and kind of fluffy. If necessary, add more club soda or water. You may use other gluten-free flours than the three listed.

To make rolls

Grease muffin tins. This will make about 18 rolls (+/-) depending upon how full you fill the muffin tins. Take the batter you have mixed up and put it into a plastic ziplock bag. Cut off one corner of the bag (about ½" or less of an opening). Pipe the batter into the muffin tins filling about ½ or ⅔ for smaller rolls, and more for larger rolls. Bake about 18 to 24 minutes or until lightly golden but not too brown. These will freeze well, and are good on day two as well. You can use English muffin rings or hamburger bun pans to make larger rolls. Smooth out the tops of the rolls with either a spatula or wet fingers.

To make Danish

Take the batter and place into a ziplock bag with a corner cut off. Pipe the batter onto a greased cookie sheet. Pipe the batter into circles; start in the center and wind around the center circle until you have made the desired size circle. This will make about 18 or more medium size Danish. Make a small indentation in the center and fill with about ¼ teaspoon of your favorite jam or jelly. Bake 18 or so minutes until the bottom starts to just turn light golden color. Let cool, then drizzle with a confectioners' glaze (see page 299). These freeze well and are delicious.

To make Waffles

Use a greased and preheated waffle iron. The waffles will be done when they start to brown just slightly. Do not overcook or the waffles will burn. These waffles freeze well and make a fast breakfast or snack.

Donut Store Coffee Rolls

Preheat oven to 350°

- 1½ cups garfava flour (or chickpea)
- 1½ cups tapioca flour
- 3 teaspoons xanthan gum
- 3 teaspoons baking powder
- ½ cup sugar
- 2 teaspoons ground cinnamon
- ½ teaspoon salt
- 4 teaspoons Egg Replacer™ dry powder
- ⅔ cup oil
- 1 cup milk substitute of any type
- 1+ cup sparkling water or club soda until the *batter is creamy*

Additional sugar and ground cinnamon as needed for topping and centers

Grease the pan you will be using. If you want large coffee rolls like those sold at the various donut stores, use either a very large muffin tin or what we use is a hamburger roll pan. Mix dry ingredients in a bowl. Add liquid ingredients and mix well. Batter will be light and kind of fluffy. If necessary, add more club soda or water.

Place a quantity of batter into a plastic food storage bag and cut off one corner on the diagonal (about ½ inch size). Place a small amount of batter in the center of the pan. Then sprinkle the center batter with both the ground cinnamon and sugar. This center mound of batter will constitute the center of the coffee roll. Once you have generously covered the center batter mound, pipe more batter into the pan swirling it around the center mound of batter. Here is where you get the coffee roll shape. If you omit adding ground cinnamon and sugar or some other spice over the mound, the swirl effect will be lost as the batter will blend together.

Top the batter with additional ground cinnamon and sugar. Baking time will be determined by the size of the pan that you use. For standard muffin tin size, bake coffee rolls for about 20 minutes. Bake larger muffin tins or hamburger roll pans for 24 or so minutes, checking for color. These freeze well, and are delightful grilled. You can also drizzle some confectioners' icing or glaze on these to make them extra sweet!

Banana Muffins

Preheat oven to 350°.

    1½ cups corn flour or other acceptable flour
    1½ cups cornstarch or other acceptable flour
    2 teaspoons xanthan gum
    ¾ cup sugar
    1 tablespoon baking powder
    ¼ teaspoon salt
    4 teaspoons dry Egg Replacer™ powder
    2 to 2½ cups mashed bananas
    ¾ cup oil of your choice
    1½ teaspoons ground cinnamon
    Dash of ground cloves

    Additional liquid to make a nice creamy batter: about ⅔ cup of water only as needed

Mix dry ingredients. Add liquid ingredients. Place into either greased muffin tins or muffin tins with baking papers. These muffins are delightful and freeze well. This recipe makes about 24 muffins with sometimes a little batter to spare which we put in an individual loaf pan. If you do not use enough liquid, you will get dense muffins. Too much liquid will not produce the best muffins either. You want a nice creamy batter that is neither too stiff nor too runny. Bake muffins in a 350° oven for 15 to 18 minutes.

Best Ever Blueberry Muffins

Preheat oven to 350°.

1¾ cups rice flour (or other gluten-free flour)
1½ cups tapioca flour (or other gluten-free flour)
1½ teaspoons xanthan gum
1 teaspoon salt
2 tablespoons baking powder
½ cup oil
½ cup mashed pear or applesauce
1 to 2 cups blueberries, either fresh or frozen
1¾ cups water (PLUS OR MINUS)
½ cup sugar
Sugar for topping

Mix dry ingredients well. Add liquid ingredients and place batter into greased mini-muffins tins or regular muffin tins. The batter consistency will be on the thick side. Sprinkle tops with sugar before baking. Bake for 15 to 18 minutes or until done. Makes 18-24 regular sized muffins or about 48 mini-muffins.

Chocolate Chocolate Chip Muffins

These delightful muffins are good enough to serve as dessert!
Children and adults just eat them right up.

Preheat oven to 350°.

2 cups gluten-free flour (your choice or use a blend)
2 teaspoons xanthan gum
1½ tablespoons baking powder
½ cup cocoa powder
¼ teaspoon salt
1 cup sugar
¾ cup oil
6 tablespoons hot water mixed with
4 teaspoons Egg Replacer™
1 to 1¼ cup rice milk or other liquid, more only if needed
½ to ⅔ cups acceptable chocolate chips

Mix dry ingredients well. Add liquid ingredients and chocolate chips. Mix well. Spoon batter into greased mini or regular sized muffin tins. Bake at 350° for 15 to 20 minutes or until done for mini-muffins. Bake regular sized muffins for 25-28 minutes or until done. These freeze well.

Flax Sorghum Sweet Potato Waffles

Preheat waffle iron

½ cup flax meal
1½ cups sorghum flour (or other flour)
1 cup corn flour or other flour
1 cup maple syrup
1 tablespoon baking powder
3 teaspoons xanthan gum
3 teaspoons Egg Replacer™
Dash of ground cloves
One 15 ounce can sweet potato purée
¾ cup oil
¼ cup water (more if necessary)

Combine dry ingredients. Then add wet ingredients, adding more water only if necessary. These were invented once our rotation diet become more solid and we changed from using cane sugar every day to the four different sweeteners that we now use. This batter will be very thick. If the batter is too runny, the waffles will come apart. If you use a different sweetener, you will need to adjust the liquid (i.e. add more water or reduce the water). Place the batter in a plastic bag with the corner cut on a diagonal. Squeeze the batter onto a greased and pre-heated waffle iron. Cook until lightly browned. Remove gently. Makes approximately 10 to 12 waffles.

Rice & Millet Pancakes

1½ cups rice flour
½ cup millet flour
1 teaspoon salt
1 ½ teaspoons xanthan gum
2 tablespoons Egg Replacer™

2 cups water
¼ cup safflower oil or other acceptable oil
¼ cup rice syrup or honey

2 teaspoons baking powder

Combine all dry ingredients together *except* baking powder. Add liquid ingredients and mix well. Add the baking powder and stir. Drop batter into a large, oiled skillet and cook on medium to medium-high heat until lightly brown. Turn pancakes over and brown on the other side.

Chocolate Chip Pancakes
Use the above pancake recipe and add either chocolate chips or carob chips to the batter.

Blueberry Pancakes
Use the above pancake recipe and add blueberries to the batter. Dry blueberries off before adding them to the batter or the water will make the batter too runny. If that happens, just add a bit more flour to thicken it up.

Half Grain Chocolate Chip Waffles

The reason that I have coined the term "half-grain" here is because while both the amaranth and quinoa flours are whole grain, the tapioca flour would not qualify as a whole grain. I have used the tapioca flour to cut the taste of the amaranth and quinoa to make them more appealing for children. If you use a whole grain flour in place of the tapioca, you will have whole grain waffles.

Preheat waffle iron
   1½ cups quinoa flour
   1 cup amaranth flour
   ½ cup tapioca flour
   1 cup sugar or other sweetener*
   1 tablespoon baking powder
   3 teaspoons xanthan gum
   3 teaspoons Egg Replacer™
   3 teaspoons ground cinnamon
   Dash of ground clove

   One 15 ounce can pumpkin or squash purée (OR 2 cups fresh squash or pumpkin, that has been baked)

   ¾ cup oil
   1 to 1¼ cup water
   ½ to ¾ cup acceptable chocolate chips

Mix dry ingredients together. Add oil and some of the water and the squash or pumpkin. You do not want this batter to be too runny. In other words, the batter should not run or drip off of your mixing spoon. Put batter into a plastic food storage bag with the corner cut diagonally and pipe onto a greased and hot waffle iron. Follow waffle iron instructions. Remove carefully as these waffles are slightly more delicate. It is most important not to add too much liquid to the batter. The water added to this recipe will also vary by how much water content is in your pumpkin or squash purée as some cooked pumpkin/squash has more water content than others. Makes 10 to 12 waffles depending on the waffle iron and batter

* Note: We use beet sugar. If using a liquid sweetener, reduce the amount of water.

Half Grain Chocolate Chip Muffins

Use the Half-Grain Chocolate Chip Waffle recipe except you will use less water for the muffins. Use ¾ cup to 1 cup water for muffins. Place muffins in a greased or paper lined muffin tin and bake at 350° for 20 or so minutes for mini-muffins or 25 to 30 minutes for regular sized muffins.

Restaurant Style Croutons

It's easy to make gluten-free, dairy-free, allergen-free croutons and they are such a nice addition to salads and some soups. These croutons can be made for any rotation day. Just use the bread or rolls from a given day. For example to have croutons for Day 1, use the rolls made with garfava and tapioca flours. To have croutons for Day 2, use rolls made from rice and millet flours.

Preheat oven to 425°.

4 cups bread cubes
¼ teaspoon onion powder
¼ teaspoon garlic powder
¼ teaspoon paprika
½ teaspoon sweet basil
½ teaspoon salt
To taste: Black pepper (go easy on this)
1 tablespoon acceptable oil

You can use any bread for this. If you are using up dried or stale bread, you will need to alter the baking time as this recipe is for freshly made bread or rolls cut into cubes. Place bread cubes in a 9" x 13" baking pan and sprinkle dry spices over the bread cubes. Drizzle 1 tablespoon of oil over bread cubes and bake in a 425° oven for 10 minutes. Remove from oven and stir. Return to oven and bake until completely toasted which will be about 20 minutes or so for fresh bread cubes. If you are watching your weight you can omit the oil. If your spices do not adhere to the bread without oil, you can lightly spray the bread cubes with a spritz of water which will help the spices adhere to the bread cubes. This may lengthen the baking time just a bit. If you have a love of other spices, you can use whatever you like. This is a general crouton recipe that we love.

Sweet Potato Chocolate Chip Muffins or Waffles

Preheat oven to 350°.

    1 cup millet or rice flour or other gluten-free flour
    1½ cups tapioca flour or other gluten-free flour
    1 cup white sugar
    1 tablespoon baking powder
    1¼ teaspoon xanthan gum
    4 teaspoons Egg Replacer™
    One 15 ounce can sweet potato purée
    ¾ cup safflower oil (or other acceptable oil)
    1 teaspoon ground cinnamon
    Dash of ground cloves
    1 to 1¼ cup water (enough to make a smooth batter)
    ½ to ¾ cup acceptable chocolate chips

Mix all dry ingredients in a large bowl and set aside. Mash the canned sweet potatoes well with a fork in a large bowl. Add oil and water and combine. Add liquid ingredients to the dry ingredients and mix to incorporate, but do not over mix. (If you can have eggs, then use 2 large eggs in place of ⅔ cups warm water and the Egg Replacer™.)

To Make Muffins:
Spoon the muffin batter into greased muffin tins. Mini muffin tins work very well with this recipe. Bake at 350° for 16 to 20 minutes for mini-muffins and 25 to 30 minutes for regular sized muffins. These freeze well.

To Make Waffles:
Place the batter in a plastic food storage bag with the corner cut off on a diagonal. Squeeze the batter onto a greased and pre-heated waffle iron. Cook until lightly browned. Remove gently. Makes about 10 waffles.

Sorghum Rolls

This is a recipe that we used for when they were on a very restricted diet after getting an allergy treatment.

Preheat oven to 375°.

2 cups sorghum flour
1 cup corn flour
1 tablespoon baking powder
3 teaspoons xanthan gum
3 teaspoons Egg Replacer™
½ teaspoon garlic salt
1 teaspoon onion powder
One 12 ounce can club soda
⅔ cup oil
¼ +/- cup water

Mix dry ingredients. Add liquid ingredients and mix well. Grease muffin tins. This will make about 18 rolls (+/-) depending upon how full you fill the muffin tins. Take the batter you have mixed up and put it into a plastic ziplock bag. Cut off one corner of the bag (about ½" or less of an opening). Pipe the batter into the muffin tins filling about ½ or ⅔ for smaller rolls, and more for larger rolls. Smooth out the tops of the rolls with either a spatula or wet fingers. Bake about 18 to 24 minutes or until lightly golden but not too brown. The baking time for the rolls depends upon the size of the rolls and the accuracy of your oven temperature. You can use English muffin rings or hamburger bun pans to make larger rolls. These will freeze well.

Hamburger & Hot Dog Rolls

To make these rolls, you can purchase special hamburger and hot dog roll pans. If you are going to be doing much baking, I highly recommend these pans. To make hamburger or hot dog rolls you simply select any of the roll recipes listed in this cookbook and pipe the batter into a greased pan. I recommend that you smooth the tops of the rolls with a spatula or a wet finger to give a more polished look. They will also be easier to slice if smoothed. If you do not have the hamburger or hot dog pans you can still make rolls in this shape. Simply pipe the batter of your choice onto a greased baking sheet and then smooth the top of the roll. Either method will work and produce a beautiful roll, however having the hot dog and hamburger bun pans will save you a lot of time. Most of the roll recipes in this cookbook will make about 8 to 10 hot dog rolls or 6 to 9 hamburger rolls which is completely driven by the size of the roll that you make.

Cloverleaf Specialty Rolls

To make the special cloverleaf rolls simply pipe 3 balls of batter into a greased regular size muffin cup or tray. The size of the balls should be somewhat uniform and will be about the size of a large marble. When the rolls bake, the three balls of batter will come together and form one nice roll. This is the way to make old-fashioned Cloverleaf dinner rolls. Any of the roll recipes in this cookbook will work great for cloverleaf rolls, and they will freeze very well in a tightly sealed ziplock bag or other sealed container. Most of the roll recipes in this cookbook will make approximately 22 to 24 cloverleaf rolls if you use the standard size muffin tin.

Savory Onion & Garlic Rolls

Use any of the roll or bread recipes in this cookbook and add ½ teaspoon onion powder, ½ teaspoon garlic powder, and 1 to 2 tablespoons minced, dried onion to the batter. If you wish you can use fresh garlic put through a garlic press. Other herbs can be added as your tastes dictate. We've used dried rosemary, oregano, basil and thyme.

MAIN DISH MEALS

Stromboli

During college I worked at the Deli and Hi-way Pizza at Penn State, which was famous for their pizza, Stromboli and Calzones. This recipe is basically almost the same as the Pepperoni Bread recipe except that it has more filling and sauce on the side.

Preheat Oven to 375°
   1 batch garfava or other roll dough
   1 medium onion, sliced
   2 teaspoons acceptable oil
   ¼ teaspoon dried basil
   ¼ teaspoon dried oregano
   1-1/2 cups grated non-dairy cheese
   1-1/2 cups sliced acceptable lunchmeat, pepperoni or other cooked meat
   1 cup of spaghetti sauce or tomato sauce flavored with herbs

Sautee onions in the oil in a frying pan over medium heat until soft and lightly browned. Spread ½ of roll dough in an oblong shape on a greased baking sheet. Top with 2-3 tablespoons of sauce, non-dairy cheese, meat, and herbs. Take remaining dough and cover the oblong shape – using a spatula to spread the dough to cover. Seal edges well with spatula or fork. Bake in a 375° oven for 25 minutes or until done. Makes one very large Stromboli or you can make smaller, individual Stromboli. Serve with sauce either on the side or with a spoonful of sauce poured over the Stromboli.

Pulled Pork

This is a relatively easy dish to make and very tasty!

Preheat oven to 300°
- **4 pounds pork roast**
- **2 teaspoons garlic powder**
- **1 teaspoon dry mustard**
- **1 teaspoon paprika**
- **2 teaspoons brown sugar**
- **1 teaspoon coarse salt**
- **2 batches of Pulled Pork Sauce (in the Sauces section)**

Preheat the oven to 300°. Mix the dry spices, salt, and sugar and rub into the meat. Roast the pork at 300° or until the internal temperature reaches at least 170° and the meat is easily separated or falling apart. If the internal temperature is reached but the meat is not yet falling apart, then lower the oven temperature to 250° and continue cooking. Total cooking time for a 4 pound roast is approximately 4 hours (2 hours at 300° and 2 hours at 250°). Either cut or pull the meat off the bone in small pieces, removing and discarding any fat. A 4-pound roast equals roughly 5 to 6 cups of pulled pork meat. You will need two batches of pulled pork sauce from this cookbook to cover this meat or about 4 cups of sauce. This recipe yields about 8 to 9 cups of Pulled Pork.

Buffalo Bites

They are quite tasty served plain and would make an excellent appetizer. Of course, you could use beef for this dish!

1 pound Buffalo ground meat (or beef or venison)
1 teaspoon paprika
1 teaspoon salt
1 teaspoon parsley
¼ teaspoon ground pepper
1 tablespoon acceptable oil
3 tablespoons acceptable bread crumbs (or roll or bread pieces, crumbled)
2 tablespoons nondairy milk substitute

In a large mixing bowl, combine meat and spices, and bread crumbs (or crumbled bread or roll pieces) and then add nondairy milk. Mix well. Shape into very small mini-meatballs and sauté in oil over medium-low heat until cooked through. This recipe makes about 35 mini-meatballs. You can make larger meatballs, however they will take longer to cook through to the center.

Better Beef & Broccoli

I tried Beef and Broccoli from several Chinese restaurants and then decided that my own version was just as good. My family agreed, and the best part was that we knew it was safe for my daughter!

1 to 1-1/2 pound of beef sliced thinly (flank steak or regular steak cut with a fillet knife)
1 Tablespoon of acceptable oil
1 red pepper chopped
2 ounces dried mushrooms (hydrated with water) or canned (drained)
3- 4 cups fresh or frozen broccoli
1-1/2 cups chopped carrots
½ onion, diced
1 clove garlic, minced
1 can of water chestnuts, drained

Sauce:
2 Tablespoons of acceptable thickener (cornstarch, tapioca, etc.)
¼ cup Bragg Liquid Amino or Soy Sauce
1 cup orange juice
1 cup broth
1 teaspoon dried ginger
2 cloves garlic, minced
1 Tablespoon vinegar or cooking sherry
1/3 cup sugar or acceptable sweetener

Tenderize your beef pieces by soaking them in 1 cup of pure water with 2 teaspoons of baking soda allowing to sit for 15 minutes. Then rinse the meat well and set aside. This process will make your meat significantly more tender. Combine sauce ingredients in a medium saucepan and cook over medium heat until thickened, then set aside. In a very large frying pan, fry the beef and onions until cooked through. Add red pepper, mushrooms, broccoli, carrots and water chestnuts and stir-fry until hot all the way through. Add garlic and quickly stir so as not to burn the garlic. Add sauce and let simmer for 2 minutes. Serve over rice. Makes 8 to 9 cups, which for us is about 5 servings.

Sweet Boy Meatloaf

This recipe will convert even the most stubborn meatloaf haters! It is delicious and unusual. I removed the milk, eggs and gluten from his old recipe and substituted with ingredients that are safe. My children ate this up and asked for seconds!

2 pounds ground beef
2 gluten-free rolls or slices of bread, torn into pieces
4 tablespoons brown sugar, packed
3 teaspoons Dijon mustard
½ cup ketchup
½ teaspoon salt or to taste
pepper to taste
½ teaspoon paprika
½ teaspoon cinnamon
½ teaspoon celery seed
pinch of ground ginger
pinch of ground cloves

Mix all ingredients together in a large mixing bowl. This will make either two standard loaf size pans or one large loaf with some possibly extra. Bake at 350 degrees for 1 hour to 1 hour and 15 minutes or until it measures done with a meat thermometer.

Wild West Chili

This recipe came about as a result of my quest to have less meat and more vegetables in our meals. We love chili, so this was a natural for us. We add the vegetables last and don't overcook them so the chili actually has a crunch to it and some added nutrition. If you like your chili hot, you'll have to kick it up a bit.

> 1 pound ground beef, buffalo or other meat
> 1 large onion, chopped
> 1-1/4 cups carrots, chopped
> 1-1/4 cups red pepper
> 1 cup chopped celery
> 2-1/2 cups cooked kidney beans (or 1- 25 ounce can, rinsed and drained)
> 2 cups tomato sauce
> 12 ounces of chili sauce
> 4 ounces of pure water
> 1-1/2 tablespoons of paprika
> 1-1/2 tablespoons of chili powder
> 1 Tablespoon sugar
> 1 large clove of garlic, minced
> 1 teaspoon of cinnamon
> dash of cloves
> Optional: 2 cups of corn (or 1- 15 ounce can of corn), additional tomato sauce

Combine beef and onion and cook over medium heat with a bit of water until the meat is fully cooked. You can cook the meat in oil, but I used water for this recipe. It lowers the fat and calories. Add kidney beans, tomato sauce, chili sauce and spices. Use the 4 ounces of water to rinse the chili sauce bottle and tomato sauce can. Cook for 20-25 minutes over medium-low heat. Then add the carrots, celery and red pepper. This makes about 11 cups of chili.

Chili On The Go-Go

This is a FAST and EASY vegetarian chili recipe that could easily be converted to be a hearty meat chili by throwing in some ground meat, poultry or turkey. I have used canned beans here for speed, however if you have more time you can soak and cook dried beans. The great thing about this vegetarian chili is that you can use any vegetables that you like or that you have on hand. The beans are interchangeable for any beans that you have on hand also! You can eat this plain in a bowl, or over rice or your favorite gluten-free grain.

1 Tablespoon oil
1 large onion, sliced
1 red pepper, cut into bite-sized chunks
4 medium carrots, peeled and sliced into bite-sized chunks
1 15-ounce can black beans, rinsed and drained
1 15-ounce can pinto beans, rinsed and drained
1 15-ounce tomato sauce
1 15-ounce diced tomatoes
1/4 teaspoon dried basil
1 Tablespoon chili powder
Dash of cinnamon
1 Tablespoons of sugar, stevia or other sweetener
Dash cayenne pepper
Salt to taste
Optional: Any other vegetables that you like or want to use up!

Sauté the onion slices in the oil over medium high heat until soft and caramelized. Add the red peppers, carrots and any other vegetables you are using. Sauté for 10 minutes over medium heat. Add the beans that have been rinsed well and drained, the tomato sauce and diced tomatoes and the spices. Cook over medium low heat for 20 minutes. This recipe as listed above will make 6-7 cups. We liked this so well that when I made it again - I doubled the recipe!

Willy's Chili

I made major modifications to our Wild West Chili so it could be eaten by a dear friend on a very restrictive diet due to surgery. Out came any celery, beans and sugar and in went whole peeled tomatoes. If I was making this for myself, I would add 2 more cups of a raw vegetable and a few more spices.

2 pounds ground beef or other meat
1 tablespoon oil
1 medium onion, chopped
2 cloves garlic, minced
28 ounce can whole peeled tomatoes, crushed in your hand
30 ounces tomato sauce
2 cups diced carrots
1 chopped red pepper
½ teaspoon cinnamon
1-1/2 tablespoon chili powder
1-1/2 tablespoon paprika

In a large frying pan brown the beef or meat and onions until well cooked. Drain off any excess fat. Add garlic, whole tomatoes (crushed in your hand), tomato sauce, red pepper and spices. Simmer for 30 minutes on medium-low to low heat making sure not to burn. Add the raw carrots at the end to give it some crunch. This will freeze well.

Luke's Beef Stroganoff

This was a recipe that my son, Luke, invented at age 14 without ever having had beef stroganoff. After I came up with the roux sauce recipe, he used the roux sauce with noodles adding beef and green beans. Pretty cool I think!

Roux Sauce (recipe in this cookbook)
1 16 ounce package frozen green beans
1 tablespoon acceptable oil
½ teaspoon garlic powder
½ teaspoon onion powder
½ teaspoon dried basil
½ teaspoon oregano
14 ounce acceptable pasta, cooked and drained
1 pound ground beef

Make 1 batch of roux sauce in a large frying pan and set aside. Cook green beans and set aside. Boil pasta according to package directions, drain and set aside. In a medium frying pan, brown the beef in the oil until well cooked, and then drain off any excess fat. Add the browned beef, green beans, pasta and herbs to the roux sauce and mix well. Heat until hot and bubbly. Makes 9 cups.

Taco Stir Fry

I made this on a wild whim as a way to stretch one pound of beef and at the same time increase the amount of vegetables we eat as a family. I was a bit apprehensive about whether it would go over. It was a declared hit with everyone except my one child who doesn't like lettuce, but who liked the topping.

1 pound ground beef, buffalo or other meat or poultry
1 tablespoon oil
1 cup chopped onion
2 cups beef or other broth
1 or more tablespoons of thickener (cornstarch, arrowroot, potato, etc.)
1 red pepper, chopped
1 tablespoon chili powder or to taste
1 tablespoon paprika or to taste
½ teaspoon Celtic salt
3 tomatoes, chopped
1 cup celery, chopped
6 cups romaine or iceberg lettuce
Crushed Tortilla chips – a few chips per serving
Optional: Non-dairy cheese or other vegetables

In a large frying pan, brown the meat and onions in the oil until the meat is completely cooked through. Add the broth, spices, salt, and thickener of your choice. Cook until the broth and spices have formed a sauce. Add red pepper, celery and reduce heat to very low. Arrange lettuce and tomatoes on individual serving places. Top lettuce and tomatoes with taco stir fry meat and vegetables. Place a few crushed tortilla chips over the top as well as any non-dairy cheese, if using. This makes about 5 servings.

Traditional Beef Stew

This is an easy recipe that I make in a slow cooker that both children and adults will love! To make it healthier you can add more vegetables than called for here. Vegetarians can skip the beef and either add tofu or more vegetables!

    1 cup beef broth or other broth
    1 cup water
    1 small onion, diced
    2 cups carrots, peeled and diced
    1-1/2 cup peas
    1 cup celery, diced
    2 large potatoes, diced
    1 pound beef, cut into small pieces
    1 clove garlic, minced
    Salt and Pepper to taste
    2-1/2 Tablespoons of your favorite thickener mixed with ½ cup water*
    1 teaspoon of dried Rosemary (or to taste)
    ½ teaspoon dried Thyme (or to taste)

This recipe may be thickened with any thickener that you normally use. You may also substitute all broth or all water for the broth and water combination listed above. Place broth and water in the bottom of a slow cooker or in a large casserole dish if baking in the oven. Add onions followed by the beef. Top the beef with the remaining vegetables. At the end of the cooking, add the thickener and cook for another 15-20 minutes. This recipe makes 6 to 7 cups.

Lightening Fast Lasagna Pie

This is a recipe that Bisquick® put out decades ago called "Impossible Lasagna Pie", which I converted to be gluten-free, dairy-free, and egg-free. Instead of using a store-bought gluten-free baking mix, you can use the Bargain Baking Mix featured in this cookbook, which will save you a good amount of money. My whole family instantly loved this fast and easy dish!

Preheat oven to 400°

- ¾ cup of the Herbed Bargain Baking Mix
- 1 cup non-dairy milk substitute
- 1 pound ground beef
- 1 tablespoon acceptable oil
- 1 cup very thick tomato sauce or some tomato paste with water added
- 1 small onion,
- 8 ounce package of acceptable non-dairy mozzarella cheese in shreds

Preheat oven to 400°. Grease a deep-dish pie plate and set aside. Brown the ground beef and onion in the acceptable oil in a large frying pan and set aside. Mix the non-dairy milk and baking mix in a medium-mixing bowl until well incorporated. Layer the ground beef, onion, tomato sauce and half of the non-dairy cheese in the pie plate. Pour the baking mix batter over the top of the ground beef mixture in the pie plate. Bake in a 400° oven for 35 to 40 minutes. Remove from the oven and top with remaining non-dairy cheese. Return to the oven and bake until the cheese is melted.

Easy Vegetable Lasagna Pie

I added vegetables to the Lighting Fast Lasagna Pie for extra nutritional value and removed the beef for a new dish, which was still a hit at our house.

Preheat oven to 400°

- **1-1/2 cups of the Herbed Bargain Baking Mix (recipe in this cookbook)**
- **1-3/4 cups nondairy milk substitute**
- **1 tablespoon acceptable oil**
- **1-2/3 cups of tomato sauce**
- **4 cups of chopped or sliced onion**
- **8 cups of thinly sliced zucchini**
- **1 cup chopped kale or spinach**
- **2 cups green beans**
- **2 cups chopped carrots**
- **12 ounces of acceptable nondairy mozzarella cheese shreds**

Preheat oven to 400°. Grease a 9"x13" pan and set aside. In a large frying pan, cook the onion and then add the zucchini and kale (or spinach) and cook for 10 minutes. Then add the carrots and green beans and cook for another 5 minutes. Mix the nondairy milk and baking mix in a medium mixing bowl until well incorporated. Layer the vegetables, tomato sauce and half of the nondairy cheese in the baking pan. Pour the baking mix batter over the top of the vegetable mixture. Bake in a 400° oven for 35 to 40 minutes. Remove from the oven and top with the remaining nondairy cheese. Return to the oven and bake until the cheese is melted. Serving size depends on how you cut it.

Gourmet Style Burgers

I invented this recipe to make burgers healthier after reading just a few chapters of "The China Study". My surprise was that my children loved them! This is definitely a way to stretch your budget and eat healthier!

1 pound beef, buffalo or other ground meat or poultry
½ small onion, chopped
1 cup carrots, finely chopped, diced or shredded
3 cups bean sprouts finely chopped = ¾ cup after chopping
    OR 1 to 1-1/2 cups greens chopped
1 clove garlic, minced
½ teaspoon Celtic salt or to taste
½ to 1 teaspoon dried Rosemary
½ cup gluten-free breadcrumbs or crushed cereal
Pepper to taste

Mix all ingredients in a large mixing bowl. Makes 6 – ¼ pound burgers. Cook as you would normally cook a burger.

Chicken Cordon Bleu

This is a classic dish that my children had never had before I made it from scratch. If you like Chicken Cordon bleu, I think you will like this rendition.

Preheat oven to 375°
> **1-1/2 pounds chicken breasts, pounded to ¼ inch thick**
> **½ pound thingly sliced ham**
> **About 1 cup nondairy mozzarella cheese shreds or sliced cheese, if available**

Coating Mix
> **1 cup acceptable cereal that is NOT sweet, crushed to about 1 ounce**
> **1 cup acceptable potato chips as measured before crushing, crushed to about ½ ounce**
> **½ teaspoon paprika**
> **1 teaspoon dried parsley flakes**

Coating Sauce
> **2 teaspoons Ener-G Egg Replacer**
> **¼ cup water**
> **½ teaspoon olive oil**
> **½ teaspoon honey**

Preheat oven to 375°. Pound chicken to ¼ inch thickness. Put a slice of ham on the flattened chicken pieces and then sprinkle cheese over the ham. Roll up and hold the shape with a long toothpick. Coat the rolled-up chicken and ham with the coating sauce and then roll in the coating mixture. Bake in a greased baking dish, uncovered, for 40-50 minutes or until the chicken reads done with a meat thermometer. We served this dish with a roux sauce (recipe in this cookbook), however many other types of sauces would work well. Serves six.

Kung Pao Chicken

This recipe was inspired by a visit to a Chinese restaurant. This is not especially spicy or hot, so if you like it hot make sure to add more spices and hot sauce. Serve this dish alone or over rice. Once you have the vegetables prepared, this is a quick stir-fry dish.

1 pound chicken, cut into small pieces
1 tablespoon acceptable oil or water
1 can water chestnuts, drained (8 ounces)
½ onion, chopped
1 tablespoon vinegar
2 tablespoons brown sugar or to taste
1 clove garlic, minced
2 teaspoons chili and garlic sauce (or other hot sauce)
3 tablespoons white wine
2 cups chicken broth or other broth
2 tablespoons of thickener of choice dissolved in ¼ cup water
1 cup julienned carrots
8 ounces of bamboo shoots
½ cup red pepper, chopped

Cook the chicken completely in a large frying pan in either a small amount of oil or a small amount of water (enough to keep the chicken from sticking). Remove the chicken and set aside. Add the onion and cook until soft (in the remaining oil or a bit of water) and then add the broth, vinegar, brown sugar, garlic, chili and garlic sauce (or hot sauce) and white wine. Stir quickly and combine all ingredients over medium heat. Add thickener of your choice and cook until desired thickness. Add chicken and vegetables and cook for 5-10 minutes. I like to make sure that the vegetables still have some crunch to them for an authentic taste. This makes about 6 cups. Serve plain or over rice or cauliflower rice.

Fast and Easy Dressing and Pork Chops

This was originally a chicken and dressing recipe that I converted. This recipe was a huge hit with everyone!

Preheat oven to 450°

10 ounces of gluten-free cereal (not a sweet cereal), crushed = about 3 cups

½ medium onion, finely chopped

2 cloves garlic, minced

5 teaspoons dried sage or to taste (2 teaspoons if using ground sage)

5 teaspoons dried thyme or to taste (2 teaspoons if using ground thyme)

1 cup water or broth

4 to 6 pork chops

Salt and Pepper to taste

Preheat oven to 450°. Lesson here on dried spices. There is a difference between ground and dried. Ground spices are more concentrated and therefore you need less to impart the flavor desired. Mix dry, crushed cereal, onion, garlic, sage, thyme and water or broth in a medium sized mixing bowl. This should be enough stuffing to stuff 4 to 6 pork chops. If you have extra stuffing, it can be baked in a separate baking dish or with the pork chops. Place pork chops in a 9" x 13" pan and stuff. I use tall toothpicks to hold the stuffed pork chops together. I add water to the bottom of the pan to provide moisture while cooking. Bake for 15 minutes at 450° to sear in the flavors, then reduce the oven temperature to 350° and bake until an oven thermometer reads done. When you reduce the oven temperature – then cover the pan with foil to keep in the moisture. Note: It is important to use a gluten-free, casein free cereal that is not sweet for this recipe.

Chicken and Dressing

This is a recipe from a friend that I modified to be free of allergens and gluten. I added some vegetables for a boost in nutrition.

Preheat oven to 350°

> **10 ounces of gluten-free cereal (not a sweet cereal), crushed = about 3 cups**
>
> **½ medium onion, finely chopped**
>
> **2 cloves garlic, minced**
>
> **5 teaspoons dried sage or to taste (2 teaspoons if using ground sage)**
>
> **5 teaspoons dried thyme or to taste (2 teaspoons if using ground thyme)**
>
> **1 cup water or broth**
>
> **3-4 Chicken breasts, cut into bite sized pieces**
>
> **1 recipe Roux sauce (from this cookbook) with ½ cup water added**
>
> **4-5 cups broccoli florets**
>
> **1 cup cauliflower florets**

Mix the gluten-free cereal, onion, herbs and water or broth together to form a stuffing and set aside. In a 9"x13" baking dish, layer the stuffing, broccoli and cauliflower. Add the chicken and cover with the roux sauce. Bake in a 350° for 1 hour or until chicken is fully cooked.

Breaded Chicken Fingers

This recipe is simple but good. A plain cereal or cracker will produce the best result.

**2-1/2 cups acceptable cereal or crackers, crushed into a fine
powder**
1 teaspoon dried parsley
1 teaspoon salt
½ teaspoon garlic powder
1 pound chicken cut into fingers, tenders or bite sized pieces

Mix dry ingredients in a medium sized mixing bowl. Dip chicken into a bowl of water and then into breading mix. Cook either by baking in a 350° oven or by frying. Cook until the chicken is completely done. This serves four (1/4 pound chicken pieces per person).

Sesame Chicken

Sesame Chicken is a popular dish at Chinese restaurants where we are never quite sure if there is MSG or peanut or tree nut contamination. Here is my version of a quick dish free of allergens. There are no leftovers with this dish in our family.

    1 to 1-1/2 pounds of chicken, cut into bite sized pieces
    2 Tablespoons or more of acceptable oil (we use sesame)
    Optional: cornstarch or gluten-free flour for coating the chicken
    Sesame Seeds for topping: about 2-3 Tablespoons

    Sauce:
    3 cups chicken broth
    ¼ cup Bragg Liquid Aminos or other soy type sauce
    2 tablespoons vinegar
    1/3 cup sugar
    2 tablespoons orange conserves, marmalade or jam
    3 tablespoons cornstarch or your favorite thickener mixed with 3 tablespoons of water
    Optional: 1 teaspoon garlic & chili sauce or dash of hot sauce

First of all note that this sauce recipe makes about three cups of sauce, which is double what you will need for the Sesame Chicken recipe. If you want extra, then use as is, if not, cut this sauce recipe in half. We love the sauce on vegetables and I make it and use it until it runs out. In a medium saucepan, combine all of the sauce ingredients and mix well. Stir over medium heat until the sauce reaches the desired thickness.

You can save calories and time by not coating your chicken with flour or cornstarch. The chicken will taste great either way. In a separate large frying pan, cook the chicken in the oil until cooked all the way through. Spoon enough sauce over chicken to cover or as desired and then top with sesame seeds. Serve chicken over rice or with rice and oriental vegetable stir-fry. Makes five servings.

Basil Chicken

I came up with this dish simply to get out of a rut with Chicken. This sauce can be used in other ways, but we use it with Chicken. It has a restaurant style gourmet flavor. It was a hit with two of my three children – it's more of an adult flavor.

1 to 1-1/2 pounds of chicken breasts
1-1/2 cups chicken broth
1 small onion, diced
2 cloves minced garlic
¼ cup cooking sherry
1 teaspoon of sugar
1-1/2 tablespoon of thickener (cornstarch or other favorite thickener)
Pinch of basil
Pinch of thyme
Salt to taste

Set aside ¼ cup of the broth. Place remaining broth, onion, garlic, sugar, basil and thyme in a medium sauce pan. Mix ¼ cup broth and thickener, and then add to the sauce pan. Heat over medium high heat until cooked through and thick. You may add more or less thickener to the sauce depending upon the consistency you prefer. Pound chicken breasts to be nice and thin. Cook either on the stove in oil or in the oven until cooked through. Cover in sauce. Serves 4 to 6 people.

Aunt Irene's Chicken & Broccoli Casserole

This recipe is from Aunt Irene Tubach, my mom's sister from Laporte, PA. I never converted it until I made the roux sauce that doubles as a creamy base without the dairy! It is a fast and easy dish to make.

Preheat oven to 350°
- 1 Roux Mixture (recipe in this cookbook)
- 2 cups of non-dairy milk – rice milk or other
- ½ teaspoon onion powder
- ½ teaspoon garlic powder
- ½ cup brown rice flour
- 1/3 cup plus 1 tablespoon non-dairy margarine or shortening
- 1 teaspoon Celtic salt

- 8 cups broccoli pieces, fresh or frozen
- 1 small onion, chopped finely
- 1 8-ounce package of non-dairy mozzarella cheese shreds (that melt)
- 2 chicken breasts cut into bite sized pieces or 2 cups leftover chicken
- 1 cup crushed potato chips for topping

To make the roux cook the margarine or shortening in a large frying pan until melted. Add flour gradually – stirring constantly as the flour and margarine or shortening makes a thick paste. Add the rice milk or other non-dairy milk 1/3 cup at a time stirring to make the mixture a creamy sauce each time before adding more rice milk. Add the onion powder, garlic powder, and salt after all the milk has been added and the mixture is creamy. The longer you cook this, the thicker it will become, so remove it from the heat after the last milk has been added and stirred in along with the spices. Grease a 9" x 13" baking pan. Line the pan with all of the broccoli, chicken and onion. Sprinkle the cheese over the broccoli and chicken. Then pour the roux mix over the broccoli and chicken. Top with crushed potato chips. Bake at 350° until the chicken is cooked through and the sauce is bubbly – about 1 hour.

Chicken Marsala

I almost called this Mock Chicken Marsala because when I made this I was aiming for Chicken Marsala, however I did not have any Marsala wine, so I made do. If you have Marsala wine, you can delete the sugar I added to compensate. This is really an adult dish. Some children will eat it and some will not. My children said they like it.

1 pound chicken breast, pounded flat
2 cups chicken broth
¼ cup finely chopped onion
½ cup Marsala wine (or ½ cup Merlot with 2-1/2 tablespoons
      sugar added)
¼ cup cooking Sherry
½ cup mushrooms (I don't use these due to allergies)

Flatten chicken breasts with a metal cooking hammer until they are nice and flat as well as thin. Cook chicken breasts in a large frying pan in the chicken broth until cooked through. Add the onion, Marsala wine, cooking sherry and mushrooms and cook over low heat until the sauce cooks down and thickens. If you are in a hurry, you can add a bit of thickener to speed things up. This makes 4 or 5 servings depending on the size of your portions.

Party Chicken and Pasta

This is a fast and easy recipe that I came up with one night when speed was of the essence. It uses the party sauce recipe that also works well with any meat or vegetables. It is a flexible recipe because you can use any type of pasta and you can use whatever vegetables you have on hand instead of the broccoli. It is easily a vegan recipe by omitting the chicken.

    1 pound chicken cut into small pieces
    1 tablespoon of acceptable oil
    10 ounces fresh or frozen broccoli
    1 medium onion, diced
    14 ounces canned or fresh cranberry sauce (whole berry or jellied)
    12 ounces of chili sauce
    8-12 ounces of cooked gluten-free pasta, drained

While the gluten-free pasta is cooking, brown chicken and onion in the oil until the chicken is completely cooked through and set aside. Combine the chili sauce and cranberry sauce in a large saucepan or stockpot and heat over medium heat until hot and bubbly. Add the broccoli and cook until the broccoli is cooked to your taste. Add the chicken and onion mixture. Add the pasta and mix well. This recipe makes 8 cups or 4 – 2 cup servings.

Tuscan Vegetable Lasagna

I invented this recipe to make a non-dairy lasagna that did not use soy. The first time I made it, we had not discovered the non-dairy cheese shreds that melt and thus I made it with just the beans listed herein. After I found the non-dairy cheese that melts – I added that, which made this recipe so much tastier!

Preheat oven to 350°
- 10 ounce package of gf lasagna noodles, cooked and drained
- 1 medium onion, minced
- 1 large carrot, shredded
- 4 cups cooked white beans or 4 – 15 ounce cans of white beans (rinsed and drained)
- 4 cups of bite-sized pieces of broccoli and cauliflower or other vegetables
- 12 ounces of tomato paste constituted to make 4 cups of tomato sauce
- 1 teaspoon garlic powder
- 1 teaspoon onion powder
- 1 teaspoon basil
- 1 teaspoon oregano
- 2 cloves minced garlic
- 1 teaspoon salt
- 8 ounces of acceptable non-dairy cheese that melts (or more)

Preheat oven to 350°. Place the vegetables in a large bowl and set aside. Puree the cooked beans in batches in a food processor with 3 tablespoons of water per batch to make a semi-creamy paste. Place pureed beans in a medium sized mixing bowl and set aside. Repeat this process until all the beans are pureed. In a separate mixing bowl, mix the 4 cups of tomato sauce with the herbs and salt. Save ¾ cup of sauce for the top of the lasagna and a handful of grated non-dairy cheese for the top as well if using. Set aside. In a 9" x 13" baking pan, place a few tablespoons of tomato sauce and spread around to cover the bottom of the pan. Then place a layer of lasagna noodles over the sauce. Next use half of the pureed beans and spread them over the lasagna noodles. Top with half of the vegetables and non-dairy cheese. Repeat this process until the ingredients are gone or the pan is full. Spread reserved tomato sauce and cheese over the top of the lasagna. Cover and bake in a 350° oven for 1 hour and 15 minutes or until hot and bubbly. This recipe freezes well.

New Style Jambalaya

This recipe was invented for two reasons. The first was that my kids were tired of our old Jambalaya recipe and the second was a way to use up leftovers! It was an instant hit with everyone and a fast and easy way to use up leftovers and get vegetables into our diet!

25 ounces of acceptable spaghetti sauce
1 pound of ground beef, chicken or other meat
1 tablespoon of acceptable oil
3 cups of zucchini, cut into pieces
4 to 6 cups of leftover vegetables, rice or other gf grains
½ cup water or more if needed

Brown the ground beef or other meat in the oil in a large frying pan over medium high heat until fully cooked. Add vegetables and/or other leftover rice or gf grains and water and heat through. Add sauce and cook until hot and bubbly. Makes about 7 cups of Jambalaya.

Jamaican Jerk Jambalaya

This recipe was completely inspired by leftovers on a beef day! It does not fit our rotation diet days very well, but it works for those occasional "what to do with the leftovers" days. It was a hit with everyone.

1/3 cup diced onion (1 small)
1 tablespoon of acceptable oil
1 chopped red pepper
2 pounds ground beef
15 ounces of whole peeled tomatoes, crushed or smashed
28 ounces of chunky tomato sauce
3 cups cooked brown or white rice
dash of cloves
½ teaspoon of thyme
¼ teaspoon of cinnamon
Celtic salt to taste
6 ounces of tomato paste
2 cups of pure water
2 cloves of minced garlic
1 tablespoon of sugar or other sweetener

Brown the ground beef and onions in the oil in a very large frying pan until cooked through. Mix the tomato paste in the two cups of water until thoroughly combined and add to the ground beef in the frying pan. Add remaining ingredients and cook until hot and simmering. Simmer for 35 to 40 minutes. Makes about 11 cups.

Italian Colcannon

I've never heard of Italian Colcannon, but I invented this recipe when I wanted to use up some cabbage from our winter CSA share and the kids told me that they did not want cabbage in a stir-fry! I knew that they liked Alberta's Colcannon (a recipe I included in this book), so why not jazz things up a bit by changing the meat, and adding tomato sauce. It was a hit!

Preheat oven to 450°

> 1 medium head of cabbage, shredded or chopped (about 8 to 9 cups)
> 1 medium onion, diced
> 12 ounces of cooked sausage, slice or diced
> 28 ounces of diced tomatoes
> 15 ounces of tomato sauce
> 1-1/2 cups of water
> 1 teaspoon of basil
> 1 teaspoon of oregano
> 1 teaspoon of Celtic salt

Make sure your sausage is cooked before you make this dish. For cooking sausage, I recommend that you boil it in a large volume of water with one tablespoon of lemon juice added to the water. Rinse and drain well before adding to this dish. Combine all ingredients in a large, deep casserole dish and stir well. Bake at 450° for 1 hour to 1 hour and 15 minutes. Makes 9 to 10 cups.

Best Ever Meatloaf

I came up with this recipe for a friend who was recovering from a health issue. My intention with this recipe was to make a standard turkey meatloaf a tad bit more nutritious by adding vegetables and some greens. It was simply delicious! This is one way to get children to eat their greens since you really can't taste them!

Preheat oven to 350°
   3 pounds of organic turkey, chicken or beef
   ½ of a medium onion, chopped
   1 large clove of garlic, minced or two smaller cloves
   ½ cup chopped greens, either bok choy, spinach or kale
   ¼ cup grated carrot
   1 teaspoon Celtic salt
   Pepper to taste

Preheat oven to 350°. This will make one very large loaf or two smaller loaf pans of meatloaf. Combine all ingredients in a large mixing bowl and mix well. Form into a loaf(s) and place in your baking pan. Bake for 1 hour and 15 to 20 minutes or until your meat thermometer reads 165-170°. You may freeze the meatloaf for later use.

Ultimate Party Meatballs

This delicious recipe comes courtesy of Heinz® Chili Sauce and Ocean Spray® Cranberry Sauce! I have made this dish repeatedly for various community functions and it is always a hit! You can make this in a large slow cooker and serve a crowd!

   2 – pounds of meatballs, cocktail size - precooked
   1 – 16 ounce can of Ocean Spray® Cranberry Sauce
   1 – 12 ounce bottle Heinz® Chili Sauce

Combine sauces and cook over medium heat – stirring until smooth. Add meatballs and cook until meatballs are heated through. Makes 30 appetizer servings or dinner for five. For larger groups, double the recipe.

Vegetable Lo Mein

I had this wonderful vegetable lo mein while out to lunch with some friends. I thought that this would be a quick and healthy meal to make at home – allergen free of course! It was an instant hit with my family! The pasta you use can make or break this dish!

1 – 10 ounce box of gluten-free spaghetti or other similar
    pasta
1 medium chopped onion
1 tablespoon acceptable oil
1 red pepper, chopped
1-1/4 cup chopped carrots
2 cups Bok Choi or other vegetable, chopped into small
    pieces
2 cups chopped zucchini or other vegetable
Sauce:
2 Tablespoons GFCF Hoisin Sauce
1 Tablespoon Bragg Liquid Aminos or soy sauce
1 Tablespoon cornstarch or other gf flour as thickener
1 teaspoon ground ginger or dry ginger powder to taste
1 Tablespoon sugar or other acceptable sweetener
1 clove minced garlic
1 cup chicken, beef or vegetable broth

Mix all ingredients for the sauce and set aside. Bring a large stockpot of water to boil for the pasta. While the water for the pasta is coming to a boil, in a large frying pan, sauté the onion in the oil. After the onion is nice and soft, add the red pepper, carrots and bok choy. Cook vegetables until soft. Cook the pasta in the boiling water according to directions and then drain well. Add cooked pasta to the cooked vegetables. Add the sauce ingredients and cook until slightly thickened. Makes 7 to 9 cups of vegetable lo mein. The pasta you use can make or break this dish. I used a fortified gluten-free pasta that practically dissolved in the water while cooking, and was just terrible. If you use Nappa Cabbage, which I frequently do when it is available, I increase the spices because Nappa Cabbage has less flavor than Bok Choy.

Vegetable Paprikash

When we began to look for more ways to increase our vegetable intake, one obvious way was to convert recipes that we liked that contained meat or poultry and to substitute vegetables for the meat or poultry. This will come out similar to a vegetable lo mein, but with a Paprikash taste due to the spices used.

> 2 cups chopped carrots
> 4 cups summer squash or zucchini (or 8 cups Bok Choy or Nappa Cabbage)
> 2 cups chopped green peppers
> 1 large onion, chopped
> 1 tablespoon acceptable oil
> 3 tablespoons paprika
> ½ teaspoon dried thyme
> 1 teaspoon ground marjoram
> 1 ½ to 2 teaspoons salt or to taste
> black ground pepper to taste
> 2 cloves garlic, minced
> 3 tablespoons acceptable thickener or more (arrowroot, cornstarch, gf flour)
> 4 cups vegetable broth
> 2 – 10 ounce packages acceptable spaghetti pasta, cooked and drained (break spaghetti noodles half before cooking)

Cook the pasta in a large stockpot, drain and set aside. Fry the carrots, zucchini (or Bok Choy or squash), green peppers, and onion in acceptable oil in a very large frying pan over medium high heat until the onion is cooked through. Cook the vegetables to your desired softness. Add 2 of the 3 cups of broth to the frying pan reserving 1 cup. Add the paprika, thyme, marjoram, salt and pepper to the vegetables and broth in the frying pan. Mix well. Add the minced garlic. Add the 2 tablespoons acceptable thickener to the reserved broth and mix well and add to the vegetables. Heat until hot and thickened. Add the vegetable mixture to the pasta in the large stockpot and stir to incorporate. Makes about 12 cups.

Beef Paprikash

Use 1 pound of ground beef in place of the carrots and zucchini. All other ingredients remain the same. Follow directions for Vegetable Paprikash.

Green & Bean Veggie Burgers

This is a recipe I invented to use up an abundance of organic greens that had accumulated in our freezer from our CSA coop. If you don't have a lot of greens, you could cut the recipe in half. Made in the quantities listed, this recipe will make between 10 and 13 good size veggie burgers – more if you make smaller size burgers. My children really enjoy these and will eat them sans bun with just a bit of ketchup. They freeze quite well.

> 4 cups chopped greens, if using frozen greens use only 3 cups and make sure they are very well drained
> 4 cups drained white beans (or 2 – 15 oz. cans of white beans)
> 1 medium onion, chopped or diced
> 1 cup chopped carrots
> 2 cloves garlic, minced
> ½ red pepper, chopped
> 3 cups of gluten-free dry cereal, crushed
> 3 cups of gluten-free puffed millet or other acceptable puffed cereal
> ½ cup crushed potato chips
> ½ teaspoon thyme
> ½ teaspoon paprika
> ¼ teaspoon ground sage
> ½ teaspoon cumin
> ¼ teaspoon black pepper

Place the greens, chopped vegetables and spices in a large mixing bowl. Add the crushed cereal, potato chips and puffed cereal. Mix well and then form into individual patties. This recipe makes between 10 and 13 good size veggie burgers. You can either bake the veggie burgers in a 350° oven until hot (about 25 to 30 minutes), or you can fry on top of the stove until warmed through. These freeze well. Makes between 10 and 13 large size burgers or 15 or more smaller ones.

Black Bean Burgers

I invented this recipe to use up squash from our coop! The first attempt at this burger recipe yielded a stuffing like consistency, which became a stuffing recipe with a little tinkering. This makes a large amount, so you may want to cut the recipe in half until you know you like it or if you are cooking for one or two.

   3 cups cooked, drained and mashed black beans (or a 25
      ounce can)
   1 medium onion, finely diced
   2 cups cooked and mashed squash
   2 cups finely chopped carrots
   2 cloves garlic
   1 teaspoon salt
   black pepper to taste
   3-1/2 teaspoons dried rosemary
   1 tablespoon dried thyme
   Optional: dash of cayenne pepper
   6 cups puffed gluten-free, casein-free cereal
   4 cups dry, lightly crushed gluten-free, casein free cereal or
      bread crumbs (not sweet)

Place rinsed and drained black beans in a large mixing bowl and mash either by hand or with a potato masher. Add cooked squash, herbs, onions and carrots and mix well. Add remaining ingredients and mix well. Make sure the cereal or crumbs are not sweet. Makes 10-13 veggie burgers depending upon the size you make. You could also use dry seeds like sesame seeds or ground sunflower seeds in this recipe.

Sassy Sausage Simmer

Necessity is the mother of invention or so the saying goes. This is a recipe I came up with to use up some pork in the freezer and other leftovers in the fridge. The children loved this as is, and true to tradition, I would spice it up if just for myself.

1-1/2 pound of cooked, organic sausage
30 ounces of tomato sauce
10 ounces fresh or frozen chopped bok choi
1-1/2 cups diced onions
½ cup chopped celery
1 cup chopped tomatoes
2 tablespoons sugar or other sweetener
1 teaspoon dried basil
1 teaspoon dried oregano
3 cups cooked rice

This recipe can be made in a slow cooker or on the stove or even in the oven. Place all ingredients in either a slow cooker or in a large saucepan or baking dish and cook until hot and bubbly. If you are using fresh or frozen sausage, cook this separately in a large stockpot of water with at least 16-20 cups of pure water and a tablespoon of lemon juice. Skim the sum as it cooks. Cook for at least one hour and drain before adding the sausage to the rest of the recipe. Makes about 10 cups.

Jo Holcombe's Barbecue

*This was my Grandmother's recipe for barbecue or "sloppy joes"
as we called it. My Mother made it often when we were growing up
and it was a family favorite. My Aunt Irene Tubach, my Mom's sister,
made it when we went to Lake Mokoma for our annual trip, and it
was the first time our gluten-free son had ever had it. He was about
14 months old at the time and he loved it! He still likes it! While this
recipe will be either a hit or a miss with children, adults usually love
it.*

> **3 pounds ground beef**
> **3 pints chili sauce**
> **1 to 2 small onions, finely chopped (depending on your**
> **preference)**
> **¼ teaspoon ground cloves**
> **½ teaspoon ground cinnamon**
> **1 tablespoon vinegar**
> **1 tablespoon dry mustard powder**
> **1 teaspoon sugar**
> **To taste: salt and pepper**

Fry the meat and onions in some type of fat or oil. Drain off excess
fat after the meat and onions are cooked. Add the chili sauce and
spices. Simmer slowly for 1 hour. This is a large amount of barbecue,
however it freezes very well. Make it and freeze what you don't eat
for another meal or two.

General Tso's Chicken

This is a recipe that we love. But if you get General Tso's Chicken from your local Chinese restaurant it isn't going to be organic, and it will most likely contain monosodium glutamate (MSG). Here is a recipe to make at home.

Sauce for Chicken:
> ¼ cup cornstarch (or other gluten-free flour)
> 2 tablespoons pure water
> ½ teaspoon dry ground ginger
> 1 clove garlic, minced
> ⅓ cup sugar
> ¼ cup Bragg™ Liquid Aminos (or soy sauce)
> 1 cup chicken broth
> 2 tablespoons vinegar
> 2 tablespoons sherry or cooking wine
> ¼ teaspoon cayenne pepper

Poultry:
> 1½ pound boneless chicken, cut into cubes or pieces
> ½ cup cornstarch (or other gluten-free flour)
> Oil for frying

Additional Ingredients:
> 2 cups broccoli
> 1 cup green onions OR ½ cup diced onion
> 4 small dried hot peppers OR
> 2 tablespoons dried hot pepper flakes
> 3 cups cooked rice, *if serving over rice*

Note: cornstarch is intentionally listed twice in the ingredients section as it is used in two placed. To make the sauce for this recipe, place all of the sauce ingredients into a container or jar with a lid and shake well to dissolve the cornstarch. Set this aside until later. Place the chicken in water to moisten so that the cornstarch will adhere to it. Using a plastic food storage bag to coat the chicken works well. Fry the chicken in oil at 350° until crispy. Drain. To finish the sauce, heat 1 tablespoon of oil in a skillet and fry the onions, peppers and broccoli for about 3 minutes. Add sauce mixture. Cook until thick stirring frequently. Add chicken and cook just long enough to heat through. This dish is typically served over rice.

Spicy Chicken Fingers

My children love this coating mix for chicken fingers! These chicken fingers can be either baked, fried, or grilled depending upon your preference for cooking. The level of spices in this recipe will work for many children. If you love spicy food, you may increase the spices in this recipe.

> 1 to 2 pounds chicken breasts, sliced into chicken finger size pieces
> 1 cup water
> 2 tablespoons amaranth flour (or other gluten-free flour)
> 4 tablespoons tapioca flour (or other gluten-free flour)
> 2 tablespoons quinoa flour (or other gluten-free flour)
> 1 teaspoon dried parsley flakes
> 1 teaspoon paprika
> 1 teaspoon onion powder
> 1 teaspoon garlic powder
> ½ teaspoon lemon peel
> 1 teaspoon salt
> To taste: black pepper

Optional:
> To taste: cayenne pepper (up to ¼ teaspoon)

Mix the flours and spices together in a small mixing bowl and set aside. Cut chicken breast into chicken finger size pieces. The larger the pieces, the longer the cooking time will be. We have small children, and we typically cut our chicken breast into pieces the size of your thumb or pinky. Dip the chicken pieces into water or other liquid and then coat with the spicy flour mixture. If you are frying the chicken fingers, they are then ready for frying. If however, you are baking or grilling the chicken fingers, you will need to dip them again in water or liquid or spritz with water or oil to moisten the spicy coating mix. Bake, grill or fry until completely cooked. These freeze well.

Macaroni Doodle

The idea for this dish came from the desire of my children to have macaroni and cheese. It uses a roux for a base, which I had not made for a very long time. While this recipe is easy to make, it does require your undivided attention for making the roux sauce.

16 ounces of acceptable pasta
½ cup gluten-free flour (brown rice*)
1/3 cup plus 1 tablespoon non-dairy margarine
2 cups non-dairy milk substitute
1 teaspoon Celtic salt
½ teaspoon onion powder
½ teaspoon garlic powder

Fill a very large stock pot with pure water and start water cooking for the pasta. When the water comes to a boil, cook the pasta according to the directions and your preferences. The next step is making a roux, which you can do while the water is boiling. In a separate large frying pan, over medium heat – cook the non-dairy margarine and flour until it is a paste. Then cook a bit longer, but not much. Gradually, add the rice milk about 1/3 cup at a time – then stir the roux. Once it becomes kind of creamy and smooth – add more milk. Continue this process until all of the rice milk has been added. Add the garlic and onion powder and salt. Stir until the sauce is a desired thickness. This makes about 7 cups of pasta.

Pizza Party

There are many different types of pizza that you can make while on a special diet. Here are some of our favorites. A pizza crust recipe can be found in the rolls, waffles, bagels and pizza crust chapter. When I make pizza, I will prepare many different toppings and let my family members make their own. When I do that, I fill several different bowls with each topping. I make the pizzas this way because everyone of my family members has their own favorite pizza type. You won't need more than a cup of the toppings. If you are only making one type of pizza, you will need more of that one topping. The leftover toppings are used the next day in either a stir-fry or a salad!

Vegetarian Heaven

Use chopped celery, red or green bell pepper, broccoli, cauliflower, garlic and shredded carrots.

Traditional Pizza

You can purchase hard salami made without nitrates, nitrites, BHA, BHT and other nasty preservatives. We use this in place of pepperoni, which is next to impossible to find sans preservatives. Top this pizza with sauce, the hard salami and a non-dairy, casein-free cheese of your choice.

Taco Pizza

For this pizza, top with your choice of tomato sauce, ground beef, chopped or sliced tomatoes, a non-dairy cheese, and bits of shredded lettuce.

Hawaiian Sky Pizza

This pizza uses sauce, chopped red pepper, broccoli pieces, tomato and pineapple chunks. It is my favorite.

Meat Lovers Delight

Top this pizza with sauce and your favorite meats. We use organic ground beef, hard salami, organic bacon and a non-dairy cheese.

Man Overboard Pizza

For this pizza, top with two or three meats of your choice, two or three vegetables of your choice, and your favorite non-dairy cheese. When we make this pizza, we will use ground beef, and preservative free salami, onions, red pepper, broccoli pieces, and non-dairy cheese. Feel free to be creative!

Margherita Pizza

Mix 2 tablespoons olive oil (or other acceptable oil) with 1 large clove of garlic that has been crushed. Drizzle the olive and garlic mixture over the pre-baked pizza crust. Thinly slice fresh tomatoes and arrange them on the pizza. Sprinkle with oregano and basil. Top with non-dairy mozzarella cheese shreds. Broil until the cheese melts.

Black Bean Lasagna

This is a leftover recipe from before I had children and I was trying to eat more vegetarian meals.

Preheat oven to 350°.

One 10 ounce package of gluten-free lasagna noodles
Two 15 ounce cans black beans (drain & rinse)
Nonstick cooking spray
½ cup chopped onion (1 medium onion)
½ cup chopped red pepper (½ of a pepper)
2 cloves garlic, minced
Two 15 ounce cans of tomato sauce
Two 16 ounce packages firm tofu, drained well and puréed
with 8 tablespoons of water)
¼ cup non-dairy sour cream topping

Cook lasagna noodles. Mash 1 can of beans. Coat a large skillet with cooking spray. Add onion, pepper and garlic. Cook over medium heat. Add mashed and un-mashed beans & tomato sauce. Heat through.

Purée the drained tofu, and if using, the non-dairy cream cheese and then set aside. Spray a 9" x 13" baking dish. Arrange 3 noodles on the bottom and top with ⅓ of the bean mixture, then ⅓ of the Tofu mixture. Repeat next 2 layers ending with the bean mixture. Cover and bake for 1 hour or until done. It should be hot and bubbly the whole way through. Top with a dollop with non-dairy sour cream. Let stand 10 minutes before serving.

Lisa's Mexican Pie

This is another recipe from before I had children and I was doing more vegetarian cooking.

Preheat oven to 375°.

Sauté in a frying pan:
   1 large onion, finely chopped
   2 cloves garlic, mashed or minced
   1 red pepper, chopped
   2 zucchini, sliced thinly

Sauté the above ingredients until they are soft. The remaining ingredients are:

   3 gluten-free tortillas
   1 cup refried beans
   1 to 1½ cups salsa
   ½ cup non-dairy sour cream

In a 9" pie plate, place one soft tortilla. Cover with ¾ cup refried beans spreading to cover evenly. Cover with ½ of the sautéed vegetables and ½ of the salsa. Place a second tortilla over the mixture and repeat the layers of refried beans and veggies. Use the third tortilla to cover the pie. As much as possible, press the top tortilla to meet the second layer. Place 2 to 3 tablespoons of salsa on top of the pie. Cover with either parchment paper or foil and bake for about 30 minutes or until hot and bubbly. Top with non-dairy sour cream.

Shepherd's Pie

We make this recipe in a large, deep casserole dish or in individual servings using small (7 ounce) glass baking dishes or small pie plates (4 ½" to 5"in diameter). This will make 10 to14 mini-Shepherd's Pies depending upon which size dish you use. If you make the mini-Shephard's Pie, it will require more mashed potatoes due to the increase in surface area, so we usually make a double-batch.

Preheat oven to 375°.

3 pounds ground beef
1 onion, finely diced
2 tablespoons oil
1 cup carrot, shredded or finely diced
1 cup celery, diced
1 cup frozen peas
5 tablespoons Worcestershire sauce*
Two 15 ounce cans of tomato sauce
3 tablespoons sugar
To taste: salt and pepper

* Contains fish and soy – omit if necessary

Mashed Potato Topping:

5 cups water
2 teaspoons salt
3 tablespoons oil
3 cups instant potato flakes (about 8 to 10 ounces)
OR
Homemade mashed potatoes

Please note if you reduce the amount of ground beef that this recipe calls for, please reduce the tomato sauce accordingly or it will be too "soupy". Brown the onions in the 2 tablespoons of oil. Then add the ground beef and brown. Drain the fat and any liquid from the beef. Add tomato sauce, sugar, Worcestershire sauce, carrots, celery and peas and cook over medium-low heat until the carrots and celery are soft. If you are in a rush, you can microwave or cook the carrots and celery separately. However, if you have finely chopped the carrots and celery, it will not take long to cook them. While the beef mixture simmers, mix up the mashed potato topping. The topping should be creamy, that is not too stiff and not too runny.

Place the beef, tomato & vegetable mixture in a deep casserole dish or pan and top with the mashed potatoes. We use a casserole dish that is about 4½" deep by 9" in diameter. We make our individual Shepherd's pies in small white Pyrex oven crocks and in small metal pie pans (about 4" diameter). Containers of this size will hold about ⅔ cup of the meat mixture. Then top with a layer of mashed potato topping. If you like a lot of mashed potatoes, then you will want to double the mashed potatoes called for in this recipe. Bake for about 45 to 60 minutes or until the Shepherd's pie is bubbling and hot. If you are making individual Shepherd's pie containers, you will also want to increase the mashed potatoes because it will take more mashed potatoes to cover all the mini pies. You may make this recipe without the vegetables if necessary; it just won't be as flavorful.

Vegetarian Shepherd's Pie

You can use just about any vegetables that you like for your Shepherd's Pie! Here is just one way to make it with vegetables. I made this for a dinner guest who just loved it..

For the Beef, substitute the following or your choice of other vegetables:
   1 large or 2 medium zucchini sliced in half-moon pieces
   2 red peppers, diced
   4 stalks celery, diced
   3 large carrots, chopped or diced

Reduce tomato sauce to one can, and add 2 tablespoons of tomato paste to the one can of tomato sauce. The reason for doing this is that the vegetables add a good deal of liquid when they cook. If you use the Shepherd's Pie recipe above without making any modifications, the result will be a soupy Shephard's Pie. Follow above recipe directions.

Hearty Pot Pies

This is a great recipe for children! The two great things about this recipe are that you can use up what you have on hand and that they freeze well. By deleting the meat and substituting more vegetables of your choice, this dish easily becomes a vegetarian meal. If you don't have individual pot pie containers I would recommend that you invest in them. You can find individual glass containers at your local discount store made by manufacturers like Pyrex and Corning, which are ideal for individual pot pies. While it may seem like it is more work to make individual pot pies, there is less waste. You may also find individual metal pie plates (4 ½" to 5" in diameter) that work well, however they cannot be reheated in microwave ovens. One large, deep casserole dish also works very well with this recipe.

Preheat oven to 375°.

Ingredients (with liberal substitutions allowed):
   1½ cups carrots, diced or chopped
   1½ cups celery, diced or chopped
   1 large onion very finely chopped (about 1 cup)
   1 large potato chopped into small pieces
   2 pounds turkey, beef, chicken or pork(cut up into small
       pieces or ground)
Additional vegetables as you choose:
   ½ to ¾ cup frozen peas OR
   ½ to ¾ cup broccoli
Broth:
   32 ounces broth of your choice
Thickening agent:
   2 tablespoons cornstarch, tapioca or potato starch mixed
       with
   ½ cup water
   To taste: salt and pepper
   1 to 2 cloves garlic, mashed (or through a garlic press)
   2½ tablespoons acceptable oil
Topping:
   1 batch pie crust

Sauté or brown meat and onion in oil until the meat is fully cooked. Sauté carrots and celery over medium heat until soft. In a separate saucepan, boil potatoes until done. Mix ½ cup broth with 2 tablespoons cornstarch or other thickening agent. Add to meat and onion mixture and cook over medium-low heat until thick. Add potatoes and vegetables to meat and gravy mixture and then spoon into the individual pot pie containers or into a deep casserole dish. The size casserole dish we use is 4½" deep by 9" in diameter. Top with a pie crust topping. Make sure to cut steam vents in the pot pie tops before baking in a 380° oven. Bake until the crust is very lightly browned, about 40 to 45 minutes for the individual pot pies and slightly longer for a large casserole dish. This makes more than a family of five can eat at one sitting, which is why we frequently make individual pot pies and freeze the extras.

Vegetarian Tamale Pie

This is a holdover from decades ago when I was eating less meat. It is a nice vegetarian dish.

Preheat oven to 400°.

4 cups water
1½ cups yellow cornmeal
¼ teaspoon salt

1 cup cheese substitute, grated (optional)

Cooking spray
1 cup onion, chopped
2 teaspoons dried oregano
1½ teaspoons chili powder
15 ounce can black beans (rinsed & drained)
16 ounce can pinto beans (rinsed & drained)
One 14¾ ounce can no-salt-added cream-style corn
6 tablespoons non-dairy sour cream

Combine 4 cups water, cornmeal, & salt in a large saucepan and bring to a boil. Cook cornmeal mixture over medium heat for 5 minutes or until thick, stirring constantly with a whisk. Stir in cheese substitute if using. Pour half of mixture into a 9"x13" baking pan or dish that has been <u>coated</u> with cooking spray.

Sauté onion until soft. Add spices, beans and corn. Cook for 1 minute. Spoon bean mixture evenly over the cornmeal crust. Drop remaining cornmeal mixture on top. Bake in a 400 oven for 30 minutes or until set. Top with sour cream.

Pork Chops in Raisin Orange Sauce

This is a family recipe that I modified to be gluten free. My grandmother, Jo Holcombe gave it to my mom, Jean Gottas.

4 pork chops
3 tablespoons gluten-free flour for coating
1 tablespoon fat of any type
To taste: salt
1 or 2 oranges
4 tablespoons sugar
1 tablespoon cornstarch
⅛ teaspoon ground cinnamon
Dash of ground cloves
1¼ cups hot water
1½ cups orange juice
¼ cup raisins

Roll pork chops in flour and brown in the fat on both sides in a large skillet. Sprinkle with salt. Set aside. Peel and section the oranges and put several sections on each chop. In a saucepan, mix the sugar, cornstarch, and spices. Add water and lemon juice and simmer until thick. Add the raisins and then pour over chops. Cover and simmer 1 hour. Serves 4. This is an excellent recipe and worth the effort.

Stuffed Cabbage Rolls

This is a flexible recipe because if you are vegetarian, you can eliminate the meat in this recipe and substitute your favorite mix of vegetables or a pilaf.

Preheat oven to 350°.

1 cup chopped onion
1 to 1½ pounds pork sausage or ground beef
1 tablespoon acceptable oil
1 head cabbage
1 teaspoon salt
To taste: pepper
One 26 ounce jar tomato sauce or your favorite sauce topping

To make this recipe you will need to remove the outer first layer of cabbage leaves. To remove the cabbage leaves from the head, place the head of cabbage in a large stockpot of boiling water for 2 to 3 minutes or until the first layer of leaves are loosened. Remove the cabbage from the boiling water and with a knife, gently remove the outer layer of leaves. Immediately place those leaves back into the boiling water and blanche them for 2 to 3 minutes. Remove the cabbage leaves from the boiling water and immerse them in a bowl of cold water to stop the cooking process.

Place the cabbage head back in the boiling water to loosen the next layer of leaves. Repeat the process until you have more than 12 or 15 large cabbage leaves. How much filling your cabbage rolls will hold depends in part on how large the head of cabbage head is. To prepare the filling, salt and pepper the meat and brown the onion and meat in the oil over medium high heat until the meat is fully cooked.

Place 1 to 2 tablespoons of meat filling in the center of each cabbage roll and fold in all of the sides to make a neat package. Place the cabbage roll with the folded side down in a greased baking dish. Repeat the process until all of the filling is used up. If you run out of cabbage leaves and have extra filling, you can use the leftover filling in the sauce that you will place over the cabbage rolls or you can go back and add additional filling to some of your cabbage rolls.

Cover the top of the cabbage rolls with either tomato sauce or your favorite other sauce recipe. Tomato sauce works well with stuffed cabbage rolls; however it is not the only option. Place the baking dish in a 350° oven and bake for 30 to 40 minutes or until sauce is bubbly. Rice is frequently used in stuffed cabbage rolls. We didn't use rice in this recipe because of our rotation diet days. You could easily add rice or another grain to the above recipe. Makes 12 or more cabbage rolls.

Stuffed Peppers

I think we tend to think of stuffed peppers as a more adult dish. My children however loved the idea of stuffed peppers and ate all the filling. Stuffed peppers are great because you can alter the filling to meet your dietary needs and rotation food days. The recipe here is for the more common stuffed peppers. Vegetarians can easily convert this dish to meet their needs by substituting vegetables, a grain or a pilaf for the meat or poultry.

Preheat oven to 350°.
- **4 to 6 red or green peppers**
- **1 pound ground beef, chicken, pork, or turkey (or grain pilaf or vegetables)**
- **1 diced onion**
- **1 tablespoon oil**
- **3 tablespoons Worcestershire sauce (*contains Fish & Soy, use only if tolerated)**
- **2 cups cooked rice**
- **To taste: salt and pepper**

When making stuffed peppers, I like to make the filling first. and For the stuffing for this recipe, brown the beef and onion in the oil until thoroughly cooked. Add the Worcestershire sauce, cooked rice and salt and pepper. Keep on a low heat while you prepare the peppers.

Remove the top of the pepper and gut the inside. Do this carefully to preserve the shape of the pepper. I cut a circle around the stem of the pepper as small as possible, remove the top and using a knife, remove the seeds and guts. The next step is to parboil the peppers. Fill a large stockpot with pure drinking water and bring to a boil. Drop the peppers in the boiling water one at a time and boil for 2 minutes (**See note below about parboiling times). Remove from the boiling water and plunge into cool water to preserve the shape and stop the cooking process. Then turn pepper upside down and drain on a cooling rack. Do this with each of the peppers.

Once your peppers are drained, place them cut side up in a greased baking casserole dish and stuff them with the filling. If you have any extra filling, place it around the peppers in the baking dish. Bake in a 350° oven for 15 to 20 minutes until heated through. This recipe filled

2 large and 2 medium peppers with enough leftover to fill one small to medium sized pepper. How many peppers you fill will depend not only on the size of the pepper but also how stuffed you make them.

**Because you will be baking them in the oven for 15 minutes after they are stuffed, I don't like to overdo the parboiling and have mushy peppers. You will get a feel for this after you make them the first time. Maybe you only want your peppers parboiled for 1½ minutes. Or maybe you would like yours parboiled for 3 minutes.

Smothered Peppers

Smothered peppers are stuffed peppers which you cover with tomato sauce and bake. The reason it is good to use tomato sauce is because both peppers and tomatoes are in the same nightshade family, so it works for rotational purposes to keep the foods in the same family on the same rotation day. If you are not rotating foods, feel free to use any sauce that you love. Follow all other directions.

Spinach Quiche

I first experimented with tofu to replace ricotta cheese in lasagna over 10 years ago before I had my children when I was exploring natural foods. With that success under my belt, I thought that tofu might make a good substitute for the eggs and cheeses in a quiche. I have made this quiche many times and it is a good party food for adults, although my daughter loves it at age five. If you are in a hurry, or don't have a gluten-free pie crust, you can make this dish without the crust as we have done many times!

Preheat oven to 350°.

1 pie crust recipe, prepared
1 large onion, chopped
2 tablespoons acceptable oil
3 tablespoons Bragg™ Liquid Aminos or soy sauce
1 large clove garlic, minced or pressed
2 tablespoons vinegar
½ teaspoon salt
To taste: pepper
One 16 ounce package firm tofu
10 ounces frozen spinach, thawed and very well drained (OR 8 very large handfuls of fresh spinach, with the stems removed)

Optional:
Oregano, basil, or other spices

Bake pie crust for 15 to 20 minutes in a 350° oven until just lightly browned. Do not over bake the crust. Open tofu package and drain excess water. In a food processor, purée the tofu with the 2 tablespoons of vinegar and set aside. In a large skillet sauté the onions in the oil until soft and well cooked. Add the Bragg™ Liquid Aminos or soy sauce and then the fresh or frozen spinach. Cook until the excess moisture is evaporated if using frozen spinach, or until the spinach is well wilted if you are using fresh spinach. Add the garlic and tofu mixture and allow to cook down for just about 2 or so minutes. Add the salt and pepper.

Years ago when I made this I used additional herbs like oregano and sweet basil which I've had to omit because of my daughter's food allergies. If you would like to add additional herbs, you can do this now. Pour tofu and spinach mixture into the pie crust and bake in a 350° oven for 1 hour or until the quiche seems firm. If you use frozen spinach and don't cook the excess liquid out of the spinach, this will add a great deal of liquid to the tofu mixture and increase your baking time substantially. Cover the crust of the pie if the edges get too brown with either aluminum foil, or a pie crust cover (a metal rim designed just to cover the edges of a pie crust during baking). Check for doneness using a clean metal knife. When the quiche is done, the knife will come out pretty clean. Allow the quiche to cool for 15 minutes before cutting and serving.

If you are making the quiche without the crust, simply place the spinach mixture into a greased pie plate without a crust! And bake as above.

Spinach Lasagna

I invented this recipe before I had children when I was doing my best to avoid dairy. It was easy to convert it to be gluten free. This is a great dish for dinner parties or special functions.

Preheat oven to 375°.

- 2 boxes gluten-free lasagna noodles
- 4 cups (32 ounces) spaghetti sauce
- 4 to 6 cups fresh spinach, washed & chopped (or 1 to 2 packages of frozen spinach drained)
- Two 16 ounce packages tofu, drained
- 2 tablespoons oil
- 1 to 2 cloves garlic, minced
- 1 large onion, chopped
- 1 red pepper, diced
- 2 cups carrots, chopped
- 2 cups celery, chopped

If using frozen spinach, thaw and drain and set aside. Cook lasagna noodles and drain. Lay out noodles on waxed paper with waxed paper between layers. Grease a 9" x 13" baking pan. Drain tofu. Purée tofu in a food processor with enough water to make a mixture the consistency of ricotta cheese, and set aside. Sauté the onions and red pepper in oil. Add carrots and celery and sauté until soft. Add the spinach. If using fresh spinach, cook just enough to wilt the spinach. If using frozen spinach, sauté to remove any water that did not drain off. Frozen spinach typically holds a lot of water and it will take 2-3 mintues to cook off the excess water. Add garlic and cook for only 1 to 2 minutes being careful not to scorch or burn the garlic.

Place a small amount of spaghetti sauce in the bottom of the greased pan and spread around. Place a layer of noodles on the bottom of the pan. Place a layer of the onion, pepper, carrots and celery mix over the noodles. Add a layer of spinach followed by a generous helping of spaghetti sauce. Finally, add a layer of tofu. Next add another layer of lasagna noodles and repeat the steps until you are at the top of the pan or out of ingredients.

Bake at 375° until hot and bubbly. You can make this in two 8 x 8 pans and freeze one or both if a smaller amount works for your family. I like to make this in two 8" x 8" pans and one we eat that day and one I freeze for another day. You can freeze the lasagna before or after baking it. To use frozen lasagna, simply thaw and heat until hot and bubbly.

This is a recipe you can get creative with. You can use other vegetables. You can add other spices. Have fun with it!

Beef Stroganoff

This recipe is from my Mother, Jean Gottas, who is an excellent cook, baker, home economist, Mother and Grandmother! It was easy to convert. Thanks Mom!

1 tablespoon gluten-free flour
½ teaspoon salt
1 pound beef sirloin or other tender cut (cut in ¼ inch strips)
2 tablespoons oil
½ cup chopped onion
1 clove garlic, minced (this is optional)
1 cup thinly sliced mushrooms (this is optional)
2 tablespoons GFCF margarine or fat
3 tablespoons gluten-free flour
1 tablespoon tomato paste or ketchup
One 15 ounce can gluten-free beef broth
2 tablespoons cooking sherry (or red or white cooking wine)
1 cup non-dairy sour cream

Dredge the meat in 1 tablespoon flour and salt. In a skillet, quickly brown the beef on all sides in the oil. Add mushroom if using, onion and garlic. Cook for 3 to 4 minutes or until onion is barely tender. Remove mixture from skillet. Add 2 tablespoons margarine or oil to pan drippings. Blend in the 3 tablespoons flour, add tomato paste or ketchup. Slowly pour in the beef broth stirring until mixture thickens. Return meat mixture to skillet and heat. Just before serving, stir in non-dairy sour cream and sherry. Serve over rice or gluten-free noodles. Makes 4 to 5 servings.

Marinated Flank Steak

This delicious recipe comes from an AOΠ Alum by the name of Lois Klotz whom I adore for so many reasons and in so many ways. Lois is a spectacular woman and this recipe is reflective of that.

24 hours in advance:

    1 cup acceptable oil
    ½ cup vinegar
    1 teaspoon salt
    ¼ teaspoon pepper
    2 teaspoons dry mustard
    2 teaspoons Worcestershire sauce (contains fish & soy)
    Dash of red pepper
    Dash of Tabasco™ sauce
    ¼ cup Bragg™ Liquid Aminos or soy sauce
    2 to 3 pounds flank steak

Mix the ingredients together and use to marinate the flank steak for 24 hours covered in the refrigerator. Then about 2 to 4 hours prior to cooking, bring out to room temperature and allow the meat to continue to marinate.

Cooking instructions for a flank steak: Preheat the broiler. Place the steak on a greased broiler rack and place under the broiler making sure that it is within 2 to 3 inches of the heating element. This is important. Broil for 5 minutes and then turn steak over and broil for 4 minutes on the other side. This will produce a rare meat because if you cook a flank steak to medium or well done, it will become extremely tough and difficult to eat. Carve in ¼ inch slices cut diagonally across the grain.

Veal Shanks Italian Style

This is a recipe that my Mom passed down to me.

    2 tablespoons oil
    4 shank crosscuts veal (2 to 2¼ pounds)
    1 medium onion, chopped
    1 medium carrot, chopped
    1 medium celery stalk, chopped
    3 cloves garlic, minced
    1 cup dry white wine
    1 medium ripe tomato, peeled, cored and chopped
    1 bay leaf, crumbled
    ½ teaspoon dried basil
    ½ teaspoon thyme
    ¼ teaspoon black pepper
    1½ teaspoon grated lemon rind
    1 teaspoon dried parsley

While you are assembling your ingredients place the veal in about 1-1/2 to 2 cups of pure water with 2 teaspoons of baking soda. Allow the meat to sit in the baking soda water to tenderize the meat for about 15 minutes. Then rise the meat well and dry. In a 2" deep skillet or 4 quart Dutch oven, brown the veal over high heat for about 2 minutes on each side. Transfer to a platter. Reduce the heat to moderate and add oil, onion, carrot, celery, and ½ of the garlic to the skillet. Cook, uncovered, for 5 minutes or until the onion is soft. Add the wine and boil, uncovered. Keep stirring to loosen any browned bits from the bottom of the pan (from searing the veal). Stir and boil for 5 minutes or until the liquid has reduced by half.

Return the veal and its juices to the skillet. Add the tomato, bay leaf, basil, thyme and pepper. Cover and simmer over moderately low heat for 2 hours or until the meat is tender but not falling off the bones. Add the parsley, lemon rind and remaining garlic to the skillet just before serving. Makes 4 servings.

Roasting Meats

For beginners, cooking meats can be a daunting challenge! One tool that will give you confidence and help keep you and your family safe is a good quality meat thermometer. Use the meat thermometer to gauge the internal temperature of the meats that you are cooking. A roast can look juicy and nicely browned on the outside, but can be very undercooked on the inside. Meat thermometers are sold in most kitchen stores, large retail stores and even in many grocery stores.

Undercooked meats can easily make you sick, so the following chart gives you some guidelines for cooking your meats. In roasting meats, the idea is to start roasting at a very high temperature so that you sear in the juices of the meats. You roast at 450° for 15 minutes before you turn the temperature down and continue roasting until it is cooked through. A larger, thicker roast will take longer than a thin cut of meat.

Prior to roasting your meat, you can season it with a variety of spices depending upon what you like. You can season your meat with simple salt and pepper, fresh garlic, rosemary, chives, or other herbs. Simply rub the selected spices or herbs around the outside of your meat cut before roasting.

Meat Roasting Times			
	Pork	**Beef**	**Lamb**
Roast for 15 minutes at:	450°	450°	450°
Reduce heat to:	350°	350°	350°
Continue cooking for:	18 to 20 minutes per pound	Rib Roasts & Sirloin Top Round: 20 to 25 min/lb Tenderloin Roast: 8 to 11 min/lb	Boneless: 19 min/lb Semi-boneless: 21 min/lb
Internal temperature when meat is done:	150° to 155°	Rare: 125° Medium: 130° Well Done: 145°	Rare: 125° Medium: 130° Well Done: 145°
Resting time before carving:	15 minutes		

Cooking a Turkey or a Chicken

I include how to cook a turkey in this cookbook because many people simply don't know how to cook one and would not know where to look for instructions on how to cook one. And because this is the most cost effective way for individuals who want to get hormone-free, antibiotic-free, free-range food. Buy the whole bird and cook it yourself. This saves money and time. We typically get a larger turkey so that we have turkey in the freezer to last for 2 to 3 months.

To prepare for cooking a turkey or chicken, make sure that any equipment that you use is clean. Wash your hands very well in hot soapy water before and after handling raw turkey or chicken or any meat for that matter. Remove the giblets and neck from inside the bird and rinse the outside and inside of the turkey or chicken with pure drinking water.

Preheat your oven to 325°. You may choose to rub the outside of your turkey or chicken with oil. Lightly salt and pepper the outside of the bird. Place the bird, breast side up, in a shallow roasting pan. To keep your bird moist, cover the roasting pan. To brown the turkey or chicken, remove the roasting lid (or foil) the last hour of cooking. Use a meat thermometer to check the temperature of the turkey or chicken even if the turkey comes with a pop-up thermometer. Your meat thermometer should read 175° or greater when the turkey or chicken is done cooking. The juices should be clear NOT pink. Allow to sit for 15 minutes before carving.

Roasting times are based on the weight of the turkey or chicken. These figures are given as estimates only and you should check your bird for doneness. The roasting times below are provided for a bird that contains NO stuffing. The roasting times also assume that the bird is fresh and not frozen.

VEGETABLES & SIDE DISHES

Sweet Beets

An abundance of root vegetables in our winter CSA share coupled with a Knights of Columbus Holiday party were just the combination to cause me to invent a new dish! They were a real hit with the Knights of Columbus and family.

Preheat oven to 350°

8 cups beets, peeled and sliced into pieces
salt and pepper to taste – as desired
1/3 cup sugar
¼ cup vinegar
1 cup water – more if needed

Place beets into a 9" x 13" casserole or baking dish. In a small bowl combine sugar, vinegar and water and mix well. Pour over beets, cover, and bake in a 350° oven for 1 hour or until the beets are soft. Makes 8 to 10 side dish servings.

Vegetables Au Gratin

The idea for this dish came in the form of a grocery store circular with an ad for vegetables au gratin that they sell – with gluten and dairy of course. I took this dish to a pot luck dinner on my first try and it was eaten up – all but 2 tablespoons of it!

Preheat oven to 350°
1 Roux Mixture (in this cookbook)
2 cups of non-dairy milk – rice milk or other
½ teaspoon onion powder
½ teaspoon garlic powder
½ cup brown rice flour
1/3 cup plus 1 tablespoon non-dairy margarine or shortening
1 teaspoon Celtic salt

Vegetables:
5 cups cauliflower, in bite sized pieces
4 cups broccoli, in bite sized pieces
½ cup seasoned, crushed cereal crumbs (not too sweet)
4 tablespoons water

To make the roux cook the margarine or shortening in a large frying pan until melted. Add flour gradually – stirring constantly as the flour and margarine or shortening makes a thick paste. Add the rice milk or other non-dairy milk 1/3 cup at a time stirring to make the mixture a creamy sauce each time before adding more rice milk. Add the onion powder, garlic powder, and salt after all the milk has been added and the mixture is creamy. The longer you cook this, the thicker it will become, so remove it from the heat after the last milk has been added and stirred in along with the spices. Place washed and drained vegetables in a 9" x 13" baking pan along with 4 tablespoons of pure water. Pour the roux mixture over the vegetables. Sprinkle seasoned cereal or cracker crumbs over top of vegetables. Bake at 350° until vegetables are desired texture and the sauce is bubbly – about 1 hour.

Heavenly Potatoes

The original recipe called for real dairy cheese, sour cream, butter, and gluten. It never occurred to me to even try to convert this recipe until I had perfected the "roux sauce" and realized what I could do with it. My children went wild over this dish! I have to admit this is as close as you can probably get to the real McCoy without the dairy and cheese. Not the healthiest dish – but one that will go over well at a potluck dinner or party.

Preheat oven to 350°
   1 Roux Mixture (in this cookbook)
   2 cups of non-dairy milk – rice milk or other
   ½ teaspoon onion powder
   ½ teaspoon garlic powder
   ½ cup brown rice flour
   1/3 cup plus 1 tablespoon non-dairy margarine or shortening
   1 teaspoon Celtic salt

   6 large potatoes, shredded or grated
   1 small onion, chopped finely
   1 8-ounce package of non-dairy cheese shreds (that melt)
   1 cup crushed cereal crumbs (not too sweet)
   2 tablespoons melted non-dairy margarine or shortening

To make the roux cook the margarine or shortening in a large frying pan until melted. Add flour gradually – stirring constantly as the flour and margarine or shortening makes a thick paste. Add the rice milk or other non-dairy milk 1/3 cup at a time stirring to make the mixture a creamy sauce each time before adding more rice milk. Add the onion powder, garlic powder, and salt after all the milk has been added and the mixture is creamy. The longer you cook this, the thicker it will become, so remove it from the heat after the last milk has been added and stirred in along with the spices. Grease a 9" x 13" baking pan. Place the shredded or grated potatoes in the pan along with the "cheese" shreds and mix well. Pour over the roux mix. Lightly stir pan. Top with crushed cereal crumbs (not sweet ones) that have been mixed with 2 tablespoons melted margarine or shortening. Bake at 350° until the potatoes are cooked through and the sauce is bubbly – about 1 hour.

Vegetable Bake

I revised the Heavenly Potatoes recipe by adding more vegetables to make it healthier. The results were amazing – it was still widely accepted and enjoyed by all.

Preheat oven to 350°
1 Roux Mixture (recipe in this cookbook)
2 cups of non-dairy milk – rice milk or other
½ teaspoon onion powder
½ teaspoon garlic powder
½ cup brown rice flour
1/3 cup plus 1 tablespoon non-dairy margarine or shortening
1 teaspoon Celtic salt

6 large potatoes, shredded or grated
2 small onions, chopped finely
2-1/2 to 3 cups grated carrots
1 8-ounce package of non-dairy cheese shreds (that melt)
1 cup crushed cereal crumbs (not too sweet)
2 tablespoons melted non-dairy margarine or shortening

To make the roux cook the margarine or shortening in a large frying pan until melted. Add flour gradually – stirring constantly as the flour and margarine or shortening makes a thick paste. Add the rice milk or other non-dairy milk 1/3 cup at a time stirring to make the mixture a creamy sauce each time before adding more rice milk. Add the onion powder, garlic powder, and salt after all the milk has been added and the mixture is creamy. The longer you cook this, the thicker it will become, so remove it from the heat after the last milk has been added and stirred in along with the spices. Grease a 9" x 13" baking pan. Place the shredded or grated potatoes, onions, and carrots in the pan along with the "cheese" shreds and mix well. Pour over the roux mix. Lightly stir pan. Top with crushed cereal crumbs (not sweet ones) that have been mixed with 2 tablespoons melted margarine or shortening. Bake at 350° until the potatoes are cooked through and the sauce is bubbly – about 1 hour.

Applesauce

My mom used to make homemade applesauce when I was growing up. I recently made applesauce because of an abundance of apples from our CSA coop. It was easy to make and was a fantastic use of the excess apples.

8 cups of sliced apples, cut into pieces*
**Water to cover, about 3 cups depending upon the size pan
    you use**

*We don't use the skin unless we know that the apples are a zero spray as opposed to a low spray apple. If you have organic apples or are not concerned about any pesticides or sprays, by all means use the skin of the apple, which will add to your applesauce. Place the apples in a medium stockpot and cover with water. Bring to a boil and then reduce heat and cook over medium low heat until desired consistency. You can speed up the process of making this applesauce by using a higher heat, but watch the pan if you do this. You can have thick and chunky applesauce or a more refined and pureed applesauce. This cooks down to about half for a chunky type of applesauce. Makes 3-1/2 to 3-2/3 cups.

Rosemary Infused Summer Medley

Oh what to do with all that summer squash and scallions besides freeze them for later use? The purpose of this recipe was to make a dish that used summer squash that my children would eat. Mission accomplished with a bang! This makes a large amount, so you may want to cut the recipe in half. We will eat most of this at one meal.

8 cups sliced or chopped summer squash or zucchini
2 cups chopped scallions
2 cups diced carrots
2 cups diced red peppers
2 teaspoons dried thyme
dash of paprika
1 teaspoon dried rosemary
salt and pepper to taste

Place the oil in a large frying pan over medium high heat, add the summer squash or zucchini, red peppers, carrots and scallions. Stir-fry over medium high eat for 3-5 minutes. Add herbs and salt and pepper to taste. Serve hot plain as a side dish or with pasta or rice. Makes about 6-1/2 cups.

Turnip French Fries

Noah looked up recipes for turnips on the Internet and found that French Fries was one suggested use. He then invented this recipe to mask the taste of the turnips! Not a bad idea if you are serving them to children!

2-3 Turnips (to serve 3-4 people)
Acceptable oil
Thyme
Basil
Sage
Salt & Pepper

For a family of five, we will use 3 turnips. That will not give you a large quantity of French Fries. Imagine a turnip is just like a potato. Wash the turnips and cut into French Fry pieces. Drizzle a light amount of oil over the French Fries and then use the herbs and salt and pepper to taste. Bake in a 450 degree oven until done. If you continue to cook the French Fries, they will get soft.

Whipped Squash

I came up with this dish for a potluck dinner when I was thinking of how to use up our abundance of winter squash! It went over extremely well at the potluck dinner. Guests thought that it was whipped sweet potatoes!

4 cups cooked squash (about 2 small to medium sized squash)
2 Tablespoons of pure water, if needed
2 Tablespoons of maple sugar or other sweetener

Place cooked squash in a mixing bowl and add water and maple sugar or other sweetener. Mix until creamy. Bake at 350 degrees until hot and steamy.

Candied Parsnips

I can honestly say that I never ate parsnips growing up or even as an adult! This recipe idea came from a woman at my CSA coop pick up. It is fast and easy and it tastes a bit like candy!

2-1/2 cups of parsnips cut into bite-sized pieces
1 to 2 tablespoon of brown sugar
1 tablespoon of acceptable oil

You can increase or decrease the amount of brown sugar you use in this recipe based on your dietary needs and requirements. You can also use a substitute sweetener although that will change the taste slightly. Place all ingredients in a small baking pan and mix well to coat. Place in a high oven (450 degrees) until the parsnips are soft. I use a broiler for the last few minutes to caramelize the sugar. With a high heat and brown sugar, you must be careful or it will burn, so watch this dish closely. Makes 5 – ½ cup servings.

Alberta's Potato Bake

The general idea for this recipe came from my friend Pat. This is a dish that her mother, Alberta, used to make. It could be used as a main dish.

Preheat oven to 450°

> **2 cups chopped onion**
> **1 medium head of cabbage, shredded or chopped into small pieces (10-12 cups)**
> **12 ounces of organic bacon (no hormones, preservatives or chemicals)**
> **4 medium potatoes, cut into bite size pieces**
> **1-1/2 teaspoon oregano**
> **3-1/2 cups of water**
> **salt and pepper to taste**

Place all ingredients in a large and deep baking or casserole dish. Mix well and bake in a 450° oven for 1 hour to 1 hour and 15 minutes. Stir several times while baking. I must add that I never got the recipe from Pat, so I hope that this does her mom's recipe justice! Makes 9 cups.

Jo Holcombe's Baked Beans

This is my grandmother's recipe for baked beans passed down to me by my mother, Jean Gottas. Much to my surprise, my children really loved these beans! If you are making this for a large crowd, you may want to double the recipe.

Preheat oven to 350°

1 pound dried beans, soaked in pure water overnight
¾ cup brown sugar
1 teaspoon dry mustard
1-1/4 cup ketchup
1 medium to large onion, diced
3 cups bean juice (what's left in the pan from cooking with
water added, if necessary to make 3 cups)
3 tablespoons molasses
6 to 8 ounces of bacon, cut into small pieces
1 teaspoon Celtic salt
Pepper to taste

Boil the beans for 1-1/2 to 2 hours or until soft making sure that you have plenty of water in the pan as it will cook down and reduce while cooking. You will most likely need to add water to the bean while they are cooking unless you start with a lot of water. Do not drain the beans when they are done cooking, rather use that liquid as an ingredient for the beans. You want to have about 3 cups of bean juice to start with for this recipe. If you are not sure how much bean juice you have, you can measure it, and add sufficient water to make 3 cups of juice. Preheat oven to 350° as the beans finish cooking on the stovetop. Add remaining ingredients and bake in the oven for 2-1/2 to 3 hours. Make sure that the beans do not boil. If they start to boil, reduce the oven temperature so that they are cooking but not boiling. Makes 7 cups of beans.

Fruit Gelatin

This recipe a natural, preservative free, dye free, no sugar added food that is an excellent food for someone who has been sick or is post-op or otherwise on a restricted diet. I have included it because there are many who don't realize how quick and easy it is to have a food like this. Children will especially enjoy making and eating this food.

½ **cup cold water**
½ **ounce of unflavored gelatin**
3 cups fruit juice
1 teaspoon to 1 tablespoon of lemon juice

For this recipe to taste great, you must use a juice that tastes good plain. If a juice is too tart for you to drink it straight up, then it won't make a good gelatin. Of course, you could use a tart juice and just add sugar to the juice to make it acceptable. To chill the water, I add an ice cube for a few minutes to the ½ cup of water and then remove the ice cube prior to adding the gelatin to the water. Place the gelatin in the cold water and let the gelatin dissolve. Set the gelatin aside. In a medium saucepan, heat the fruit juice just to the boiling point and remove from heat. Add the gelatin and lemon juice to the fruit juice and stir well. Refrigerate until set. Serve with fresh fruit and or whipped topping.

Mediterranean Rice

*I inadvertently made too much rice one afternoon for another dish –
way too much rice! I came up with this dish to ensure that the extra
rice would get eaten. It was an immediate hit!*

3 cups cooked rice
14 ½ ounces diced tomatoes
1 small onion, diced (about ½ cup)
1 tablespoon acceptable oil
Celtic salt to taste
**2 tablespoons finely diced spinach, kale or other green (very
    tiny pieces)**
2 tablespoons Taco Seasoning (see recipe in this book)

In a large skillet sauté the onion in the oil over medium high heat until
completely soft and thoroughly cooked. Add the taco seasoning and
stir to incorporate. Add the diced tomatoes, salt if using, and cooked
rice and stir well cooking over medium low heat. Add very finely
diced spinach, kale or other greens and stir to incorporate. It should
be emphasized that the greens should be very finely chopped. I used
a food processor, which yielded the tiniest pieces you could imagine.
Heat through and serve. This can be a side dish, or you can add black
beans for a more filling main dish. This makes 3 cups.

Quinoa Pilaf

I'll be honest, I do not like quinoa! I made this recipe on a whim because I needed a new food on our 'quinoa' day. Much to my surprise, we all liked it – even me the quinoa hater! It just goes to show that a little onion and flavorings can work wonders!

½ **cup quinoa grain**
¼ **cup chopped onion**
½ **cup chopped red bell pepper**
½ **cup chopped celery**
2 **cups pure water**
dash of Celtic salt

Rinse quinoa grain and pick out any stones or unsavory grains. Then place all ingredients in a medium saucepan and cook over medium heat for 25-30 minutes. The quinoa grain will absorb the water and become slightly larger. This makes 2 to 2-1/4 cups.

Fried Green Tomatoes

At the end of the growing season our CSA had some green tomatoes. Rather than let them ripen, I decided to introduce my children to a childhood recipe I remembered.

    4 large tomatoes or several smaller tomatoes
    1 tablespoon Ener-G egg replacer mixed with ¼ cup water
    3 tablespoons non-dairy milk
    2/3 cup gluten-free flour of choice
    salt and pepper to taste
    1 cup crushed cereal (not sweet) or dry breadcrumbs
    oil for frying

Place Ener-G egg replacer mixed with water in a small bowl. Place the non-dairy milk in second separate bowl and set aside. Mix the flour and salt and pepper and place in a third bowl. Place the breadcrumbs or dry crushed cereal in a fourth bowl. Slice the tomatoes to desired thickness – thinner slicing will facilitate faster cooking. Dip each slice of tomato into the egg replacer and then into the flour bowl. Next place the slice of tomato into the non-dairy milk bowl and then into the crushed cereal or breadcrumbs bowl. Fry the tomato over medium heat until cooked through. Place on a paper towel to drain.

Party Pasta Salad

This is a family favorite and a recipe you will recognize. This recipe is really only good on the day it is made. Do not make it ahead or the pasta will dry out in my humble opinion and I am not kidding on this! If you can't make it the day you are serving it, don't bother!

> 16 ounces acceptable pasta cooked and drained
> ½ cup Italian salad dressing
> ½ cup chopped scallions
> 1 cup chopped or grated carrots
> 1-1/4 cup grated zucchini
> Optional: black olives, celery, bits of non-dairy cheese,
>   cherry tomatoes

Mix pasta, vegetables and salad dressing in a large bowl. If additional optional ingredients are used, increase amount of Italian salad dressing used. Refrigerate and use the same day. This pasta salad is to be made and eaten in the same day. The gluten-free pastas do not have the same staying power as gluten pasta. Makes about 8 cups.

Bok Choy Stir Fry

If necessity is the mother of invention then the need for using Bok Choy from our organic coop was the mother of this recipe being born. Vegetarians can omit the bacon and use their favorite oil in place of the bacon fat.

½ package of nitrate and nitrite free, hormone and chemical free bacon
1 large head of cauliflower broken into small pieces
1 small onion, chopped
6-8 stalks of bok Choy, chopped
½ of a red pepper, chopped
salt to taste
1-1/2 teaspoons of dried rosemary or to taste
1/3 to ½ cup of water
1 tablespoon reserved bacon fat

Cook the bacon in a large frying pan and set cooked bacon aside. Reserve 1 tablespoon of the bacon fat and use in the frying pan to cook the onion until soft and brown. Add red pepper, cauliflower, rosemary, bok choy and water. Cook until flavors meld and the cauliflower gets cooked until desired softness. Makes about 7 cups depending on the size of the head of cauliflower.

The Baltimore Casserole

*This is a recipe that I invented simply to use up our CSA produce –
namely an abundance of carrots and cabbage from our winter share.
We were shocked and delighted at how this dish came out! I have
served it to many guests who thought it was excellent as well. It is
a fantastic way to get healthy vegetables into your diet. We use a
non-dairy, melting cheese in this dish, and I can tell you that the non-
dairy cheese makes all the difference in the world in this recipe. My
children were studying the Baltimore Catechism while I was naming
this dish, which gave rise to the name.*

Preheat oven to 350°
   3 to 4 cups shredded carrots
   1 large onion, finely chopped
   3 cups cooked rice
   1 teaspoon Celtic salt
   4 to 5 cups grated cabbage (or more)
   8 ounces non-dairy mozzarella cheese shreds
   ½ to ¾ cup water

Place shredded carrots, onion, cabbage and cooked rice in a very large
mixing bowl and mix well. Sprinkle salt over top and mix again. Place
slightly over half of the mixture into a 9" x 13" or larger baking pan or
casserole dish. Then place about ¾ of the shredded non-dairy cheese
over the casserole. Add remaining shredded vegetables and cover
with the non-dairy cheese that remains. Pour water over casserole and
cover. Bake in a 350° oven for 45 minutes or until all ingredients are
cooked through and steaming hot. The first time I made this, I poured
about a cup or more of herbed tomato sauce over the top before I
baked the casserole dish. It smelled like lasagna in the house and was
delicious. However, for reasons that I can't explain, my family likes
it better without the herbed tomato sauce, which is why I listed it as
optional.

Rustic Potatoes and Spinach

I was looking to use up spinach and potatoes from our CSA. We were all pleased with this dish!

¾ cup sliced leeks (about 1 medium)
4 cups red potatoes (or other potatoes) cut into bite sized
    pieces
2 cups fresh spinach leaved, chopped or torn into little pieces
1 ¼ cups vegetable broth or water
Salt to taste
Pepper to taste
Additional water as the potatoes cook

Place all ingredients in a large frying pan and cook over medium low heat, stirring often so it does not burn. Add water as needed as the liquid cooks down. Cook until the potatoes are cooked. Cooking time will vary with the size of potatoes. This makes about 4 cups.

Garlic Rosemary Roasted Potatoes

This was a recipe that I invented to use up potatoes and onions from our CSA coop.

2 medium onions
5 cloves garlic ~ or more
1 red pepper, chopped into pieces
6 medium potatoes, diced (about 2 to 2 ¼ cups)
Olive Oil or other acceptable oil
Salt to taste
½ to ¾ teaspoons dried rosemary

Mix all ingredients in a large baking pan (9" x 13") and broil or roast until potatoes are cooked through, stirring every 5 – 6 minutes. Cooking time will vary in direct relationship to the size of the potato pieces. Approximate time for broiling or roasting (450º) for 45 to 50 minutes.

Vegetable Stir Fry

Vegetable Stir-fries are easy and fast to make and are versatile because you can use the vegetables that are either in season or that you have on hand. With this stir-fry recipe you can eat it plain, with a tablespoon or two of Bragg™ Liquid Aminos or soy sauce, any commercially made sauces on the market, or the General Tso's sauce recipe included in this section with the General Tso's Chicken recipe.

2 tablespoons acceptable oil
1 large onion, sliced into wedge-shaped slices
1 large red pepper, cut into strips and then cut in half
5 cups fresh or frozen vegetables

Here is one mix that we often use:

2 cups carrots
1 cup celery
1 cup broccoli
1 cup cauliflower
1 clove garlic, minced

Wash and prepare the vegetables. If using broccoli and cauliflower, cut into bite sized pieces. Cut remaining vegetables on a diagonal for a more appealing dish. Put the oil in a large skillet and heat over medium high heat. Add onions and fry for about 2 to 3 minutes. Add all remaining vegetables except the garlic and sauté until crisp-tender. If your vegetables still retain some of their crispness, you are retaining more of the vegetable enzymes, which are good for you. This can be served as a side dish, or over rice or any other cooked grain as a main dish.

Vegetable Fried Rice

This recipe is for basic fried rice, which our family loves. You can vary this recipe by adding meat, chicken or additional vegetables.

3 cups cooked rice
5 tablespoons acceptable soy type sauce
⅓ cup onion , finely chopped
½ cup carrots, diced
¼ cup peas
2 cloves garlic, minced
2 tablespoons of acceptable oil

Sauté the carrots and onions in the oil until soft. Remove pan from heat and add peas, minced garlic, soy type sauce, and rice. Over medium heat, stir fry the rice mixture until heated through.

Pork Fried Rice

This is another family favorite.

3 slices bacon or cooked pork cubes
3 cups rice, cooked and cooled
½ cup peas, fresh or frozen
**½ cup canned miniature corn on the cob ears (or just plain
  corn)**
To taste: salt and pepper

In a large frying pan, fry bacon until fully cooked. Remove and drain bacon. Crumble bacon and set aside. In the frying pan containing the bacon drippings add the rice, vegetables and bacon and fry over medium high heat until heated through. Salt and pepper to taste. You may add soy sauce or Bragg™ Liquid Aminos but they are optional because the bacon and bacon drippings add a lot of flavor to this fried rice. You can substitute pork cubes in place of the bacon. If you are substituting cooked pork, you will need to add a little oil to this recipe.

Eggless Scrambled Eggs

It is amazing how much this dish looks like scrambled eggs. The most important aspect of making this dish is not to add too much turmeric (an uncommon spice that is yellow). Turmeric gives the tofu the color of scrambled eggs, but don't be heavy handed because it does add flavor. This dish is just great with the optional ingredients of vegetables, and the non-dairy cheeses available these days.

1 pound firm tofu
1 tablespoon of acceptable oil
To taste: salt and pepper
Dash of turmeric
Optional:
Sautéed vegetables (onions, peppers, broccoli, cauliflower)
Non-dairy vegetarian cheeses, shredded

Open package of tofu and drain excess water leaving the block of tofu. In a large skillet or frying pan, add oil and bring to a medium heat. Add tofu to frying pan by crumbling into chunks with your hands. Add salt and pepper to taste and just a dash of turmeric. Stir fry until the tofu is heated all the way through and the coloring of the turmeric is blended throughout. If necessary, you can add more turmeric, but only if the "eggless" scrambled eggs need more coloring. If you use the non-dairy vegetarian cheeses, you may want to place the grated or mashed cheeses over the tofu and place under the broiler as this frequently produces the best "melting" of the non-dairy cheeses.

Cole Slaw

This recipe avoids the mayonnaise typically used in cole slaw with a simple syrup and vinegar instead. It is tasty but different than mayonnaise based cole slaw.

1 head cabbage, grated or shredded(or 1½ bags of shredded cabbage)
1 medium onion, chopped
1 red pepper, chopped
1 yellow pepper, chopped
1 orange pepper, chopped
1 cup shredded carrot
½ cup sugar
½ cup white vinegar
¼ cup of acceptable oil
½ teaspoon celery seed
¼ teaspoon dried mustard

In a saucepan, combine sugar, vinegar, oil, celery seed and dry mustard and bring to a boil. Boil for 2 minutes until sugar is dissolved and remove from heat. Let cool. Process cabbage into bite-sized pieces by using a hand grater or a food processor to shred or grate. Place cabbage, chopped peppers and the shredded carrot in a large bowl. Pour the sugar and vinegar mixture over the cabbage mixture and allow to marinate in the refrigerator overnight. Mix well before serving.

German Potato Salad

German potato salad is normally free of dairy and is delicious. This is a large quantity.

8 to 10 large potatoes boiled in skins and peeled while hot
12 strips bacon fried crisp
2 medium onions
2 teaspoons salt
4 tablespoons sugar
½ cup diced celery
⅔ cup cider vinegar or white vinegar
4 tablespoons potato starch or other thickening agent or flour, dissolved in ⅓ cup water
2 cups water

While the potatoes are boiling and the bacon is frying, dice the onion and celery. Sauté the onion and celery in the bacon fat when the bacon is done. When the onions and celery are cooked, remove from the pan and make the sauce for the potato salad in the remaining bacon fat. Combine the vinegar, water, sugar, and salt and cook over a low heat. In a small bowl, combine the potato starch (or substitute thickener) with the water to dissolve. Add to the sauce mixture and cook, stirring while it thickens. Peel and cut the potatoes into slices. Add the sauce mixture, crushed or crumbled bacon, sautéed onion and celery to the potatoes. This is delicious hot or cold. This is a party or family size recipe. If you are cooking just for one or two I would cut this recipe in half.

Baked Butternut Squash

This is an easy food to prepare and it is an excellent side dish for dinners as well as a great baby food. If you make this for your infant or toddler, you can then freeze the baked butternut squash in ice cube trays or other small portions and take out just the right amount when it is feeding time. Butternut squash has a slightly sweet taste, and you may find it palatable scooped right out of the shell.

Preheat oven to 375°.

1 butternut squash

Optional:

You may oil the outside of the squash (we do NOT do this, however some people do)

If you want to, you can add sugar, brown sugar or any sweetener that suits you (I don't add any sugar to squash when it is cooking)

Wash and dry the squash and cut in half lengthwise. Remove the seeds and place open side down in a baking dish. Place in a 375° oven and bake for 1 to 1½ hours depending upon the size. When it is completely soft and tender it is done. Scoop out the insides discarding the shell.

On great way to use squash is for muffin and waffle recipes, which I have included in this book. Squash adds nutrition, great taste, and is a welcome addition to baked goods.

Beets

Yes, I had to include a recipe for beets because most people don't know how to cook beets or what to do with them. It's all a learning process and I didn't know how to cook beets years ago either! How to get your kids to eat beets? Try the Mock Ranch Dip featured in this cookbook! All three of my children will eat beets with a little of the mock Ranch Dip we make. The cooked beets will keep in your fridge for about 3 days. The uncooked (raw) beets however will keep in your fridge for weeks and weeks. So, just cook what you will eat.

Cut off the tops of your raw beets and place in a large pan of water. Bring to a boil and cook until a sharp knife can be inserted easily. Large to medium sized beets will probably need to be boiled for about 1 hour. Watch the pan and add water as needed. Cool beets slightly and then peel outer skin. Beets can also be cooked in the oven. Wrap washed beets with greens removed in aluminum foil and back at 400° until cooked through using a knife or potato tester to check for doneness. Beets can be cooked at a lower temperature as well it will just take longer. Beets can scorch in the oven so it is important to check them every 20 or so minutes.

Scalloped Potatoes

What? Scalloped potatoes without dairy and gluten? Yes! You can have delicious scalloped potatoes without the dairy and gluten!

Preheat oven to 375°.

6 to 7 large potatoes, washed well
2 tablespoons oil
4 tablespoons acceptable flour (rice, or tapioca)* (see note below about flour choice)
2 cups nondairy milk substitute
To taste: salt and pepper
1½ tablespoons minced, dried onion

Wash and peel the potatoes, and soak in pure water while you proceed. If you have never made scalloped potatoes, the basic recipe is to layer peeled and thinly sliced potatoes with slabs of fat and to sprinkle flour, salt and pepper to each layer. In this gluten-free and dairy-free version of scalloped potatoes we are using liquid oil (since the slabs of fat melt anyway) and gluten-free flour. It *does matter* which gluten-free flour you use and *it does matter which liquid* you will use because certain gluten-free flours and dairy-free beverages will alter the taste of the scalloped potatoes.

In a large greased casserole or glass baking dish place a single layer of peeled and sliced potatoes on the bottom of the dish. Lightly sprinkle this layer of potatoes with salt and pepper, a pinch of the dried onion flakes and the gluten-free flour you have selected. Then place a second layer of peeled and sliced potatoes on top of the first layer. Repeat the sprinkling of salt, pepper, minced onion and flour. Continue this layering process until all potatoes are used up. Pour oil over the potatoes and then fill the casserole dish with your non-dairy milk substitute. Add enough milk substitute to come up to the top of the potatoes.

Bake the potatoes in a 375° oven for 60 minutes stirring occasionally. Your potatoes will be done when a knife goes through them easily. The reason that I recommend thinly sliced potatoes is because they will bake more quickly. If you have used thicker slices, you will need to bake your scalloped potatoes longer.

Notes:

*I have recommended rice or tapioca flours for this recipe because they are about as tasteless as you can get. It doesn't mean that these are the only two flours that you can use. I have made this recipe with garfava flour and it tasted great! The only negative about this recipe using garfava flour was that the potatoes turned out a little browner in color because garfava flour is darker in color. So, my recommendation for the rice or tapioca flours is not just for taste but also for the sake of appearance.

**Many of the non-dairy beverages will add sweetness or other flavors to foods. So, you may have to compensate if you use a sweetened or stronger flavored beverage.

Restaurant Style Broiled Home Fries

If you can eat potatoes, this is one way to dress up a bland food. I got the idea from a restaurant as the name implies.

5 washed potatoes, (peel if desired), sliced thinly
1½ tablespoons acceptable oil (you can use more if desired)

Select one of the following spices:

Lisa's Special Seasoning Salt (recipe is in this book)

OR your choice of:
Rosemary, basil and parsley
Paprika, cayenne pepper, garlic and onion salt

Or use acceptable commercial seasoning mixes as you
tolerate them

Do you want spicy home fries? Or perhaps home fries with just a hint of flavor? Choose one of the seasoning options and sprinkle over the potatoes. Broil until done, approximately 30 minutes depending on how you slice your potatoes stirring occasionally so they do not burn.

DRESSINGS, DIPS & SAUCES

Ranch Dip

While traveling I picked up an organic packet of Ranch Dip mix, which was actually not very tasty. That lead to the invention of this recipe! This is fast and easy to make and you can use this recipe with non-dairy sour cream or regular sour cream!

¾ to 1 teaspoon onion powder
¾ to 1 teaspoon garlic powder
1-1/2 teaspoon salt
2 tablespoons parsley
1 to 1-1/2 teaspoons of sugar
8 ounces of non-dairy sour cream

Mix all spices together with non-dairy sour cream or other base.

Gourmet French Dip

I was at a fairly fancy restaurant when they served this delicious bean dip for the bread. It was amazing. Not having the recipe, I have no idea what they put in their bean spread except for beans. This dip was a hit with everyone in my family on the first try. We use if for fresh vegetables, to spread on gluten-free crackers or on bread (rolls in our house).

1-1/2 cups cooked white navy beans or 1 – 15 ounce can of
    navy beans, rinsed and drained
2 tablespoons of olive oil
1 clove of garlic, minced
salt to taste
1/4 plus teaspoons of dried basil (just a dash more than ¼
    teaspoon)

Place all ingredients into a food processor and pulse or blend until smooth. Taste test it to see if you want to add more spices. I personally would use more spices, however this is the recipe that my family rated top notch. Serve with fresh vegetables, bread or rolls or chips. Makes just over 1 cup.

Chicken or Turkey Gravy

Gravy is not that hard to make. If you have never made it, try it at least once. I'm sure you'll be surprised at how easy it is to make from scratch.

3 cups of chicken or turkey drippings or broth
1 teaspoon of salt
2-1/2 Tablespoons Cornstarch or other thickening agent

If you are using chicken or turkey drippings, use a piece of cheesecloth to strain out any pieces of meat or fat. Place the strained drippings or broth in a medium saucepan. Add cornstarch to ¼ cup of cold water and mix until there are no lumps. Add to broth or drippings and cook over medium high heat until thickened. If you prefer thicker gravy, you can add more cornstarch or other thickening agent.

Giblet Gravy

If you never know what to do with the neck and giblets from your turkey or chicken, try this recipe for delicious gravy.

1 chicken or turkey neck
giblets and other organs
6 cups of pure water
1 teaspoon of salt
¼ onion, sliced into large wedges
2 Tablespoons Cornstarch or other thickening agent

Place the giblets, organs and neck in a medium sauce pan with the water and cook over medium low heat for 1 to 1-1/2 hours. Remove the neck, giblets and other organs. Strain the remaining liquid through clean cheesecloth or very clean tea towel or other such cloth. Wash pan out and return strained liquid back into the clean pan. You will have about 1-1/2 cups of giblet broth. Add cornstarch to ¼ cup of cold water and mix until there are no lumps. Add to giblet broth and cook over medium high heat until thickened. If you prefer thicker gravy, you can add more cornstarch or other thickening agent.

Everybody's Salsa

I named this Everybody's Salsa because even my daughter would eat it! Why? Because it lacks the jalapeño peppers that make regular salsa too hot and spicy for her. This is a great way to use up an abundance of tomatoes during the summer.

   **4 cups fresh tomatoes, diced (approximately 5 medium
      tomatoes)**
   6 ounces tomato paste
   1 tablespoons sugar
   2 cups onion, chopped
   ½ teaspoon salt
   1 tablespoon vinegar (optional)
   ½ teaspoon garlic powder
   ½ teaspoon onion powder
   1 tablespoon parsley

In a large bowl, combine all ingredients together and mix well. The flavors of this will meld together in a few hours. If you like or can tolerate jalapeño peppers, feel free to add them. This recipe makes about 4 ½ cups of salsa.

Mango Peach Salsa

I had a version of this at a party and I just fell in love with the taste! When peaches came into season in our CSA, it was the right time to try my hand at this. This version is not overly spicy or sweet – so you can add more kick or sweetness as desired.

> **2 cups fresh, chopped tomatoes (about 3 medium tomatoes)**
> **1-1/2 cups diced mango**
> **1 cup diced peaches**
> **1-1/2 cup onion**
> **1 cup green onions**
> **1 tablespoon red wine vinegar**
> **1 tablespoon lemon juice**
> **3 tablespoons sugar**
> **2 tablespoons tomato paste**
> **¼ teaspoon xanthan gum**

Mix all ingredients together in a large mixing bowl. This recipe makes 5-1/2 cups.

Peachy Salsa

I invented this recipe because I had lots of ripe peaches and tomatoes from our CSA cooperative! On the first try, which is a miracle of sorts we had a salsa that we loved and in fact ate all up within twenty minutes. A bit of tinkering, however, made it even better! We do not make this with much of a kick, but you are obviously welcome to. Also, I do not add sugar since the peaches are naturally sweet.

1 ½ cups diced fresh peaches
1 ½ cups diced fresh tomatoes
2 teaspoons dried parsley
1 cup chopped onion
½ teaspoon Celtic salt
Dash of cayenne pepper or hot sauce or to taste
Optional: 2 tablespoons tomato paste

Mix all ingredients in a medium size-mixing bowl. The tomato paste is listed as optional because the first time I made this, it did not occur to me to include the tomato paste and it was delicious! The tomato paste will give it a more "store-bought" consistency in my opinion. This recipe makes about 3-1/2 cups. If it is not sweet enough for you then you can add sugar to taste.

Old Fashioned Salsa

I made this recipe to use up tomatoes from our abundant CSA cooperative! Most commercial salsa products contain sugar. If you use stevia as the sweetener it is more diet friendly to diabetics and those watching their sugar. Remember you only need a very tiny amount with stevia! Be careful when adding your "kick". I added too much fresh, chopped cayenne pepper to one batch and it was HOT!

   2 cups fresh chopped tomatoes
   ½ cup finely diced fresh green pepper
   1 cup diced onion
   1 clove garlic, minced
   3 tablespoons tomato paste
   2 teaspoons vinegar
   salt to taste
   dash of stevia or sugar to taste
   dash of cayenne pepper, hot pepper sauce or hot peppers to
       taste

Combine all ingredients in a medium-sized mixing bowl. If you are using fresh, chopped cayenne pepper from your garden or coop, my suggestion is to chop it very, very fine and add a little bit at a time. When making your own salsa – a word to the wise – add the hot peppers or cayenne peppers just a bit at a time! This recipe makes about 3 cups.

Guacamole

My children tried an organic guacamole one day at the grocery store. My children loved it. Eventually, I thought we should try to make it from scratch – why not! This is an easy recipe with few spices. Feel free to add more spices as your tastes dictate.

2 ripe avocados, peeled and seeded, cut into chunks
2 teaspoons vinegar (optional)
½ teaspoon garlic powder
½ teaspoon onion powder
Salt and Pepper to taste

Combine all ingredients in a food processor and blend until smooth and creamy. Eat immediately or freeze. Guacamole will turn brown quickly when exposed to air, so if you are not going to eat all of the guacamole, place the guacamole in a plastic bag with the air removed and freeze. This makes 1 cup.

Sweet & Sour Sauce

Here is a quick sweet and sour sauce that you can make using organic ingredients without preservatives and additives.

½ cup pineapple juice
3 Tablespoons acceptable oil
2 Tablespoons brown sugar
1 teaspoon salt
½ teaspoon pepper
¼ cup apple cider vinegar (or other mild vinegar)

Combine all ingredients in a medium saucepan and cook over medium high heat. Once the ingredients come to a rolling boil, reduce heat and simmer for 5-7 minutes. This makes about ¾ cup of sauce.

Red Sweet & Sour Sauce or Dressing

The inspiration for this recipe comes from two sources both of which are store bought bottled sauces. Some of the commercially made sweet and sour sauces contain artificial food dyes, potassium sorbate, and sodium benzoate. This provides a nice, low cost alternative without the not so hot ingredients. This sauce took about 10 attempts to get the flavor to match the bottled sauce because I did not add enough sugar. It was shocking to me how much sugar it took to get the perfect flavor match to the commercial sauces that my children loved. I'm not advocating that this is a healthy sauce, just a better alternative to some commercial sauces.

1 cup ketchup
¾ cup sugar or other sweetener
1-1/2 tablespoon oil
3 tablespoons water
2 tablespoons vinegar
1-1/2 teaspoon celery seed
¼ teaspoon garlic powder
½ teaspoon parsley flakes

Place all ingredients in a medium saucepan over medium heat. Cook for 10 to 15 minutes to thicken slightly and meld the flavors. The taste of this sauce will change as it cools and varies if the sauce is hot or cold. Makes about 1 cup. While this is not my favorite sauce because of the high amount of sugar, my children love it – I often make a double batch of this.

Basil Sauce

I came up with this dish simply to get out of a rut with Chicken. This sauce can be used on chicken or vegetables. It has a restaurant style gourmet flavor. It was a hit with two of my three children.

1-1/2 cups chicken broth
1 small diced onion
2 cloves minced garlic
¼ cup cooking sherry
1 teaspoon of sugar
1-1/2 Tablespoon of thickener (cornstarch or other favorite thickener)
Pinch of basil
Pinch of thyme
Salt to taste

Set aside ¼ cup of the broth. Place remaining broth, onion, garlic, sugar, basil and thyme in a medium sauce pan. Mix ¼ cup broth and thickener, then add to the sauce pan. Heat over medium high heat until cooked through and thick. You may add more or less thickener to the sauce depending upon the consistency you prefer. This makes 1-1/2 cups of sauce.

Pulled Pork Sauce

This is quick to make and will store in the fridge for a week or more.

¼ cup vinegar
1/8 cup acceptable oil
½ cup honey
7 oz. tomato paste
½ cup water
1 teaspoon lemon juice
½ teaspoon Worcestershire sauce
Salt & Pepper to taste

Mix all ingredients together until combined well. Use with pulled pork. Makes 2 cups.

Hot Wings Sauce

I made this recipe to make Buffalo chicken wings. Some of the bottled sauces to make wings contain preservatives (chemicals), which we like to avoid.

½ teaspoon salt
1/8 teaspoon pepper
2 Tablespoons acceptable oil
2 Tablespoons red hot sauce
½ teaspoon white vinegar
dash of xanthan gum

Mix all ingredients in a shaker bottle or dressing bottle and shake well to mix. Use over chicken wings or as a dipping sauce. Makes ¼ cup sauce.

Meat Marinade

This is a simple recipe I came up with to marinate meat!

¼ cup oil
3 Tablespoons Worcestershire Sauce
1 teaspoon garlic powder
1 teaspoon onion powder

Mix all ingredients and slather over the meat. Let the meat soak in this marinade for several hours or overnight before cooking. This recipe makes about ¼ cup of marinade, so if you have a lot of meat or a really large cut, you may need to double the recipe.

Fruit Salad Dressing

This is a nice dressing if you want a fresh fruit cocktail without a heavy syrup.

½ cup lime juice
½ cup honey or other liquid sweetener (like agava nectar)
Pinch of ginger

Mix all ingredients together and pour over fruit. When adding the ginger, less is more. You can always add more ginger. Let flavors meld together for a few hours and taste. Then you can add more ginger if desired. Makes about one cup dressing.

Balsamic Vinaigrette Dressing

It is difficult to find soy-free salad dressings that are also free of other allergens. I came up with this dressing for our spring salad bonanza with our CSA organic cooperative. I used a small amount of stevia to cut the bite of the balsamic vinegar. The flavor of this dressing is much better on day two or three when the flavors have melded. Caution on the cayenne pepper – too much will result in a dressing that leaves your mouth hotter than you might like! I usually double the recipe so I don't have to make it as often. This is definitely one of those adults only recipes – most children won't like this.

1/3 cup pure water
1 tablespoon olive oil or other acceptable oil
1 tablespoon balsamic vinegar
1 tablespoon apple cider vinegar
1/8 teaspoon of stevia powder or sugar to taste
dash of Celtic salt
1 clove garlic, minced
dash of onion powder
dash of black pepper
tiny, tiny amount of cayenne pepper
dash of xanthan gum or about 1/8 teaspoon

Combine all ingredients and mix well. I mix this up in a glass cruet, the kind that Good Seasons® Salad Dressing still sells. This makes about ½ cup of dressing. You may want to double the recipe if you like it as much as I do.

Hearty Italian Dressing

I invented this recipe for those of you who have trouble with soybean oil! Many salad dressings contain soybean oil, which can be troublesome to say the least! This is also a great way to save money since the better salad dressings can be expensive!

1 cup filtered water
2/3 cup olive oil or other acceptable oil
1/3 cup white vinegar
dash of stevia or sugar to taste
2 tablespoons pureed roasted red peppers
1 tablespoon roasted red pepper, finely chopped
¼ teaspoon salt
¼ teaspoon garlic powder
1 clove garlic, minced
dash of onion powder
dash of dry mustard powder
dash of cayenne pepper
dash of ground black pepper
dash of oregano
¾ teaspoon xanthan gum

Mix all ingredients well. Makes about 2 cups of dressing. Refrigerate to meld the flavors before using.

Fast and Easy Italian Dressing

I came up with this recipe when I was out of my favorite dressing and I didn't have the roasted red pepper that my first Italian Dressing calls for! Made with olive oil and stevia, this dressing can suit allergy and diabetic needs. You might like this more than the Hearty Italian Dressing.

1/3 cup vinegar
1/3 cup acceptable oil
1/3 cup pure water
1 teaspoon oregano
½ teaspoon basil
½ teaspoon dried rosemary
¼ teaspoon onion powder
1 teaspoon dried parsley
1 clove garlic, minced
dash of stevia (or sugar to taste)
dash of cayenne pepper
black ground pepper to taste
dash of Celtic salt
dash of xanthan gum

Mix all ingredients in a dressing bottle or shaker and shake well to incorporate. This makes about 1 cups of dressing.

Roasted Red Pepper Vinaigrette

I came up with this recipe to knock-off a commercially made dressing that contained milk. I wanted one without milk for obvious reasons! It took some tweaking to get the texture and taste to mirror the store-bought brand, which is what my son wanted. It is a great dressing, however you have to have red peppers on hand to roast or purchase roasted red peppers, which adds to the cost and preparation time.

½ cup water
1/3 cup acceptable oil
¾ cup roasted red pepper puree
1 tablespoon vinegar
dash of stevia (or sugar to taste)
1 tablespoon roasted red peppers, finely diced
1 tablespoon tomato paste
¼ teaspoon salt
½ teaspoon onion powder
dash of black ground pepper
dash of xanthan gum
¼ teaspoon garlic powder

You can either roast your own red peppers and then puree in a food processor, or you can purchase roasted red peppers and puree them in the food processor. I've done both. If you roast your own red peppers, you will need to add some liquid to the food processor. The store-bought roasted red peppers will typically come in a jar with liquid surrounding the red peppers, and thus they will already have liquid and should not require any additional liquid. Mix all ingredients in a blender and blend until all the ingredients are incorporated. This recipe makes about 1-1/2 cups.

Hot Bacon Dressing

I decided to make hot bacon dressing for an abundance of greens that we received from our CSA cooperative, the Native Offerings Farm. This dressing can also be used with potatoes to make a hot potato salad. This is not a recipe most children will like.

6 ounces of nitrate, nitrite, chemical and hormone free bacon
1 cup water
¼ cup vinegar
dash of salt
1 small onion
2 teaspoons celery seed
4 tablespoons sugar
1 tablespoon bacon fat from cooking the bacon
1-1/2 tablespoons acceptable thickener and ¼ cup water

Chemical free, hormone free, nitrate and nitrite free bacon is available in more and more grocery stores and health food stores. Cook bacon in a large frying pan over medium low heat. Bacon without all of the chemicals seems to burn easier, so watch the bacon carefully and remove from pan when cooked. Reserve 1-2 tablespoons of bacon fat for cooking the onion. Set the cooked bacon aside for use later. The rest of the bacon fat may be frozen for later use or discarded. Fry the onion in the reserved bacon fat. When the onion is fully cooked, add remaining ingredients except for cooked bacon. Make dressing in the frying pan stirring constantly. When dressing is complete, add crumbled bacon. Serve hot over fresh spinach or other green salad or over potatoes. Makes about 1 cup.

1000 Island Dressing

Oh my gosh – I am so excited about this salad dressing because it does not contain mayonnaise! It tastes just like the bottled dressing I used to buy, but without the additives and preservatives – and at a much lower cost!

½ cup oil
1 tablespoon apple cider vinegar
1 teaspoon salt
1 teaspoon dry mustard
½ cup ketchup
4 tablespoons sweet relish
2 tablespoons finely diced onion
1 teaspoon xanthan gum
1/3 cup non-dairy milk substitute
3 tablespoons sugar
1/3 cup water plus 3 tablespoons water

Mix all ingredients in a blender and blend until well incorporated. This makes 2 cups of dressing.

Poppyseed Dressing

My Mom served this delicious salad dressing at a holiday meal! I felt that I wouldn't be able to convert it because it contained mayonnaise. I was shocked and elated when I created this recipe. Truth be told – this was not the recipe I was shooting for! How do you like that!

½ cup oil plus 3 tablespoons
½ teaspoon salt
2 tablespoons apple cider vinegar
¾ cup nondairy milk substitute
½ teaspoon xanthan gum
2 ½ teaspoon Stevia
1 ½ teaspoon sugar
2 tablespoons poppyseeds

Blend completely in blender. Makes about 2 cups.

Asian Sauce

I invented this sauce to go on a stir-fry when we got tired of the same old stir-fry sauce we were using. Much to my surprise, my children liked it. As usual, I would spice it up a bit for adults only because it is too bland for me..

2 cups beef broth
2 large clove garlic, minced
½ cup pure water
2 to 3 tablespoons of acceptable thickener (gluten-free flour, cornstarch, etc.)
Salt to taste
4 teaspoons ground ginger (or more)
3 tablespoons brown sugar

Mix water and thickener in a small bowl or measuring cup and set aside. Place the beef broth, garlic, spices, and sugar in a medium saucepan and stir over medium heat until the sugar is dissolved. Add the thickener and continue cooking over medium to medium high heat until thickened. Remove from heat and serve over your favorite dish. This recipe makes about 2-1/2 cups and will keep in the fridge for a few days to almost a week.

Roux Sauce

I came up with this sauce when my children kept asking for macaroni and cheese. They did not start doing this until a commercially made gfcf macaroni and "no cheese" dish came out that we purchased at the store. The issue with the commercially made dish was not the ingredients but the cost. This sauce expanded our food dish options in ways I never dreamed. This sauce is the basis for the Macaroni Doodle Dish (mac and cheese), and is used in several dishes that formerly contained cream sauces or lots of milk and cheese.

½ cup gluten-free flour (brown rice*)
1/3 cup plus 1 tablespoon non-dairy margarine
2 cups rice milk or non-dairy milk substitute
1 teaspoon Celtic salt
½ teaspoon onion powder
½ teaspoon garlic powder

In a large frying pan, over medium heat – cook the non-dairy margarine and flour until it is a paste. Then cook a bit longer, but not much. Gradually, add the rice milk about 1/3 cup at a time – then stir the roux. Once it becomes kind of creamy and smooth – add more milk. Continue this process until all of the rice milk has been added. Add the garlic and onion powder and salt. Stir until the sauce is a desired thickness.

Refried Beans a la Natural

I always wanted to make refried beans – don't ask me why! I didn't fry these in oil after the beans were done cooking, which saved time and calories.

    3 cups pinto beans, rinsed and drained
    10 cups pure water
    1 large onion, finely chopped (about 1 cup)
    1 large clove garlic, minced
    2 teaspoon Celtic salt

Rinse beans well in pure water, stirring the water to wash the beans. Rinse and drain the beans. Place the beans and water in a large stockpot over medium high heat. Add chopped onion, garlic and salt. Cook on high for about 15 minutes, then reduce the temperature to between low and medium and cook until the beans are completely cooked through and soft. This will probably take about 1-1/2 hours. You will have plenty of water left from cooking unless you cook over heat that is too high. Once the beans are completely cooked, drain off almost all of the water, which should be at least 2 cups of the bean juice and set aside. If you don't drain sufficient juice off the beans, they will be soupy. Using a potato masher, mash the beans well. If you need to add any of the bean juice, do so sparingly. This makes about 4-1/2 cups of beans.

Cranberry Sauce

My Mom always makes homemade cranberry sauce for the holidays! This is fast and easy and perfect for so many dishes.

    1 cup sugar
    1 cup water
    1 package fresh whole cranberries

Mix the sugar and water in a medium saucepan. Bring to a boil and stir until the sugar is dissolved. Add the cranberries; return to a boil. Reduce heat and boil gently for 10 minutes, stirring occasionally. Remove from heat and cool completely. Refrigerate. Makes about 2 ¼ cups.

Raspberry Sauce

This is a recipe for a smooth raspberry sauce without the seeds and pulp and this is NOT the recipe for raspberry cake filling although the ingredients are similar.

2 cups raspberries (fresh or frozen, thawed)
1 tablespoon lemon juice
½ cup sugar or other sweetener
⅓ cup water

In a small saucepan combine the sugar and water and bring to a boil over medium high heat. This is the process of making a simple syrup which is sugar and water. Stir constantly until the sugar is completely dissolved which may take 5 minutes. Add the raspberries and cook for 2 more minutes, stirring constantly.

Remove from heat and run through either a blender or a food processor to purée. Then pour the raspberry mixture through a fine wire mesh strainer over a medium bowl to remove the solids and seeds. Press the raspberry mixture through the mesh strainer with the back of a spoon to extract all of the liquid. You can save the raspberry "pulp" from the strainer for raspberry ice cream if you don't mind the seeds.

Add the lemon juice to the raspberry liquid that you collected from the straining process and allow to cool completely before serving. This makes approximately 2 cups. If you are not going to use the sauce in the next three days, freeze it for longer storage.

Lemon Marinade

This is an easy recipe to use with chicken.

¼ cup safflower or other oil
½ teaspoon garlic powder
¼ teaspoon lemon pepper
1 teaspoon parsley flakes
½ teaspoon paprika
1 teaspoon lemon juice

Mix well and refrigerate. Use within a week.

Homemade BBQ Sauce

¾ cup ketchup
2 tablespoons oil
1 tablespoon vinegar
2 tablespoons honey
2 teaspoons water
1 large clove garlic
¼ teaspoon xanthan gum

Mix all ingredients together. If you can tolerate a lot of garlic or are a garlic lover, you can add more than one clove. If you cannot tolerate commercial ketchup or afford the more expensive organic ketchups, you can use a mix of tomato paste and water in place of the ketchup, but you will need to add more sweetener to compensate. This makes about ¾ cup of sauce. We usually double or triple the recipe.

Fresh Barbecue Sauce

There are lots of commercially made barbecue sauces around these days. If you are looking for something a little bit fresher than bottled sauce, here is one more recipe for you.

> **2 tablespoons oil**
> **½ cup onion, chopped**
> **3 tablespoons Worcestershire Sauce**
> **1 clove garlic, minced**
> **2 full bottles chili sauce (or a double batch of chili sauce recipe*)**
> **¼ cup apple cider vinegar**
> **¼ cup sugar or other sweetener**
> **¼ cup water**
> **To taste: ground pepper**
> **½ teaspoon paprika**
> **¼ teaspoon chili powder**

Sauté the onion in a large frying pan in the oil until it is very soft. Reduce heat to low and add minced garlic, chili powder, paprika, and fresh ground pepper. Sauté quickly and constantly as garlic is easy to scorch. Sauté for 2 minutes. Remove from heat and add the remaining ingredients. Return to heat and simmer over low to medium low heat for one hour. Makes about 3½ cups.

*If you do not tolerate commercial chili sauce, you can use a double batch of the chili sauce recipe included in this cookbook.

Chili Sauce

I invented this recipe when my daughter required foods that were organic and free of preservatives. It is so much more economical to make some of these foods from scratch!

6 ounces organic tomato paste
1 cup pure drinking water
¼ cup sugar or other acceptable sweetener
2 tablespoons vinegar
1 teaspoon salt
1 tablespoon dried onion flakes
1 teaspoon garlic powder
½ teaspoon onion salt

Dissolve the tomato paste in the water and then add remaining ingredients. Cook slowly for 15 to 20 minutes. Makes 1½ cups. Double if using for barbecue.

Mom's Spaghetti Sauce

My spaghetti sauce with a boost of nutrition in the form of added carrots and celery.

2 cups carrots, coarsely chopped
1 cup celery, coarsely chopped
2 cups onion, coarsely chopped
2 tablespoons olive or other acceptable oil
4 cloves garlic, minced (large cloves)
2 tablespoons dried basil
2 tablespoons dried parsley
2 tablespoons dried oregano
12 ounces tomato paste
13 cups tomato sauce
1 cup packed brown sugar

This recipe makes about 15 cups depending upon how long you simmer down the sauce. Sauté onion, carrots, celery in oil in a large stockpot over medium high heat until soft. Add garlic and stir for 1 minute. Add dried spices and sauté 1 more minute. Add tomato paste and tomato sauce and brown sugar. Simmer over low to medium heat for 1 + hour.

Mama Mia Spaghetti Sauce

1¾ cup finely chopped onion
½ cup diced carrots
1 red pepper, diced
2 cloves garlic, minced
¾ cup finely chopped celery
2 tablespoons olive or other oil
1½ tablespoons oregano
1 tablespoon basil
1 tablespoon parsley
4 tablespoons brown sugar
4 cups pure drinking water
24 ounces tomato paste
56 ounces canned tomatoes
1 to 2 teaspoons salt

This recipe makes about 7½ cups or more of spaghetti sauce depending upon how long you simmer it. Sauté onion, carrots, and celery in oil in a large stock pot. Sauté until soft, then add garlic and stir for 2 minutes. Add dried spices and sauté one more minute. Add remaining ingredients and simmer for 1 to 2 hours.

Oriental Salad Dressing

The idea for this salad dressing was to make a knock-off from a chain restaurant that was too high in calories for my tastes. I used stevia to reduce the sugar.

½ cup plus 1 tablespoon acceptable oil
1 tablespoon apple cider vinegar
½ cup liquid non-dairy milk substitute
¼ teaspoon xanthan gum
1-1/2 teaspoon stevia powder (or sugar to taste)
1-1/2 teaspoon Dijon-style mustard
1-3 tablespoons water (or to the desired consistency)

Mix all the ingredients in a blender and mix well. You can add the water, 1 tablespoon at a time, to achieve the desire consistency. Without the water this will be very thick. Makes about ¾ cup if you use 3 tablespoons.

Zero Calorie Raspberry Vinaigrette

I invented this recipe to reduce the sugar and avoid preservatives. We love this dressing!

½ cup white vinegar
2/3 cup water
½ teaspoon xanthan gum
¾ teaspoon stevia
½ cup raspberries

Blend all ingredients in a blender. Makes about 1-1/2 cups.

Fat-Free & Sugar Free Italian Dressing

I came up with this to reduce sugar and fat and avoid the preservatives in many dressings.

1/3 cup acceptable vinegar
1/3 cup pure water
Black pepper to taste
¼ teaspoon xanthan gum
Dash of garlic powder
Dash onion powder
¼ teaspoon dried oregano
¼ teaspoon dried basil
Dash of cayenne pepper
¼ teaspoon dried thyme
Stevia to taste , about ¾ teaspoon plus or minus
Pinch of salt

Blend all ingredients together in a blender. Makes between 2/3 and ¾ cup.

Peach Vinaigrette

This is fantastic when you have fresh peaches and perfect for those watching sugar in their diet.

1/3 cup cider vinegar
2/3 cup pure water
½ teaspoon xanthan gum
¾ teaspoon stevia
Dash of salt
½ cup peaches

Puree in a blender until creamy. Makes ab out 1-1/2 cups of dressing.

Dijon Vinaigrette

I created this to have more salad dressing options in our house free of allergens with reduced sugar and fat.

½ cup organic cider vinegar
2/3 cup pure water
½ teaspoon xanthan gum
¾ teaspoon stevia
Dash of salt
3 teaspoons of Dijon mustard

Mix all ingredients well Makes 1-1/4 cups.

Healthy 1000 Island Dressing

This recipe is for those who want a zero sugar and no fat dressing without preservatives.

¾ cup pure water
1/3 cup organic apple cider vinegar
1-1/2 tablespoon tomato paste
Dash of salt
½ teaspoon garlic powder
½ teaspoon onion powder
1 teaspoon lemon juice
Dash white pepper
¼ teaspoon Worcestershire sauce
¼ + teaspoon xanthan gum
¼ + teaspoon stevia powder

Mix all ingredients together well. Makes about 1-1/2 cups.

Cowboys Dip

This is one of our original recipes from back in the day.

12 ounces non-dairy sour cream
2 tablespoons dried parsley flakes
¼ teaspoon onion salt
¼ teaspoon garlic salt
¼ teaspoon special seasoning salt (recipe in this cookbook)
Dash of paprika

Add all ingredients to the non-dairy sour cream and mix well. This dip is great with chips and fresh vegetables.

Mock Ranch Dip

My son, Luke, was the inspiration for this dip mix. We think it is absolutely delightful!!

- **12 ounces non-dairy sour cream**
- **2 teaspoons sugar**
- **½ teaspoon salt**
- **To taste: fresh ground pepper (e.g. 8 grinds of a small pepper mill)**
- **1 to 2 teaspoons vinegar**
- **½ teaspoon garlic powder**
- **½ teaspoon onion powder**
- **Dash of xanthan gum**
- **1 tablespoon minced dried onion flakes**
- **1 tablespoon dried parsley (further crushed in your hands)**
- **1 large garlic clove (either smashed or put through a garlic press)**
- **2 tablespoons water (add this last, and only to desired consistency)**

In a small mixing bowl, combine all ingredients. Stir well. Refrigerate for 2-3 hours before serving to meld the flavors. This dip is great for chips, fresh vegetables, meats and crackers. Makes 1½ cups of dip.

Noah's Mock Cheese Sauce

When my son, Noah was six years old he invented this recipe. It really is quite good? If you cannot have the real thing this is a great substitute.

This recipe is for an individual serving.
> **2 slices non-dairy "cheese**
> **Dash of salt and pepper**

Optional:
> **Dash of cayenne pepper**
> **Dash of garlic or onion powder**

Tear cheese slices into pieces and place in a microwavable bowl. Add salt and pepper and any of the optional spices. Cover bowl with waxed paper and microwave for 10 seconds. If not melted, microwave for 10 seconds more. Microwaves vary greatly in power and your time will be determined by your microwave power. Stir in spices. Use as a chip dip or for crackers. This can also be poured over tortilla chips for nachos.

French Onion Dip Mix

This recipe was inspired by my desire to have an onion dip like the one we used to have in the "good old days". This dip's flavors meld overnight, so it will have a stronger flavor the second day, so make sure you make it one day before you need it for optimal taste!

12 ounces non-dairy sour cream
4 tablespoons dried onion flakes or bits
1 teaspoon onion powder
1 teaspoon onion salt
1 tablespoon sugar
1 large clove of garlic, minced

Mix all ingredients together. For the "mock sour cream" for this dip, use whatever non-dairy sour cream you can tolerate. Instead of the non-dairy sour cream, you could substitute pureed chickpeas.

Chili and Garlic Sauce

The reason I made this recipe was to eliminate the preservatives found in most chili and garlic sauces. It took an awful lot of tries to get this right in terms of consistency, taste and heat. This sauce is used in a few recipes in this cookbook.

5 tablespoons of water
3-1/2 tablespoons of vinegar
3 ounces of tomato paste
1 tablespoon of cayenne pepper or crushed peppers
1-1/2 tablespoons of sugar
6 cloves of garlic, minced
Dash of salt
½ teaspoon of garlic powder

Mix all ingredients well to incorporate. This makes about ¾ cups of sauce.

Smashing Fruit Dip

This is a surprisingly simple dip that tastes excellent with fruit!

12 ounces non-dairy sour cream
3¾ tablespoons packed brown sugar

Mix well and refrigerate. The flavors will meld overnight or in a period of several hours, so the taste improves with some time. If you are using a sour cream brand that comes in an 8 ounce size, you will use 2½ tablespoons of packed brown sugar to the 8 ounces of sour cream. You can make individual serving portions if needed, and here are the proportions:

Eggless Mayonnaise

With the new foods commercially available now, you can purchase non-dairy mayonnaise made without eggs. This recipe is offered to the few who cannot tolerate soy, canola, or the other ingredients in the commercially available eggless mayonnaise. This recipe is nothing like mayonnaise made with eggs and dairy ingredients, but it is an acceptable substitute.

1 teaspoon salt
½ teaspoon paprika
¼ teaspoon dry mustard
Dash of cayenne pepper
1 teaspoon plain gelatin
½ cup cold non-dairy milk substitute
½ cup hot non-dairy milk substitute
4 tablespoons lemon juice

Combine gelatin and ½ cup cold milk and dry spices. Mix well. Add ½ cup hot non-dairy milk substitute and lemon juice and refrigerate until well chilled, 2 to 4 hours. Remove from the refrigerator and beat until fluffy in an electric mixer or with a rotary whisk. Chill again for 2 to 4 hours and then remove and beat one more time. Refrigerate until needed. You will need to stir this very well before using, and you may need to thin it a little bit with some lemon juice or water if the consistency is too thick for you. Makes about 1 cup.

Sassy Salad Dressing

This salad dressing is definitely not for everyone. But if you like a sweet and sour type dressing, then this one may just hit the spot. You can alter the tartness or sweetness by changing the vinegar to sugar ratio.

⅔ cup sugar, or other sweetener
1 cup vinegar
½ teaspoon white pepper
1 tablespoon chives
1 teaspoon salt
2 tablespoons Worcestershire sauce
½ cup olive oil (or other acceptable oil)
1 small onion, finely chopped
½ teaspoon paprika
2 teaspoons prepared mustard

Place all ingredients into a blender and mix well. This recipe keeps well in the refrigerator for about 1 week. It is excellent on raw spinach and lettuce greens. Makes about 1½ cups.

Celery Seed Dressing

I have had this recipe for decades. I love it although it can be made healthier with a sugar substitute.

½ cup sugar or other sweetener
1 teaspoon dry mustard
1 teaspoon salt
1 tablespoon grated onion
⅓ cup vinegar
¾ cup acceptable oil
1 tablespoon celery seed

Combine sugar or other sweetener, mustard, salt, onion, and vinegar in a blender and mix well. Add oil and blend again. Add the celery seed and pulse just to mix well. Makes about 1 cup.

Ranch Dressing

I invented this for salads so we could have a soy-free dressing that the kids would enjoy. The thickening agent in this dressing is xanthan gum. You will need a blender to make this recipe as it thickens with the whirling motion of the blender. Don't be alarmed if you mix it up and it seems too watery. You can add more xanthan gum, but I would not add more until you have blended it in the blender.

½ cup pure drinking water
⅓ cup acceptable oil
¼ cup milk substitute
1 tablespoon sugar or other sweetener
1 tablespoon brown rice syrup
1 teaspoon apple cider vinegar
1 teaspoon white or red wine vinegar
1¼ teaspoon garlic powder
1¼ teaspoon onion powder
½ teaspoon Dijon mustard
1 teaspoon lemon juice
1 teaspoon dried parsley flakes
Dash of ground black pepper
¼ teaspoon xanthan gum, Blend and use ¼ teaspoon more, only if necessary to thicken

Note: You can substitute other natural sweeteners, if needed, as long as you understand that they will alter the taste. Therefore, if you are using other sweeteners (like honey), you may need to adjust your spices. And if you are using a flavored milk substitute you will have to adjust the recipe to compensate for the flavor.

Combine all ingredients in a blender and blend for 1 to 2 minutes. Add more xanthan gum, only if necessary to thicken to your desired consistency. Store in an airtight container in the refrigerator. Makes about 1 cup.

Strawberry Vinaigrette

This recipe was Noah's idea and he was there to taste test the first go at it. This is nice for fresh spinach, salads, or as a dipping sauce for fresh veggies.

½ cup acceptable oil
2 tablespoons red wine vinegar
2 tablespoons sugar
5 large fresh strawberries (more if your berries are small)
Dash of salt
To taste: ground pepper

Combine all ingredients in the blender and purée until smooth. Refrigerate until well chilled. If you are using smaller strawberries, use more than five.

DESSERTS, CAKES, COOKIES & SWEET TREATS

Gloria's White Wedding Cake

The inspiration for this recipe goes to Gloria, a dear friend, and an amazing woman – hence the name! I had given up on ever creating a white, egg-free cake until Gloria asked for help for her nieces wedding. I created this recipe just for Gloria and I think of her every time I make it. If you change the flour mix, it will change the texture and result of the baked good. It is a delicious cake that freezes well.

Preheat oven to 350°
> 1 1/2 cups white rice flour (I used a mix of white and brown rice flour - half each)
> 1 1/2 cups of tapioca flour
> 2 teaspoons of xanthan gum
> 1 1/2 cups sugar
> 2 Tablespoons baking powder
> Pinch of salt
> ½ cup or 8 tablespoons of non-dairy margarine substitute at room temperature
> 4 teaspoons of Ener-G® Egg Replacer (dry powder)
> 2 teaspoons vanilla
> 1 1/2 cups rice milk
> Extra rice milk: 1 to 4 tablespoons, as needed

Preheat oven to 350 degrees. Grease and flour two 8-inch round baking pans and set aside. Measure all of the dry ingredients into a large mixing bowl and set aside. Take your margarine and cut it into small pieces and add to the dry ingredients. Cut the margarine into the flour mixture until it is very, very well incorporated into the dry ingredients. Add 1 1/2 cups of rice milk and the vanilla. Start to mix the batter. Then add a little less than 1/2 cup of additional rice milk. The batter for this cake will be very thick. It will not drip off of a spoon. It will hold it's shape pretty well. You may need a bit less milk if you are light on your flour measurements.

Mix well, but do NOT OVER MIX your batter. You will probably see small lumps of margarine in the batter, which is fine. Place the batter into your prepared pans and bake for 20 to 35 minutes or until done. Oven temperature is very important. A hotter or cooler oven will change both the baking time and results. This recipe produced a nice, moist cake. Because we used organic sugar and organic vanilla (both browner in color than clear vanilla or bleached sugar), our cake was not a pure white color. For cupcakes, bake for 25 to 2 8 minutes or until done. This recipes makes 24 to 26 cupcakes if using about ¼ cup batter per cupcake.

Chocolate Applesauce Cake

One of my friends was telling me about an egg-free applesauce cake her family made, which had raisins and spices in it. That conversation gave me the idea for this recipe. I took out the spices and raisins and added chocolate for flavor. It took me several tries since I invented this from scratch. My first two attempts did not have enough sugar or applesauce. I hit is just right on the fourth try! This freezes well.

Preheat oven to 350°
   1-1/4 cup Garfava flour
   ½ cup tapioca flour
   ½ teaspoon salt
   2 teaspoons baking soda
   1-1/2 teaspoon xanthan gum
   ¼ cup cocoa powder
   Dash of cloves
   ½ cup margarine or acceptable oil
   1-1/2 cup sugar (3/4 cup white and ¾ cup brown)
   1-1/2 generous cups applesauce (a tad bit over 1-1/2 cups)
   1 teaspoon vanilla

Preheat oven to 350°. Grease and flour a Bundt pan or 2- 8 or 9 inch round pans and set aside. Measure the flours, salt, baking soda, xanthan gum, cocoa and cloves into a small mixing bowl and set aside. Mix the margarine or fat and sugar and cream together in a large mixing bowl. Add the applesauce and vanilla and mix well. Add the flour mixture and mix just enough to incorporate all ingredients. Do not overmix. Place the cake mixture into the baking pan(s) and spread out to fill the pan(s). For a Bundt cake for 50 to 60 minutes or until done, for 2 round cake pans bake 25 to 35 minutes. This recipe makes excellent cupcakes. The baking time for cupcakes is 23 to 27 minutes or until done. Watch closely while baking and check for doneness at appropriate times. Baking time will depend slightly on rack placement and pan size. If you use a 9" x 13" pan, you will get a cake that is only about one inch tall, so be forewarned that this is not formulated to make a 9" x 13" cake. This recipe will make about 20 cupcakes.

Bakery Frosting

Yes, you can get frosting at home that is very much like what you would get from a Bakery! I highly recommend that you consider taking a Wilton® Cake Decorating Class if you are going to be baking for a gluten-free, dairy-free family member because you can learn to decorate any cake that you make and have it look just like it came from a bakery! The Wilton® Cake Decorating Classes are typically offered at crafting stores where their products are sold.

> **2 pounds confectioners' sugar (10 X or powdered sugar)**
> **1 cup shortening or solid fat (see note on this)**
> **2 teaspoons pure vanilla extract**
> **Dash of salt**
> **8 tablespoons water, more as needed**

Please note that not all shortening or "solid" fats will work for this recipe. You will get a frosting, but it will not be light and fluffy. One of the fat substitutes that we use I simply will not use in frosting. If the shortening or solid fat becomes runny, very soft or kind of melts at room temperature – that is not the fat to use in this frosting. Place powdered sugar in the mixing bowl of an electric mixer. Cut up the fat or shortening into small chunks and place on top of the powdered sugar. Add the dash of salt, and vanilla. Add the water 1 tablespoon at a time evenly around the powdered sugar. The above ratio of water to confectioner's sugar is perfect for frosting a cake. If, however, you want to make decorative flowers or trim with the frosting, you will add less water so you get a stiffer frosting.

**In the Wilton® Cake Decorating Classes you are taught the proper consistency for frostings and decorative icings. If you find that you are having difficulty spreading this frosting on your cake you can add an additional tablespoon of water or two to make your frosting spread easier on you cake.

Gently start and stop your mixer to blend the powdered sugar, shortening and water until it is well combined. Then gradually turn up your mixer speed and mix for 2 to 3 minutes until the frosting is light and fluffy.

Chocolate Bakery Frosting

Use 4 to 5 tablespoons of acceptable cocoa powder in the recipe on page 251.

Chocolate Frosting

This is a basic chocolate frosting simply using non-dairy and allergy and gluten free ingredients.

> **1 stick of acceptable margarine or other shortening**
> **4 tablespoons cocoa**
> **5 - 6 tablespoons of water or non-dairy milk substitute**
> **1-pound (16 oz.) acceptable powdered or Confectioner's**
> **   sugar**
> **1 teaspoon pure vanilla extract**
> **Dash of salt**

Combine all ingredients and beat until smooth and creamy.

Chocolate Ganache Frosting

I made this after eating out at a restaurant and seeing the dessert tray! It may not be the traditional way that Ganache is made, but this is absolutely divine!

> **10 ounces acceptable chocolate chips**
> **1 cup liquid non-dairy milk substitute**

Bring the non-dairy milk substitute to a near boil. Pour over the chocolate chips and stir very well until smooth. Pour over cake while hot or at least warm. This makes 2 cups.

Raspberry Cake Filling

I came up with this recipe when I was looking to serve a special cake for my son's Confirmation. I used this filling with the chocolate cake and the chocolate ganache frosting. It was so divine! You can use cherries in place of the raspberries.

2 cups raspberries, fresh or frozen
2 tablespoons of acceptable thickener (cornstarch, arrowroot, tapioca, etc.)
¾ cup sugar
Pinch of salt
1 ½ tablespoon lemon juice

Cook all ingredients over medium heat until thickened. This makes 2 cups. This is intended to be used as a cake filling, but could be used in other desserts.

Dreamy Chocolate Cream Pie

I got the idea for this dessert while out at a restaurant and thinking about how I could make a chocolate cream pie. It's dreamy!

1-pie crust of your choice*
1/2 to 3/4 cup melted acceptable chocolate chips
1/4 cup liquid sweetener (like agave)
16 oz. Non-dairy whipped topping
6 acceptable cookies, crumbled into LARGE chunks
More melted chocolate to drizzle over the top of the pie
(about 1/2 cup chocolate chips)

While you can use any piecrust, for this pie I recommend either crushed cracker or cookie crumbs, cereal or what we used was a marshmallow and rice cereal crust. You remember how you used to combine a rice cereal, marshmallows and some margarine to make marshmallow treats? Well you can make a batch of rice-crisp treats and the standard batch will make 2 piecrusts with some leftover for treats. I used a rice-cereal/marshmallow crust because I wanted to use up some marshmallows that had seen better days!! It is all about finding ways to use the food before it expires! Place whatever piecrust you are using in a standard 8 or 9 inch pie dish. In a large mixer, whip up the whipped topping until it is fluffy and stiff like a standard whipped cream topping. Add melted chocolate (1/2 cup to 3/4 cup) and liquid sugar and mix well.

Place chocolate topping mixture into pie plate. Sprinkle chunks of the cookies on top of the pie. Drizzle the remaining 1/2 cup melted chocolate chips over the top of the pie. There are so many ways that you can vary this pie. I plan to have fun with this over the coming winter months!! Here is the picture. The chocolate on the top of my pie was clumpy because I melted it in the same bowl as the sugar/chocolate mixture was in and that altered the consistency and drizzle factor for the melted chocolate. It still tasted fantastic!!

Decadent Chocolate Brownies

My good friend, Gloria, modified my chocolate cake recipe by reducing the water to make the cake into brownies and then sent the new recipe back to me! Thanks Gloria!

Preheat oven to 350°

> 3 cups of gluten-free flour (1-1/2 cups garfava flour and 1-1/2 cups tapioca works well)
>
> 2-1/2 cups sugar
>
> 1 teaspoon baking soda
>
> 2 teaspoons xanthan gum
>
> 1 cup unsweetened cocoa
>
> 1 teaspoon salt
>
> 1 cup oil
>
> 2 teaspoons pure vanilla extract
>
> 1 cup cold water
>
> 1 tablespoon distilled vinegar

Grease and flour a 9" x 13 " baking pan and set aside. Place the dry ingredients in a large mixing bowl and stir to combine. Add the oil, pure vanilla extract and water and mix well. Add vinegar and stir to mix. Place in your prepared baking pan. Bake for 30 to 35 minutes or until a toothpick comes out clean. Cool completely before cutting. Makes 20 – 2 inch brownies.

Best Ever Chocolate Brownie Bites

The inspiration for this recipe came from a party where regular brownie bites were being served, which contained gluten, dairy and eggs. The trick to the brownie bites is all in the directions. The basis for the recipe is the Decadent Chocolate Brownie recipe with slight changes. This recipe will give any gluten-containing brownie bite a run for the money!

Preheat oven to 350°

- 3 cups of gluten-free flour (1-1/2 cups garfava flour and 1-1/2 cups tapioca works well)
- 2-1/2 cups sugar
- 1 teaspoon baking soda
- 2 teaspoons xanthan gum
- 1 cup unsweetened cocoa
- 1 teaspoon salt
- 1 cup oil
- 2 teaspoons pure vanilla extract
- 1 cup cold water
- 1 tablespoon distilled vinegar
- ½ cup acceptable chocolate chips

Grease mini-muffin tins and set aside. This will make between 48 and 52 brownie bites depending upon how much batter you place in each muffin tin. Place the dry ingredients in a large mixing bowl and stir to combine. Add the oil, pure vanilla extract and water and mix well. Add vinegar and stir to mix. Add chocolate chips and stir to incorporate. Do not over mix.

Place batter in greased mini-muffin tins filling each cup just over halfway full. If you put too much batter in the muffin pans, the brownie bits will bake out over the top making them look like mushrooms. When you have filled all the muffin tins, pat the top of each brownie bite so it is flat and even with your fingers. This will give the finished baked good a store-bought appearance. The baking time is dependent upon whether you want soft, chewy brownie bites or crunchy brownie bites. The first time I made this recipe, I ended up with crunchy brownie bites, which I took to a memorial service. The comment made about this "experimental" recipe – was that they were like the brownies at the edges of a pan – which, if you like those kind of brownies, is great.

After repeated testing, the end result is all dependent upon baking time and handling.

For soft, chewy brownie bites, bake for 16 minutes in a 350° oven. Remove from oven at 16 minutes (this assumes that you are using an oven thermometer and your oven temperature is an exact 350°) and allow the brownie bites to sit in the muffin tins for 2 to 3 minutes only before removing them from the pans to a cooling rack. The brownie bites will continue to cook and set up during the two minutes they are in the baking tins. They will be delicate until they have cooled, so remove them very gently from the baking tins. I gently turn the baking pans upside down over a cooling rack and tap gently to remove them from the pan. Depending on the grease used to grease the pan, you may need to run a table knife around the edge of the muffin tin to release the brownie bite. They will be ready to eat once they are cooled. For crunchy brownie bites, bake for 18-20 minutes. Cool completely before eating or storing. Makes 48 to 52 brownie bites. These freeze very well.

Texas Brownie Cake

Last month my three children decided that they were "tired" of our regular chocolate so I pulled out my Mom's "Texas Sheet Cake" Recipe and one from a friend that was called "Brownie Cake" only to find that they are one and the same. I converted them to be free of gluten, dairy, and eggs and we were off! This cake has been a real hit wherever I have taken it!! It freezes well.

Preheat oven to 350°. This recipe uses a special sized pan and that is important. Use a jelly roll type pan which would measure approximately: 15" x 10" x 1 1/2" OR 15" x 10 1/2" x 1". Grease and flour your pan. Please note that different gluten-free flours will yield different results with this cake.

MIXTURE #1:
In a large mixing bowl, combine and then set aside:
- **2 cups Gluten-free flour (1-1/2 cups Garfava and ½ cup tapioca)**
- **2 cups sugar**
- **1/2 teaspoon salt**
- **1 1/4 teaspoon xanthan gum**

MIXTURE #2:
In a medium saucepan, combine and bring to a rolling boil and then set aside:
- **2 sticks of acceptable margarine or 1 cup of solid shortening**
- **1 cup water**
- **4 Tablespoons cocoa**

MIXTURE #3:
Once you have completed the above two steps, mix together in a small bowl or a 2 cup glass measuring cup:
- **1/4 cup water combined with 1 Tablespoon Ener-G egg replacer ****

Then ADD to mixture # 3:
- **1 teaspoon baking soda**
- **1/2 cup non-dairy milk substitute**
- **1 Tablespoon vinegar**
- **1 teaspoon pure vanilla extract**

Make mixtures #1 and #2 and set aside. Make mixture #3 and set aside. Add the baking soda, non-dairy milk substitute, vinegar and pure vanilla extract to mixture #3 stirring quickly. Quickly then add mixture # 2 and #3 to the first mixture and stir to combine and remove lumps. Do not overmix. Pour into your prepared shallow baking pan. Bake in a 350°oven for 20-23 minutes or until done. Watch so it does not over bake. Frost the cake while it is warm. This cake freezes well. Note: When I made this cake while I was traveling with the kids and inadvertently forgot to bring the Ener-G egg replacer, I added 2-1/2 extra teaspoons of baking soda to replace the egg replacer. That would bring the total of baking soda to 3- ½ teaspoons if you don't have the egg replacer.

South of the Border Key Lime Cheesecake

The original recipe for this dessert came from Laurette, an amazing woman who I know. I modified Laurette's recipe by removing the nut crust and coconut oil and adding more ingredients to cut the lime taste as it was too strong for us. The result is a healthy and easy dessert to make, which most people will enjoy.

> 2 cups sweet crumbs (plus 1 tablespoon oil for crust)
> 2 bananas
> 2 ripe avacados, medium
> 1 cup mango
> ½ cup agava syrup or other liquid sweetener
> 1 tablespoon acceptable oil
> 1 cup organic lime juice

To reduce calories, you can make this dessert without the crust. Place the sweet crumbs (crushed cookies, crushed graham crackers, etc.) in an 8-inch round cake pan or other baking dish or pie place. Add just enough oil to moisten and have crumbs stick together (less is more). Using a fork, push crumbs together and form a crust in the baking pan, then set aside. In a food processor, mix the bananas, peeled and seeded avacados, mango, agava syrup, and lime juice until smooth and creamy. Pour into prepared pan and freeze. Serve slightly frozen – but not too frozen. Optional toppings: Non-dairy whipped topping (see special ingredients) or extra sweet crumbs.

Berry Burst Dessert

This is a healthier frozen dessert based on primarily fresh or frozen fruit. I came up with this idea to have a second raw foods dessert for my raw foods friend Christine. The sprinkling of a few chocolate chips is completely optional as is a crust.

4 bananas
2 cups fresh or frozen strawberries
2 kiwis, peeled and sliced
2 avacados, peeled and sliced
½ cup agava syrup
2 cups raspberries
Optional: a crust and gfcf chocolate chips

If you are using a crust, place the crust in an 8" baking pan or pie plate and set aside. Place all ingredients (except for the crust and chocolate chips if you are using them) in a food processor and blend until creamy. Place in an 8" round baking pan or pie plate and sprinkle with a few chocolate chips, if using. Freeze or 6 to 8 hours or until solid.

Not Your Mother's Apple Pie

My friend Laurette served me a raw foods apple pie that was absolutely delicious. I thought it would be a great way to use up the extra apples we had from our CSA coop. Raw foodies usually use tree nuts in their piecrusts. While my first attempt at creating a crust failed miserably, I was eventually successful with this piecrust. Yes, even my children will eat this pie! What is so great about this dessert item is that it is fast and easy to make – and no baking is required!

Crust:
1 cup ground sunflower seeds
¼ cup raisins
¼ cup dried cranberries
3 tablespoons maple syrup or other sweetener
2 tablespoons water

Filling:
4 cups apples peeled and sliced thinly (about 2 very large apples)
2 tablespoons ground flax seed
2 tablespoons lemon juice
3 tablespoons maple syrup or other sweetener
Dash of cinnamon
2 tablespoons of pure water

Additional Apples:
4 cups peeled and sliced apples to layer in the pie

Mix the ground sunflower seeds, raisins, dried cranberries and maple syrup or other sweetener and water in a food processor and blend well. Pat the mixture into a standard pie plate. Layer 4 cups of apples neatly in the piecrust. Place 4 more cups of apples, flax seed, lemon juice, sweetener or sugar, cinnamon and water in a food processor and puree well. Gently spoon the pureed apple mixture into the pie plate pressing down lightly. Make sure the top of the pie is covered with the pureed apple mixture. Makes 1 apple pie.

Aunt Paulie's French Apple Cobbler

I got this recipe in July 1988 from my Great Aunt - Pauline Holcombe who was from Dushore, PA. I resurrected it when we had an abundance of organic apples. It only took minor tweaking to make it free of gluten and allergens. This is a high-sugar, old fashioned dessert and not for the health conscious except for special occasions.

> **5 cups peeled tart apples**
> **¾ cup sugar**
> **2 tablespoons gluten-free flour**
> **½ teaspoon cinnamon**
> **¼ teaspoon salt**
> **1 teaspoon pure vanilla extract**
> **1 tablespoon acceptable non-dairy margarine**
> **If not using tart apples – then add some lemon juice**

Combine above and turn into a 9" x 9" x 1-3/4" pan or a deep dish apple pie pan.

> **Topping:**
> **½ cup gluten-free flour**
> **½ cup sugar**
> **1 teaspoon baking powder**
> **dash of salt**
> **3 tablespoon acceptable non-dairy margarine**
> **½ tablespoon Ener-G Egg Replacer**
> **½ teaspoon xanthan gum**
> **¼ cup pure water**

Combine above ingredients in a medium size mixing bowl and mix by hand until smooth. Drop batter in nine parts on top of apples and then spread. Bake for 30 minutes or until apples are done.

Rustic Renaissance Tart

I came up with this recipe – you guessed it – to use up pears and quinces from our CSA! I wasn't sure if it would be edible, so I threw in some sugar to guarantee it. The kids ate it right up!

Preheat Oven to 350°
  1 pie crust
  3 quinces, peeled and grated
  5 pears, peeled and thinly sliced
  4 – 6 tablespoons sugar

Preheat oven to 350°. Place the pie crust in a tart pan or shallow pie plate. I use a shallow pie dish. Layer half of the sliced pears in the bottom. Slicing them very, very thin will help in the baking process. Place a layer of grated quince over the layer of the pears. Sprinkle with half of the sugar. Repeat layer of pears and quince. Sprinkle with remaining sugar. Note: quince will darken when exposed to air, so don't be alarmed. Top the edges of the tart or pie pan with foil to protect it from getting over baked. Bake 1 hour at 350° or until done.

Lemon Cream Pie

If you can tolerate soy – or as we do – use it for special occasions – this pie is party worthy!

Preheat oven to 350°
  1 cup ground or crushed cereal crumbs
  1 teaspoon xanthan gum
  ½ cup sugar (less can be used if desired)
  4 tablespoons acceptable non-dairy margarine

Combine above ingredients in a medium sized mixing bowl and cut margarine into cereal crumbs. When well mixed, pat crumb mixture into a deep-dish pie plate. Bake at 350° for 11 to 13 minutes or until the pie crust just starts to brown. Do not overbake. Allow to cool completely before filling. Makes one deep dish pie crust.

  4 teaspoons lemon juice
  6 ounce can of lemonade
  6 cups of an acceptable type of whipped topping

Measure out 6 cups of Rich's Whip topping that has already been whipped into a topping. Place in a large mixing bowl. Add lemon juice and lemonade. Working quickly, mix all ingredients well and pour into the crumb pie crust. Freeze immediately for 4-6 hours or until firm. Makes 1 deep dish pie. Serves 6 to 8.

Clever Chocolate Clusters

This is a recipe that I have made since early childhood. It is an exceptionally easy recipe to make for children. It is as rich as it is easy to make! It was easy as pie to convert to meet our celiac and allergy needs.

12 ounces acceptable gluten-free, dairy-free chocolate chips
2 cups acceptable cereal
½ cup raisins
½ cup acceptable pretzels, broken into pieces
½ cup sunflower seeds
1 teaspoon pure vanilla extract
Optional: omit sunflower seeds and add 1 cup acceptable
   marshmallows

Measure the cereal, raisins, pretzels and sunflower seeds into a large mixing bowl and stir well. Melt the chocolate in a double boiler and then pour over the cereal mixture. Stir quickly and thoroughly. Add vanilla and mix to incorporate. Place a teaspoon of chocolate cereal clusters on a baking sheet covered with waxed paper. Refrigerate for about 20 minutes or until firm. Makes about 2-1/2 dozen cookie treats.

Mary's Chocolate Sauce

This recipe is from Mary Cosgrove, my Dad's first cousin, who is an outstanding cook like many of my relatives! It was a cinch to convert this recipe to work for our family! Mary and her daughter, Mary Jo Saxe, are also cookbook authors!

1 tablespoon acceptable margarine
1 tablespoon tapioca flour
2/3 cup boiling water
1 cup granulated sugar
3 tablespoons cocoa
½ teaspoon pure vanilla extract

Combine all ingredients except for the pure vanilla extract in a medium saucepan and cook for 15 minutes over low heat, stirring frequently. Add the pure vanilla extract at the end of the cooking time and stir well. Makes 1 cup. Store in the refrigerator.

Old Fashioned Chocolate Sauce

I came up with this recipe as my children wanted a thicker chocolate sauce and for that reason only! A bit spoiled aren't they when it comes to food!

¾ cup pure water
1 teaspoon acceptable non-dairy margarine substitute
½ cup acceptable cocoa powder
1 cup sugar
dash of salt
1 teaspoon pure vanilla extract
smidgen of xanthan gum

Mix the water, acceptable margarine substitute, cocoa powder, sugar and salt in a medium saucepan. Cook over medium low heat for 7 to 12 minutes, stirring constantly. Cool slightly and then add the pure vanilla extract and stir to incorporate. Add the xanthan gum and mix well. Makes about 1 to 1-1/4 cups.

Hot Fudge Sauce

I am the one who likes hot fudge sauce so I had to include this!

6 tablespoons cocoa powder
3 tablespoons oil
⅓ cup boiling water
1 cup sugar

Mix cocoa powder and oil in a double boiler. Add ⅓ cup boiling water. Mix well and then add sugar. Bring to a boil. Allow to boil for 3 minutes. Cool just slightly before serving. This sauce will have to be warmed up prior to serving, as it is very thick when cold.

Old Fashioned Chocolate Pudding

This is an old-fashioned chocolate pudding recipe converted to be free of gluten and dairy. The thickness of this pudding will depend upon what type of non-dairy milk substitute you use.

2 tablespoons cocoa powder
6 tablespoons sugar
3 tablespoons acceptable thickener
1-3/4 cups non-dairy milk substitute

Mix all ingredients in a medium saucepan until well mixed. Cook over low heat until the pudding thickens to the right consistency. It will thicken slightly as it cools. Chill until it sets up. Makes 4 – ½ cup servings.

Aunt Irene's Cranberry Surprise

This is my Aunt's recipe for a delicious dessert, which my Mom actually converted to be gluten-free and egg-free!

Preheat Oven to 350°

2 cups cranberries, whole (may be either fresh or frozen)
1 ½ cups sugar
1/3 cup water mixed with 2 teaspoons Ener-G Egg Replacer
1 cup gluten-free flour
¾ teaspoon xanthan gum
¾ cup melted non-dairy margarine substitute

Preheat Oven to 350°. Grease a 10-inch pie plate and spread the cranberries evenly over the bottom of the pie plate. Sprinkle ½ cup of sugar over the cranberries. In a medium mixing bowl, combine the Ener-G egg replacer with water and add the remaining sugar. Stir well. Add flour, xanthan gum, and melted margarine substitute and mix well. Pour over the cranberries and smooth over the top. Bake for 1 hour, but check it at 45 minutes and if it is getting too brown, cover with foil for the last few minutes.

Toll House Caramel Bars

The basis for this recipe was a decadent recipe that I had forever! It was very difficult to convert to be gluten-free and dairy-free. I think it took four tries before I was satisfied. This bar cookie will be devoured by most. They are rich, but oh – so good!

Preheat Oven to 350°

> 2 cups gluten-free flours (1 cup garfava; 1 cup tapioca)
> 1/3 cup gluten-free flour – separate from the 2 cups (half and half)
> 2 teaspoons xanthan gum
> pinch of xanthan gum – separate from the 2 teaspoons
> 2 cups of crushed cereal (not too sweet)
> 1 cup packed brown sugar
> 2 teaspoons baking soda
> ¼ teaspoon salt
> 1 cup melted non-dairy margarine (2 sticks, if using stick form)
> 1 cup non-dairy caramel sauce (recipe in this book)
> 1 package non-dairy, acceptable chocolate chips

Preheat Oven to 350°. In a large mixing bowl combine the 2 cups of gluten-free flour, crushed cereal, 2 teaspoons xanthan gum, brown sugar, baking soda and salt and mix well. Melt margarine substitute and pour over the dry ingredients. Mix well. Set 1 cup of this mixture aside. Press the remaining crumb mixture into an ungreased 9" x 13" pan. Bake at 350° for 15 minutes or until lightly browned. While the crust is baking, combine the 1 cup caramel sauce, 1/3 cup gf flour and pinch of xanthan gum and stir well. Set aside. Remove from oven and sprinkle with chocolate chips. Drizzle the caramel mixture over the crust base. Sprinkle with reserved crumb mixture. Return to oven and bake for 20-25 minutes or until lightly browned.

Easy Party Mints

This recipe came from the back of a Domino's® Sugar bag. The mints are quite tasty! Thanks Domino's®. This makes a good quantity of candy – you may want to consider cutting the recipe in half unless you are having company or a party!

¼ cup acceptable margarine
2 Tablespoons water
Dash of salt
½ teaspoon peppermint extract
3 ½ to 3 ¾ cups Confectioners' sugar
Optional: natural food coloring

Combine margarine and water and place in a medium saucepan over low heat until the margarine melts. Remove from heat and add salt and peppermint extract. Add sugar gradually blending until desired consistency is reached. If you are using natural food coloring (that is food coloring made from beets, tumeric or blueberries), separate some of the candy into different bowls and add the natural food coloring – working it into the candy. Knead or roll until smooth. Mold individual candies or roll into a rope and slice. Use within a week or so. Makes about 1 pound of mints.

Gingerbread House

It is wonderful to have a gluten-free, casein-free, egg-free, nut-free and peanut-free Gingerbread House!! How exciting for all of us. I used a mold for my house which I highly recommend. If you don't have time to make your own, you can give your children some of the gluten-free graham crackers and some frosting and let them construct their own. This is what we'll do for fun over the holidays after the house we made today is gone. Here is the recipe for the gingerbread followed by a list of ideas for items that you could use to decorate your own gingerbread house.

Preheat oven to 350°
- **1 cup light corn syrup**
- **1/2 cup firmly packed brown sugar**
- **1/2 cup vegetable shortening or other acceptable shortening**
- **4 cups of gluten-free flour (I recommend using 2 different flours-see instructions)**
- **1-1/2 teaspoons of xanthan gum**
- **1 tablespoon ground cinnamon**
- **1 tablespoon ground ginger**
- **1-Stiff board or sturdy baking pan covered with foil or parchment to place your house on**
- **1 or more batches of white frosting**

Preheat oven to 350 degrees. This recipe will produce different results based on your choice of gluten-free flours. I recommend a mix of 2 cups of garfava flour and 2 cups of tapioca flour if you can tolerate those flours. Otherwise you can use any gluten-free flour mix of your choice. In a large bowl combine flours, xanthan gum, cinnamon and ginger. Stir to mix well and set aside. In a medium saucepan, heat the corn syrup, brown sugar and shortening over medium heat stirring to mix well until the mixture starts to bubble and becomes very foamy. Immediately remove from heat and pour into the flour mixture.

Quickly stir the hot sugar mixture into the flours. Try not to over mix. The dough will become pretty hot to the touch. Fill your mold with the dough and bake for between 10 to 15 minutes. My mold took about 15 minutes to bake. Remove from pan very gently onto a baking rack being careful not to break the cookie. It will harden as it cools. For my mold, I had to repeat the process two more times to get the four sides and two roof pieces. You will need one full recipe from above and a half-batch if your mold is anything like mine. This is not a recipe that will double! So if you need more than what the above recipe makes, you'll have to make it twice. I recommend rolling the dough out on a sheet of waxed paper while your mold is baking as otherwise it starts to cool in a huge ball and it is harder to fill the mold.

For glue, you can use a very stiff frosting or a frosting "glue" recipe which is basically: 1 cup confectioner's sugar, 1/4 teaspoon cream of tartar, 1/3 cup boiling water and either 1 egg or egg substitute. We have one who is highly allergic to eggs so last year I used the "glue" frosting minus the egg and used some dry powder egg-replacer in place of the egg. This year I used my basic white frosting, however I reduced the water to make it very stiff.

Ideas for Gingerbread House Decorations
There are so many different things you can use to decorate your gingerbread house. Now there are organic gummy bears free of most allergens, preservatives and artificial colors!!

1. Gluten-free pretzels
2. Candy and/or candy canes
3. Gummy bears
4. Marshmallows
5. Raisins
6. Dried cranberries
7. Chocolate chips
8. Lollipops
9. Gum
10. Cereals
11. Cookies
12. Gingerbread shapes
13. Graham crackers
14. Sunflower seeds
15. Chocolate shaped candies
16. Fruit leather
17. Frosting and more frosting

Woo-Hoo Bars

I found this recipe on the back of a regular cereal box and simply tinkered with it to make it allergen free. This recipe is easy enough to make and yet it tastes good enough that you kids and party guests will go "Woo-Hoo". One batch will go quickly!

2/3 cup corn syrup or other sweet syrup
¼ cup brown sugar
Dash of salt
1 cup ground sunflower seed butter or other tolerated butter
1 teaspoon vanilla
½ teaspoon cinnamon
2-1/2 cups acceptable rice cereal
1-1/2 cups cornflake cereal
1 cup acceptable chocolate chips

Grease a 9" x 13" pan and set aside. Measure the two cereals, cinnamon and chocolate chips into a large mixing bowl and set aside. In a medium saucepan, cook the corn syrup and brown sugar and dash of salt until it comes to a boil. Remove from heat and add vanilla and 1 cup sunflower butter, mixing quickly. Add this mixture to the dry cereal and mix well. Spread into the prepared pan.

Old Fashioned Rice Pudding

The idea or need for this came again from someone who was not feeling well. I had never eaten or made rice pudding from scratch. My first attempt at this recipe was so sweet that I couldn't even eat it! I also used too much rice milk on the first go. This will appeal to the masses, however if you have a real sweet tooth, you will probably want to add more sugar than is directed.

   2 cups cooked rice
   3 cups rice milk
   ¼ cup sugar or sweetener
   2 tablespoons margarine or acceptable margarine substitute
   1 tablespoon pure vanilla extract
   pinch of Celtic salt

Place all ingredients into a medium saucepan and cook over medium heat, stirring constantly. This is one recipe that you will want to watch. Lower heat if needed to prevent burning or scorching. Cook for about 45 minutes or until desired thickness.

Chocolate Tapioca Pudding

This is an easy dessert item that you might like if you like tapioca pudding. Not everyone in my house likes tapioca pudding – even chocolate flavored.

½ cup sugar
3 tablespoons tapioca granules
5 tablespoons acceptable cocoa powder
1 tablespoon acceptable oil
2 teaspoons Ener-G Egg Replacer®
¾ cup non-dairy milk substitute
1 teaspoon pure vanilla extract

Combine all ingredients except for vanilla in a medium sauce pan and stir well. Cook over medium heat until the pudding thickens up. Add vanilla. Remove from heat and cool. This will thicken slightly more as it cools. Serve cold. This recipe makes about 3 cups of pudding.

Caramel Sauce

This is the final caramel sauce recipe that I perfected for use in the Toll House Caramel Bars recipe in this book. This is much more creamy than the Hot Caramel Sauce recipe – also in this book. Unlike the Hot Caramel Sauce recipe, this caramel sauce does not need to be hot. This will work for cookie and dessert recipes that call for caramel sauce as well as over ice cream.

½ cup light brown sugar, firmly packed
½ cup white sugar
½ cup light corn syrup
3 tablespoons non-dairy margarine substitute

Mix this and set aside:
½ cup non-dairy milk substitute
2-1/2 to 3 additional tablespoon of non-dairy margarine
    substitute

Place the sugars, corn syrup and margarine substitute in a medium saucepan and stir over medium heat, stirring constantly until the sugar crystals are dissolved. Then remove from heat and add the non-dairy milk and the 2-1/2 to 3 additional tablespoon of non-dairy margarine and stir until combined. Return to heat after adding the nondairy milk and margarine and cook stirring constantly until well combined. It is very important to cook this just until the sugar crystals are dissolved or your sauce will be grainy. Once, when I didn't cook the sauce long enough, I put it immediately back on the heat (before adding the nondairy milk and margarine) and cooked it longer. That worked one time. The surest thing is to make sure that the sugar is dissolved. This sauce thickens a lot as it cools. Makes 2 cups.

Hot Caramel Sauce

Oh boy was this a great learning experience! I wanted a caramel sauce as a topping for our non-dairy ice cream for sundaes and also for making a toll house bar recipe. My first attempt yielded a grainy mixture that was a bomb. I put it back on the stove and kept adding to it and cooking it. By the time I was done, I had an edible caramel sauce ~ but no idea what the quantities were for each ingredient! Yep. Take two on the caramel sauce. After some more changes, this is a great sauce for ice cream, desserts, and even fresh, raw apples – but it has to be served HOT. When cooled, this is too thick to be edible.

½ cup light brown sugar, firmly packed
½ cup white sugar
¼ cup light corn syrup
3 tablespoons non-dairy margarine substitute

Mix this and set aside:
¼ cup non-dairy milk substitute
1 additional tablespoon of non-dairy margarine substitute

Place the sugars, corn syrup and margarine substitute in a medium saucepan and stir over medium heat, stirring constantly until the sugar crystals are dissolved. Then remove from heat and add the non-dairy milk and the 1 additional tablespoon of non-dairy margarine and stir until combined. It is very important to cook this just until the sugar crystals are dissolved or your sauce will be grainy. Once, when I didn't cook the sauce long enough, I put it immediately back on the heat (before adding the liquid Dari-Free® and margarine) and cooked it longer. That worked one time. The surest thing is to make sure that the sugar is dissolved. This sauce will thicken as it cools.

Chocolate Brownies

This is a brownie recipe from my childhood that I converted to be allergy free and gluten free.

Preheat oven to 350°.

2 sticks margarine
4 ounces GFCF unsweetened baking chocolate
2 cups sugar

4 teaspoons Egg Replacer™ powder mixed with
½ cup water

2 teaspoons vanilla extract
1½ cups GF flour mix (use ¾ cup each of two different flours)
1 teaspoon baking powder
1 teaspoon salt
1 teaspoon xanthan gum

In a medium saucepan, combine the margarine and baking chocolate and heat on LOW until melted. Stir in the sugar and mix well. Let pan cool slightly, about 5 to 10 minutes while you grease and flour a 9" x 13" baking pan. Mix the water and egg replacer and mix very well to remove all lumps. Strain the egg replacer mixture through a wire mesh strainer to remove any remaining lumps. After the saucepan has cooled a little, add the strained egg replacer. Stir in the vanilla extract. Mix the dry ingredients in a separate bowl, and stir well. Then add to the saucepan mixture, stirring only as much as needed to combine. Do not over mix. Pour into the prepared baking pan and bake for 25 to 30 minutes (or more) until a toothpick comes out clean, and the top springs back slightly when touched.

Sugar Cookie Cut-Outs

These can be used on any rotation day depending upon what flour you use. The type of flour used will dramatically alter the taste. In this recipe I have listed rice or millet in combination with tapioca for a very bland flour mix.

Preheat oven to 350°.
   1 cup white sugar
   2 tablespoons oil
   4 tablespoons warm water mixed with
   4 teaspoons Egg Replacer™
   1½ teaspoons vanilla extract
   ¾ cup rice or millet flour (or any other acceptable flour)
   1 cup tapioca flour
   1 teaspoon xanthan gum
   1 teaspoon baking soda
   2 teaspoons baking powder (or cream of tartar)
   2 tablespoons water

Mix sugar and oil. In a separate bowl, mix the warm water with the dry Egg Replacer™ powder and stir until it is very thick and creamy. Add the Egg Replacer™ to the sugar/oil mixture and mix well. Add the vanilla extract and stir well. Then add all of the dry ingredients and mix well. Add the water last and only if needed. Divide the dough in fourths and refrigerate wrapped in waxed paper or plastic for 1 to 2 hours.

Remove 1 section of dough from refrigerator and roll the dough out between 2 sheets of waxed paper dusted with tapioca flour. Cut out with cookie cutters and place on an ungreased baking sheet. Sprinkle with acceptable baking colored sugars or white sugar. Bake very tiny cookies for 6 to 7 minutes and larger cookies for 9 to 12 minutes. These will not turn brown or golden but will remain pretty "white" in color. If you over bake these, they will be very crisp and hard. Properly baked, they will have a soft texture, but will not fall apart. These travel well and freeze well. You can also use a confectioners' frosting if you want a more festive cookie.

Moran Spice Cake

This is a family recipe that originates in the depression era when milk and eggs were often in short supply. I converted it to be gluten-free. Other shortening can be used as allergies permit.

Preheat oven to 350°.

> 1 cup lard (or other acceptable shortening)
> 2 cups water
> 1 to 2 cups raisins
> 1 teaspoon ground cinnamon
> ½ teaspoon ground cloves
> 2 cups white sugar
> 3 cups gluten-free flours (use a mix of flours)
> 1 tablespoon baking powder
> 1 teaspoon baking soda
> 2½ teaspoons xanthan gum

Combine shortening or lard, water, raisins, all spices, and sugar in a saucepan. Simmer for 10 minutes but do not boil or you'll end up with a candy base! Remove from heat and let stand until cool.

Grease one 9" x 13" baking pan. Combine the flour, baking soda, baking powder, and xanthan gum in a small bowl. When the saucepan mixture is cool, add the flour mixture to the liquid and stir until combined well. Pour the batter into your greased baking pan and bake for 45 minutes or until the center is done.

Delicious Chocolate Cake

This makes one great chocolate cake, and it is easy to mix up. This recipe does not work well with some flours like amaranth, sorghum and quinoa. For this recipe I would suggest the rice, tapioca, or potato flours and maybe even the garfava flour.

Preheat oven to 350°.

   3 cups gluten-free flours (for example 1½ cups rice flour and
        1½ cups tapioca flour)
   2 cups white sugar
   1 teaspoon salt
   2 teaspoons baking soda
   ½ cup unsweetened cocoa powder
   2½ teaspoons xanthan gum
   ¾ cup vegetable oil
   2 tablespoons distilled white vinegar
   2 teaspoons vanilla extract
   1¾ cups cold water

Combine all the dry ingredients in a large mixing bowl. Add liquid ingredients and mix well. Pour into a 9" x 13" ungreased baking pan. Bake for 30 to 40 minutes or until cake tests done with a toothpick or cake tester or if top bounces back if touched lightly with your finger. This cake freezes well. Promptly freeze any leftovers. Bake for 22 to 25 minutes for cupcakes. Makes 24 cupcakes. These cupcakes freeze well.

Carrot Cake

For this recipe, I took the family spice cake recipe and altered it to make a carrot cake.

Preheat oven to 350°.

> 1 cup lard (or other acceptable shortening)
> 2 cups water
> 2 cups grated carrots
> 1 teaspoon ground cinnamon
> ½ teaspoon ground cloves
> 2 cups white sugar
> 3 cups GF flour mix (use a mix of whichever flours you can tolerate)
> 1 tablespoon baking powder
> 1 teaspoon baking soda
> 2½ teaspoons xanthan gum

Optional:

> ½ to 1 cup raisins

Combine shortening or lard, water, carrots, all spices, raisins (if using) and sugar in a saucepan. Simmer for 10 minutes but do not boil or you'll end up with a candy base! Remove from heat and let stand until cool. Grease one 9" x 13" baking pan. Combine the flour, baking soda, baking powder, and xanthan gum in a small bowl. When the saucepan mixture is cool, add the flour mixture to the liquid and combine well. Pour the batter into your baking pan and bake for 45 minutes or until the center is done. Cool cake completely and then frost with the non-dairy cream cheese frosting recipe included in this section.

Non-Dairy Cream Cheese Frosting

This is the perfect addition to the carrot cake recipe included in this cookbook! We love this frosting.

16 ounces powdered or confectioners' sugar (10X), sifted
One 8 ounce container of non-dairy cream cheese
1 teaspoon of vanilla

Place powdered sugar in a mixing bowl. Place the non-dairy cream cheese in chunks on top of the powdered sugar. Add the vanilla. Very slowly mix in the lowest speed of your electric mixer until the cream cheese blends with the powdered sugar. Gradually increase the speed of your mixer and blend frosting until it is creamy. I recommend sifting to reduce the lumps in your frosting. Otherwise, you'll need to mix the frosting longer to remove any lumps in the sugar. Refrigerate frosting until ready to use, and refrigerate any cake that you use this frosting on as you would with a regular cream cheese frosting.

Sun Blossom Cookies

This is the famous peanut butter with a Hershey Kiss in the center converted to be free of allergens and gluten. Instead of a Hershey Kiss in the center, you can mound up some chocolate chips or chocolate chunks.

Preheat oven to 375°.
Sift together:
- **1¾ cups gluten-free flours**
- **1½ teaspoon baking soda**
- **½ teaspoon salt**
- **1½ teaspoons xanthan gum**
- **1 tablespoon Egg Replacer™**

Cream Together:
- **½ cup acceptable margarine**
- **½ cup acceptable non-nut butter (soy, sunflower, etc.)**

Add:
- **½ cup white sugar**
- **½ cup brown sugar**

Add:
- **1 teaspoon vanilla extract**
- **3 tablespoons non-dairy milk substitute or water (more as needed but spairingly)**
- **¼ cup gluten-free/dairy-free chocolate chips**

Beat well. Add dry ingredients to wet ingredients. Shape by teaspoon into balls. Roll in sugar and place on an ungreased baking sheet. Make a small indentation in the center of the cookie before baking. Bake for 8 to 9 minutes. Remove from oven and place a few gluten-free/dairy-free chocolate chips in the center of the cookie. Return to the oven and bake for 2 to 3 minutes. These cookies freeze well.

Hershey's® "Perfectly Chocolate" Chocolate Frosting

This recipe comes from the back of a Hershey's® Cocoa Powder can, and with minor changes it becomes a useful recipe to us.

1 stick (½ cup) margarine or acceptable substitute
⅔ cup Hershey's Cocoa
3 cups powdered sugar
⅓ cup acceptable milk substitute
1 teaspoon vanilla extract

The directions on the cocoa powder said to melt margarine and stir in cocoa. Then alternately add powdered sugar and milk substitute, beating until spreading consistency. I found that just mixing it all in an electric mixer was sufficient without melting the margarine. Add an additional tablespoon of water if necessary to get the proper frosting consistency. Makes about 2 cups.

Molasses Cookies

This is a family recipe converted to be free of gluten and allergens. These keep well in an airtight container and freeze well.

Preheat oven to 350°.
- **2 tablespoons olive oil (or other acceptable oil)**
- **⅔ cup sugar**
- **½ cup molasses**
- **4 tablespoons hot water mixed with**
- **5 teaspoons Egg Replacer™**
- **1¼ cups tapioca flour (full cups)**
- **¾ cup potato starch (full ¾ cup)**
- **1 teaspoon baking soda**
- **1 teaspoon xanthan gum**
- **½ teaspoon salt**
- **½ teaspoon ground ginger**

Mix together oil and sugar. Then add molasses and mix well. Add the remaining ingredients and mix well. This dough will <u>not</u> appear as if there is enough liquid when you start mixing it. Don't panic; continue to mix by hand until dough comes together. Form small balls and place on an <u>ungreased</u> cookie sheet. Slightly flatten the balls and top with white sugar. Bake about 7 to 9 minutes depending upon the size cookie you have made. Over baking will give you hard cookies which are not nearly as nice as the soft ones. This recipe makes about 26 to 30 cookies of a smaller size.

Best Banana Chocolate Chip Cookies

My grandmother Josephine Holcombe used to make these excellent banana oatmeal chocolate chip cookies, which contained gluten. I think she'd be surprised at how similar this conversion is to her original recipe. We use puffed millet in place of the oatmeal. These cookies freeze well.

Preheat oven to 350°.

- 1 cup white or brown sugar (or ½ cup of each)
- 1 cup shortening or other margarine
- 4 tablespoons hot water mixed with
- 5 teaspoons Egg Replacer™
- 3 mashed bananas
- ½ teaspoon salt
- ¾ teaspoon ground cloves
- 1 teaspoon ground cinnamon
- 1 teaspoon vanilla extract
- 1 teaspoon baking soda
- 2 cups gluten-free flour mix (full cups)
- 2 cups puffed millet (full cups)
- 1 cup gluten-free chocolate chips
- 2 teaspoons xanthan gum

Cream together shortening and sugar. Add egg replacer and bananas. Then add in dry ingredients and vanilla extract and mix well. You may need to add a bit more flour if your cookies flatten out too much. Drop onto greased cookie sheets and bake 7 to 9 minutes depending upon the size of your cookies. These should be a soft cookie, not crispy or crunchy. This is an excellent way to use up old bananas.

Soft & Chewy Chocolate Chip Cookies

Preheat oven to 350°.

> 2½ cups gluten-free flour blend (bland flours make the best cookie)
> ½ cup gluten-free baby rice cereal
> 1 cup white sugar
> 1 cup brown sugar, firmly packed
> 1 cup acceptable margarine, softened
> 4 tablespoons hot water mixed with
> 1½ tablespoons Egg Replacer™ (or 2 eggs)
> 1½ teaspoons vanilla extract
> 1 teaspoon baking soda
> 1 teaspoon salt
> 1 teaspoon xanthan gum
> 5 to 10 ounces acceptable chocolate chips

Make sure your margarine is at room temperature. If you can use eggs, use two and delete the 4 Tablespoons of hot water. Place all ingredients except for the chocolate chips into a mixing bowl. With your mixer, blend at the lowest speed until the dough begins to incorporate. Then gradually increase the speed of your mixer, and beat on high for about 3 or so minutes. You can also mix this by hand although it is more difficult. Refrigerate the cookie dough for at least 1 to 2 hours (a must for the best cookies). Also, make sure to use an oven thermometer to ensure that your oven is 350° and not higher (lower your oven temperature accordingly if your oven runs hot).

Spoon the cold dough onto ungreased baking sheets and bake for 8 to 10 minutes, but no more than that. If your cookies flatten like pancakes, check your oven temperature because it is probably off. One other thing you can try if your cookies flatten is adding more flour to your dough, refrigerate and try again. These will be just like the "mall" cookies that contain all those no-no ingredients. They will be nice and chewy & soft. If they are crunchy, you over baked them or your oven temperature is too high.

Lemon Bars

This is a recipe from my mom, Jean Gottas which has been converted to be gluten-free. If you can tolerate eggs, I would use them for the topping.

Preheat oven to 350°.

Crust:
> **2 cups gluten-free flour mix (lighter flours work best in this recipe; rice, tapioca, cornstarch, or potato)**
> **½ cup sugar**
> **1 cup acceptable margarine**

Combine above and pat into a greased 9" x 13" pan. Bake for 20 to 25 minutes (more or less depending on your true oven temperature). While this is baking, mix up the following:

Topping:
> **1 cup hot water mixed with**
> **7 tablespoons Egg Replacer™ (see note below)**
> **5 tablespoons lemon juice**
> **2 cups sugar**
> **1 tablespoon gluten-free flour**

When the pan comes out of the oven, pour the egg replacer mixture over the crust immediately. Return to the oven and bake for 15 to 20 minutes. Bake until the edges start to brown lightly. Remove from the oven and sift confectioners' sugar over the top while the pan is <u>HOT</u>!

Note: If you can tolerate eggs, then use 4 eggs in the topping and delete the 1 cup water and the 7 Tablespoons egg replacer.

Ultimate Chocolate Chip Cookies (Double Batch)

Just about everyone will enjoy these chocolate chip cookies!

Preheat ovem to 375°.

1½ cups butter flavor shortening or other shortening
2½ cups brown sugar, firmly packed
4 tablespoons non-dairy milk substitute
2 tablespoons vanilla extract
6 tablespoons hot water with
7 teaspoons Egg Replacer™ (or 2 eggs)
3½ cups gluten-free flour
2 teaspoons xanthan gum
1½ teaspoon baking soda
2 teaspoons salt
2 cups gluten-free chocolate chips

Cream together shortening and brown sugar until smooth. Add milk and vanilla extract and mix well. Add Egg Replacer™ and mix until smooth. In a large bowl, mix flour, baking soda, xanthan gum and salt together. Add to wet ingredients. Stir in chocolate chips. Refrigerate cookie dough for at least an hour or two or until well-chilled. On an ungreased cookie sheet, bake 8 to 10 minutes for chewy cookies, 11 to 13 minutes for crisp cookies. Makes about 6 dozen 3-inch cookies.

Super Sugar Cookie Cut-Outs

Bland gluten-free flours will provide a better flavor than some of the stronger flours.

Preheat oven to 375°.

1¼ cups white sugar
1 cup shortening or margarine, softened
6 tablespoons hot water mixed with
5 teaspoons Egg Replacer™ (or 2 eggs)
¼ cup light corn syrup or brown rice syrup
1 tablespoon vanilla extract
3 cups gluten-free flour
2½ teaspoons xanthan gum
1 ½ teaspoon baking powder
1 teaspoon baking soda
½ teaspoon salt

Cream the sugar and shortening in a mixing bowl and beat until creamy. In a separate bowl, mix the hot water and dry powdered Egg Replacer stirring to remove lumps, and adding it to the sugar and shortening mixture. Add the vanilla extract and syrup. Combine the remaining dry ingredients and add to the shortening/sugar mixture gradually. Divide the dough into 4 pieces. Wrap each piece in waxed paper and refrigerate for at least 1 hour (or place in the freezer for 15 to 20 minutes). Roll out between 2 sheets of waxed paper that have been dusted with a light coating of gluten-free flour. Cut out your favorite cookie shapes with floured cookie cutters. You can sprinkle decorator sugars on the cookies before baking if you do not intend to frost the cookies. Bake on an ungreased baking sheet. The baking time will depend completely on the size of the cutout AND how thick you roll the dough! The larger and thicker the cookie, the longer the baking time. The time will vary from 4 to 9 minutes. Whatever you do, do not over bake! Cool cookies on a cooling rack. You may then frost as desired. This recipe makes 3 to 4 dozen cookies, depending on the cookie size.

Chocolate Pudding

2 cups non-dairy milk
¼ cup sugar
2 tablespoons cocoa powder
Dash of salt

To thicken:
3 tablespoons gluten-free flour mixed with
½ cup non-dairy milk

In a saucepan, heat the 2 cups non-dairy milk, sugar, cocoa and salt until the sugar is melted and all the ingredients are well combined. In a separate measuring cup or bowl, mix the flour and ½ cup of non-dairy milk until well blended. Add the non-dairy milk and flour mixture to the saucepan and cook until the pudding is thick and creamy stirring constantly. It will thicken just a bit as it cools. If you desire pudding that is firmer, you can increase the flour by 1 tablespoon or more. Makes five ½ cup servings.

Black Bottom Cupcakes

This is a favorite recipe that I converted to be gluten-free, dairy-free and egg-free. The original recipe came from a friend. If you make these in mini-muffin pans, they make adorable sweet treats suitable for any party or festive gathering.

Preheat oven to 350°.

Line mini-muffin pans with baking papers and set aside. You will also need some mini-chocolate chips for this recipe.

Batter One:

One 8 ounce container of acceptable non-dairy cream cheese
⅓ cup sugar
2 tablespoons hot water combined with
3 teaspoons Egg Replacer™ (or 1 egg)
⅛ teaspoon salt

Beat Batter One ingredients together until well combined and set aside.

Batter Two:

1½ cups gluten-free flour
1 cup sugar
⅓ cup cocoa powder
1 teaspoon baking soda
1 teaspoon xanthan gum
½ teaspoon salt

In a separate bowl, sift Batter Two ingredients together.

Add to Batter Two:

1 cup boiling water
½ cup oil
1 teaspoon vinegar
1 teaspoon vanilla extract

Beat Batter Two ingredients together until well combined. Fill mini-muffin baking pans ½ full with Batter Two. Top each muffin with ½ to 1 teaspoon of Batter One. Then top each muffin with 6 to 8 mini-chocolate chips if desired. Bake for about 20 to 25 minutes or until done. Makes about 48 mini-size cupcakes.

Mock Peanut Butter Cookies

This is a family recipe for peanut butter cookies converted to be FREE of peanut butter, gluten, dairy, and eggs. They could easily pass for peanut butter cookies.

Preheat oven to 350°

1¼ cups gluten-free flour
1 teaspoon baking powder
½ cup margarine or solid shortening
½ cup white sugar
½ cup brown sugar, packed
2 tablespoons hot water mixed with
3 teaspoons Egg Replacer™ (or 1 egg slightly beaten)
1¼ teaspoons xanthan gum
½ cup acceptable non-nut butter (soy, sunflower, or other)

Sift dry ingredients together twice. In a large bowl cream margarine and both sugars until soft and blended, but not fluffy. Add Egg Replacer™ (or egg) and non-nut butter and mix well. Add dry ingredients and mix well. Make balls of dough the size of a walnut or so and roll the balls of dough in sugar. Place on an ungreased baking sheet and then press the ball of dough with a fork twice to make a crisscross pattern on top of the cookie. Bake for 12 or so minutes. Do not over bake. These cookies do not brown. Makes about 3 dozen cookies depending upon the size of the cookie.

Non-Dairy Cheesecake

This makes a great cheesecake for those of us who do not eat dairy. You can make it with or without a crust. A crumb crust recipe is provided, however you can make it without the crust. This recipe is best made in a spring form pan designed for cheesecakes so that you can remove the cheesecake from the pan easily. If you don't have a spring form pan, you can simply cut slices from your baking pan and remove the slices from the pan individually. It is best not to store the cheesecake in the pan. This recipe is to be used with an 8" or 9" spring form cheesecake pan with a removable bottom.

Preheat oven to 350°.
Crumb Crust
> **1½ cups gluten-free cereal crushed into crumbs either by hand or with a food processor**
> **2 teaspoons xanthan gum**
> **⅓ cup sugar**
> **6 tablespoons acceptable oil (or solid shortening*)**
> **1 to 2 teaspoons ground cinnamon**

If you can use a solid shortening or margarine in the crust, you will get a better result. If using a solid shortening or margarine, use just ¼ cup. Mix crumb crust ingredients together well, and press firmly into your spring form or baking pan. Use either a rolling pin or the bottom of another baking pan, plate, or other hard, flat surface to mash the crumbs together. The crumbs should be pressed very well together. If they are not, your crust will fall apart and be crumbly. Bake in a 350° oven for 10 to 12 minutes. Do not over bake. You do not need to brown the crust. After removing the crust from the oven, increase the heat to 375°

Cheesecake First Layer:
> **16 ounces non-dairy cream cheese**
> **¾ cup sugar**
> **½ teaspoon vanilla extract**
> **¼ teaspoon xanthan gum**
> **½ teaspoon salt**

Mix all first layer cheesecake ingredients listed above until creamy. Place on top of crumb crust if you are using one, or directly in your cheesecake baking pan or other 8" or 9" square baking dish if you are not. Bake in a **375° oven** for 45 minutes (note higher temperature). While this is baking, mix up the second layer.

Cheesecake Second Layer:
> **12 ounces non-dairy sour cream**
> **4 tablespoons sugar**
> **½ teaspoon vanilla extract**
> **⅛ teaspoon salt**
> **¼ teaspoon xanthan gum**

Mix second layer ingredients well and pour on top of the cheesecake after it is done baking. Return the cheesecake to the oven and **increase the oven temperature to 425°.** Bake for 30 minutes. Allow to cool and then refrigerate overnight before serving.

White Frosting or Filling

¼ cup shortening
1 teaspoon milk substitute
4 tablespoons gluten-free flour
1 teaspoon vanilla extract
4 tablespoons hot water
 5 teaspoons Egg Replacer™
1- 16 ounce box powdered or confectioner's Sugar

Combine the hot water and Egg Replacer and mix well. Then add the shortening, milk substitute, flour, vanilla and mix well. Then add the powdered sugar and beat well.

Confectioners' Icing or Glaze

This is the recipe that we use for the Danish recipes included in this book. It is fast and easy. We make it in smaller batches so it is fresh.

2 cups powdered or confectioners' sugar
1 teaspoon vanilla
2 tablespoons pure drinking water
Pinch of salt
Optional:
1 to 2 teaspoons of margarine

Mix all ingredients and stir until smooth and creamy. This makes about 1 cup of icing or glaze. You can add a few drops of water to make your icing thinner. If you add too much water and your icing becomes too runny, simply add more powdered sugar one tablespoon at a time. To apply icing or glaze to Danish, place icing in a plastic bag with one corner cut off on a diagonal. Cut off a tiny diagonal as you can always increase the size of the whole in the bag. Pipe the icing over your Danish or other treat in a swirling or zig-zag pattern.

Whoopie Pies or Moon Pies

Who can resist two chocolate cookies with a white creamy filling? These cookies freeze well. We typically freeze them without the filling, but you can do it either way.

Preheat oven to 350°.

> 1 cup shortening or margarine
> 2 cups sugar
> 6 tablespoons hot water mixed with
> 2 tablespoons Egg Replacer™
> 1 cup milk substitute "soured": add 2 teaspoons baking soda
>   to 1 cup non-dairy milk substitute
> 1 cup hot water
> 1 teaspoon baking powder
> 4 cups gluten-free flour
> 1 cup cocoa
> 3½ teaspoons xanthan gum

Mix above ingredients in order as listed. Drop by teaspoonful onto a baking sheet. Bake for 10 minutes. When cool, use white frosting in between two cookies. You can use one of the frosting recipes in this cookbook, or you can use any frosting recipe that you like. This recipe makes a lot of whoopie pies, so you may want to cut the recipe in half until you are sure that you like them! These do freeze fairly well.

Grandma Jo's Perfect Pie Crust

This is adapted from my grandmother's pie crust recipe. It works every time.

Preheat oven to 450° (if baking ahead of time)
- **3 cups sifted gluten-free flour mix**
- **1¼ cups shortening**
- **4 tablespoons hot water mixed with**
- **5 teaspoons Egg Replacer™**
- **1 teaspoon vinegar**
- **1 teaspoon salt**
- **5 tablespoons cold water (must be cold!)**
- **2 teaspoons xanthan gum**

Add the xanthan gum to the flour mix. Add salt. Cut shortening or lard into the flour mixture until crumbly. In a separate bowl, beat Egg Replacer™ and water. Add vinegar and salt to the egg replacer mixture. Then add to flour mixture. Add cold water and form dough. Roll out between 2 sheets of waxed paper. Makes 2 double pie crusts.

To bake an unfilled shell, prick before baking. Place in the oven for 10 to 12 minutes or until lightly browned. You can protect the edges from over-browning by covering them with aluminum foil strips or commercially available pie crust rings.

Savory Quinoa Crust for Pot Pies & Quiche

I adapted my Grandmother's pie crust recipe to the rotation diet we were using at the time and added some spices to offset the quinoa taste. Quinoa is not my favorite grain if you couldn't tell.

1½ cups quinoa flour or other flour
1½ cups corn starch, tapioca flour, potato flour or rice flour
1 cup shortening or lard
2 teaspoons xanthan gum
1 teaspoon onion powder
2½ teaspoons garlic powder
1 teaspoon vinegar
4 teaspoon Egg Replacer™ mixed well with
4 tablespoons hot water

5 tablespoons cold water

Add the xanthan gum to the flour mix. Add salt. Cut shortening or lard into the flour mixture until crumbly. In a separate bowl, beat Egg Replacer™ and water. Add vinegar and salt to the egg replacer mixture. Then add to flour mixture. Add cold water and form dough. Roll out between 2 sheets of waxed paper. Makes 2 double pie crusts. Follow pot pie (see page 160) or quiche (see page 168) recipes for baking directions.

To bake an unfilled shell, prick before baking. Place in a preheated 450° oven for 10 to 12 minutes or until lightly browned. You can protect the edges from over-browning by covering them with aluminum foil strips or commercially available pie crust rings.

Apple Crisp

Preheat oven to 375°

Crisp Mixture:

    1½ teaspoon ground cinnamon
    ½ cup tapioca flour
    1 cup garfava flour
    ¾ cup brown sugar, packed
    ¾ teaspoon xanthan gum
    **¼ cup acceptable solid shortening OR 6 tablespoons
        acceptable oil**

Mix the above dry ingredients and then add 6 tablespoons oil. If you can tolerate a solid shortening of any kind, use ¼ cup or more of that cut into the flour mixture instead of the oil. Set the mixture aside while you prepare the apples.

    5 cups peeled, sliced apples
    3 tablespoons lemon juice

Mix the apples with the lemon juice. Place the apples in a glass pie plate. Top with crisp mixture. Bake for 30 minutes. Remove from oven and add ½ cup of pure water. Stir apple crisp to mix well and return to the oven for 15 more minutes. This may be served hot or cold.

Apple Crisp Take Two

A second take on apple crisp that uses cereal.

Preheat oven to 350°

- ¾ cup gluten-free flour
- 1 cup crushed acceptable cereal
- ¾ cup brown sugar
- ½ teaspoon xanthan gum
- ½ cup plus 1 tablespoon nondairy margarine
- 5-6 cups apples, peeled and sliced

Preheat oven to 350°. Grease a 7"x12" baking dish and layer the apples in the baking dish. Mix the dry ingredients well and then cut into the nondairy margarine until it is a fine crumbly mixture. Place the crumb mixture over the top of the apples. Bake for 40 minutes or until done.

Peach Crisp

I created this recipe to use up organic peaches and nectarines that were not ripe but had some nasty bad spots. I happened to have some leftover freshly grated zucchini from making zucchini bread so it all came together.

Preheat oven to 350°

> ¾ cup gluten-free flour (1/2 cup garfava and ¼ cup tapioca)
> 1 cup crushed acceptable gluten-free cereal
> 1/3 cup brown sugar
> 1/3 cup white sugar
> 1 teaspoon xanthan gum
> ½ cup nondairy margarine
> 1 cup zucchini shredded (or other fruit)
> 4 cups peaches and nectarines, peeled and diced

Preheat oven to 350°. Grease a 7" x 12" baking dish. Layer the peeled and sliced peaches, nectarines and zucchini in the baking dish. Mix the dry ingredients and then cut the margarine in until it is a fine crumb mixture. Place the crumb mixture on top of the fruit and bake for 40 minutes or until done.

Cherry Pie

This is a great beginner recipe if you are teaching your children to bake. It is simple, and assuming you've helped them out with the crust, it's a real winner. My Mom taught me to make cherry pie when I was very young and once you've done it, you are struck by how easy it is.

Preheat oven to 450°.

> **One 16 ounce can sour cherries (water packed sour cherries; NOT canned cherry pie filling)**
> **3 tablespoons cornstarch (or other thickening agent)**
> **1 cup sugar**
> **Pinch of salt**
> **1 tablespoon lemon juice**
> **Dash of lemon extract (optional)**
> **Dash of natural food coloring (red)**
> **1 gluten-free pie crust – topping is optional**

Drain cherries and place the cherry juice in a medium size saucepan. Add sugar, cornstarch, salt, and lemon juice as well as optional ingredients. Increase heat to medium high stirring at all times. Once the cherry juice is thickened, add cherries to saucepan. Place filling into pie shell and bake. You can top your cherry pie with a crust topping, make lattice topping (strips of pie crust dough woven together and used for a topping), or leave your pie without a topping. Place pie in a 450° oven for 10 minutes. Reduce heat to 350° and bake for 40 minutes or until golden brown.

Strawberry Pie

Once we started getting strawberries from our local organic farmer came the question what would we do with all of the strawberries? Strawberry pie and strawberry ice cream are two great answers to that question.

2 quarts fresh strawberries, tops removed
1 cup sugar
3 tablespoons cornstarch or other flour for thickening
½ cup water
Pinch of salt
1 tablespoon oil
1 tablespoon lemon juice
1 gluten-free pie crust, baked and cooled

Bake a single gluten-free pie crust for 10 to 12 minutes or until lightly golden and set aside to cool (see page 301). In a medium saucepan dissolve the cornstarch in the water and set aside. Then sort the berries into excellent and less than excellent condition setting aside the strawberries in mint condition. Mash up the secondary strawberries and place in the saucepan with the cornstarch. Add the sugar, salt, oil and lemon juice. Cook over medium heat stirring constantly until mixture is thick. Remove from heat and allow to cool. In the meantime, cut the best strawberries in half. When the saucepan mixture is cold, stir in the remaining strawberries. Place in the baked pie shell and chill before serving.

Marshmallow Cups &
Mock Peanut Butter Cups

These are too cute and very exciting for children and for those adults who remember the days of Reese's Peanut Butter Cups and Mallow Cups which are now taboo due to allergies! I served little cups at our Valentine's Day party and our guests thought they tasted just like the real (peanut butter) thing! These are excellent for children who want to fit in, but can't have dairy, peanut butter, soy or other ingredients.

You can either purchase a special mold or you can use regular or mini-sized muffin tins. I like using the mini-muffin tins lined with mini baking papers.

1⅓ cups to 1½ cups of acceptable chocolate chips
2 to 3 tablespoons of acceptable filling, either non-nut butter or an acceptable marshmallow substitute (recipe for marshmallows is in this book)

This recipe will make 24 mini-sized marshmallow or Mock peanut butter candy cups. Line 24 mini-muffin tins with baking papers and set aside. Place ½ cup of chocolate chips in a small glass bowl and microwave for 25 seconds. Remove and stir well. They may not look like they're melted but they will have begun to melt. Return them to the microwave for another 15 seconds to finish melting the chocolate. Place ½ teaspoon of chocolate in each muffin tin. Use the back of a spoon or rubber spatula to press the chocolate up the sides of the baking papers or mold. Once chocolate is uniformly pressed against the sides with a thin layer on the bottom, repeat with next muffin tin.

When you run out of chocolate, place another ½ cup in the glass bowl and repeat the above process to melt the chocolate chips. Once the chocolate cups are formed, place the chocolate in the freezer for 5 to 7 minutes to mold. Remove from freezer and fill with filling. Then top with final layer of chocolate to complete the candy.

For Marshmallow Cups:
Fill center with ¼ to ½ teaspoon of acceptable marshmallow filling. Melting marshmallows does not work well to fill these candy cups because the marshmallow is too sticky to get into the cups before it cools and becomes unmanageable again. Top with a final layer of melted chocolate. Place in the refrigerator until chocolate is hardened. These store best in the refrigerator.

Mock Peanut Butter Cups:
Fill center with ¼ to ½ teaspoon of acceptable non-peanut butter. Top with a final layer of melted chocolate across the top. Place in the refrigerator until chocolate is hardened. These store best in the refrigerator.

Hard Candy or Lollipops

It is not difficult to make your own hard candy, but you do need a candy thermometer. Candy thermometers are sold at the craft stores in the Wilton Baking section or at better cooking stores. You will also need flavoring for your candy. We special ordered ours on-line, however you can get candy flavors at craft stores and specialty kitchen stores.

There are now natural colorings that you can use instead of the traditional food colorings. The natural food colorings are made from foods that are rich in color like beets and blueberries. These do not add flavor to your candy. I recommend that you have hard candy molds which are sold on-line and in craft and baking stores. There are two different kinds of candy molds. One is for melted chocolate only and the other can be used for melted chocolate OR hard candy. The molds used for hard candy are made of a different material to withstand the heat of the hot candy when you first mold it. The candy molds suitable for melted chocolate only are not to be used with making hard candy.

1 cup pure drinking water
2 cups organic sugar
¾ cup light corn syrup
1 tablespoon oil
1 teaspoon candy flavoring
Optional:
Natural food coloring

All hard candies become sticky unless individually wrapped. Instead, we place our finished candy in a hard plastic storage container separated in layers by waxed paper. This has worked very well. Grease your candy molds and set aside. This candy recipe made a fair amount of candy. It made more than 12 lollipops (4 to 6 of which were very large), and many smaller candies. If you run out of molds you can pour a small amount of the candy onto an oiled cutting board while keeping the rest of the candy on low heat. Cut the candy on the cutting board into squares or pieces with a knife or scissors and roll into balls.

Boil 1 cup of water in a large heavy pan. Remove from heat. Add sugar, light corn syrup and oil and stir until dissolved. Return pan to heat and bring to a boil. Cover the pan for about 3 minutes so that the steam washes down any crystals from the pan. Remove the lid from the pan and insert the candy thermometer. Cook the sugar mixture to what is called the "hard-crack" stage, about 300°.

Remove from heat and cool to about 160°. If you are using food coloring, add it now. Add candy flavoring now. Suggested flavors include ¼ teaspoon oil of peppermint or cinnamon, 1 teaspoon of oil of orange, lime or wintergreen, or other flavor of your choice. We have used bubblegum and cotton candy flavors too. Pour the candy into the candy molds or shape as directed above.

Chocolate Syrup (Corn-Free)

Being corn free is extremely difficult for many reasons. We used this to also avoid preservatives in commercially made syrups.

Single Batch	Double Batch
1 cup sugar	**2 cups sugar**
½ cup cocoa powder	**1 cup cocoa powder**
Dash of salt	**2 dashes of salt**
1 cup water	**2 cups of water**
Optional:	
1 teaspoon of vanilla extract	1 teaspoon of vanilla extract

Mix the sugar, cocoa, and salt in a saucepan. Add the water and mix well. Bring to a boil stirring constantly, then reduce the heat and simmer for 2 or 3 minutes. Be careful not to burn. Chocolate scorches easily so don't leave this unattended. Remove from heat and add vanilla extract if using it. Once the syrup is cool, store in the refrigerator. This can be used to make chocolate milk, milkshakes, or poured over ice cream. A single batch makes about 1 cup. Syrup can be made thicker by reducing the amount of water used.

Homemade Marshmallows

If you can eat corn and tolerate food dyes, store-bought marshmallows are much easier than making your own. I made marshmallows very few times after finding other alternatives that my children could tolerate.

2 tablespoons gelatin
¼ cup cold water
¾ cup boiling water
2 cups sugar
⅛ teaspoon salt
1 teaspoon vanilla extract
Confectioners' sugar

In a medium bowl soak the gelatin in the cold water until all of the water has been absorbed by the gelatin. Boil the sugar and water in a medium saucepan until it reaches the soft-ball stage which is about 238°. Add vanilla and salt to your gelatin mixture. Pour the sugar and water syrup over the gelatin slowly beating the gelatin constantly with a fork or wire whisk until it is cool and thick. Grease a shallow baking pan and then lightly dust with confectioners' sugar. Turn the marshmallow mixture into the prepared baking pan and smooth out the top. Dust the top with confectioners' sugar. Let sit overnight. Cut the marshmallows into squares the next morning and dust with confectioners' sugar. If you can't use confectioners' sugar due to the corn or cornstarch, you can make your own. The recipe for confectioners' sugar follows this one.

Corn-Free Confectioners' Sugar

The reason some people cannot tolerate confectioners' sugar is because corn or cornstarch is frequently added to prevent caking. While making confectioners' sugar from scratch is not difficult, it is not something that I enjoyed or did often. To make confectioners' sugar at home you simply use cane or beet sugar in granular form and whirl it in a blender until it is powdered.

½ cup light raw sugar or white sugar (or beet sugar)

Whirl in a blender until powdered.

ICE CREAMS, SORBETS AND FLAVORED ICES

Ice Cream

This recipe requires the use of an automatic ice cream maker.

24 to 28 ounces acceptable nondairy milk
½ cup sugar or other sweetener
1 tablespoon Egg Replacer™ dry powder
1 tablespoon oil
½ teaspoon of xanthan gum
½ teaspoon vanilla extract
Pinch of salt

Place all ingredients into a blender and mix well. Transfer to a container and store in the refrigerator until very cold, about 2 hours. You can also place in the freezer for 30 or more minutes. Once it is very cold, pour it into your automatic ice cream maker and process until it is very thick then place in the freezer. For flavoring options, use any of the six flavoring listed in the next recipe for a more gourmet ice cream result.

Luke's Ice Cream Squall

There is a well-known fast food ice cream shop that makes fun ice cream beverages. My son loves them, but unfortunately dairy really doesn't sit well with him or as well as we would like! This was his attempt to create a similar frozen shake using our non-dairy ice cream.

> 1 cup non-dairy ice cream
> 1/8 cup non-dairy milk substitute
> Additional special treat ingredient: choose 1
> 2 acceptable chocolate cookies or 2 tablespoons acceptable candy pieces

Blend all ingredients in a blender. Makes 1 cup. This can be flavored many different ways! Have fun being creative!

Blueberry Ice Cream

You will need either a juicer that can handle frozen bananas for this recipe or one of the new gadgets that puts out frozen fruit sorbets or ice cream.

> 1 frozen banana (skin removed before freezing)
> 5 tablespoons frozen blueberries

Place half of the frozen banana in the juicer, set up to process a frozen banana, and process through the juicer catching the ice cream in a container as it comes out of the juicer. Add the frozen blueberries, and then the second half of the banana. This will come out as a soft serve ice cream and can be eaten as is or you can freeze it to have a hard ice cream. This recipe makes one cup.

Low Sugar Ice Cream

With the use of stevia this is more viable for people who have to watch their sugar.

20 ounces of Non-dairy liquid
2 teaspoons of stevia or other acceptable sweetener
½ teaspoon xanthan gum
1 teaspoon of pure vanilla extract
1 tablespoon acceptable oil

When making non-dairy ice cream, remember that the blander the oil, the better tasting the ice cream will be. I try to use safflower oil for non-dairy ice cream we make instead of some of the stronger tasting and smelling oils. Mix all ingredients in a blender and blend well. Refrigerate for 4-6 hours. Place in an ice cream maker and process for 5 to 6 minutes or until very thick. Makes about 3 cups of ice cream.

Chocolate Ice Cream
Add ⅓ cup chocolate syrup to the liquid ingredients. Follow above directions.

Mint Chocolate Chip Ice Cream
Follow above recipe deleting the vanilla and adding instead 1 teaspoon of mint extract, and several drops of green food coloring. After the ice cream is nearly done, add ½ to ¾ cup crushed or chopped chocolate chip pieces.

Chocolate Chocolate Chip Ice Cream
Use base recipe omitting the vanilla extract and adding ⅓ cup chocolate syrup to the mixture instead. Follow recipe instructions above adding ½ to ¾ cup chopped or crushed chocolate chips at the end of the ice cream making session.

Gourmet Chocolate Ice Cream
Add ⅓ cup chocolate syrup to the liquid ingredients, and in place of the vanilla extract, use 1 teaspoon of cherry extract. This will give your chocolate ice cream some pizazz and a bit of mystery.

Raspberry Ice Cream
Omit vanilla extract and use 1 teaspoon of raspberry extract or flavoring instead. Add 1 cup to 1 ½ cups of fresh or frozen raspberries and follow above directions.

Cookie Dough Ice Cream
Add chunks of unbaked cookie dough to your ice cream after it is a soft custard and before it is frozen in the freezer. You will use about 1 cup of cookie dough, which should be added in teaspoons to your soft custard. This is delicious!

Peaches and Cream Ice Cream

I invented this recipe just to have a variety in our dessert arsenal. How this recipe will taste is driven by how sweet or peachy your peaches are! Some peaches have more flavor than others.

1 frozen banana (skin removed before freezing)
1 cup frozen peaches

Place half of the frozen banana in the juicer or other device equipped to do this and set up to process a frozen banana, and process through the juicer catching the soft serve ice cream as it comes out of the juicer in a container. Add the frozen peaches, and then the second half of the banana. This will come out as a soft serve ice cream and can be eaten as is or you can freeze it to have a hard ice cream. This recipe makes one cup.

Chocolate Chocolate Chip Ice Cream

This was me playing around in the kitchen to see just how far I could go with frozen banana ice cream. If you are avoiding all dairy, this is pretty good and much healthier for you.

3 frozen bananas (skins removed before freezing)
1-1/2 tablespoons of acceptable cocoa powder
1 to 2 tablespoons acceptable chocolate chips
Dash of organic and pure peppermint extract

Place one frozen banana in the juicer, set up to process a frozen banana, and process through the juicer. Catch the banana ice cream in a bowl or container as it comes out. Add the chocolate chips, cocoa powder and pure peppermint extract to the ice cream after it has come through the juicer. This will come out as a soft serve ice cream and can be eaten as is or you can freeze it to have a hard ice cream. This recipe makes about one and a half cups.

Lemon Ice

This is one of my children's favorites. It is a treat on a hot summer day. You can use another acceptable sweetener than sugar if needed.

> 1 cup sugar or other sweetener
> 2 cups pure drinking water
> Dash of salt
> 2 teaspoons fresh lemon zest (children may not like this
>   ingredient)
> ½ cup lemon juice

Place the sugar and water in a medium saucepan and heat over medium heat until it comes to a light boil. Reduce heat and cook for 2 minutes. Remove from heat and allow to cool completely. Add the salt, fresh lemon zest and lemon juice. Stir well, and place in a container in the freezer for several hours.

Lime Ice

This has significantly less sugar than the Lemon Ice above. It is harder to scrape out of the container, yet it is very refreshing on a hot day!

> 4 Tablespoons lime juice
> 4 Tablespoons sugar or other sweetener
> 1½ cups pure drinking water

Mix ingredients well and freeze. Stir after the lime ice has been in the freezer for two or so hours and then re-freeze. Because this is an ice, you will need to use a scraper, fork, or sharp blade to scrape the ice out to serve.

Cranberry Ice

8 ounces of pure cranberry juice*
8 ounces of pure drinking water
4 tablespoons sugar or other sweetener

*This recipe adds sugar because pure cranberry juice is very tart. If you are using diluted or sweetened cranberry juice, then you can decrease or eliminate the sugar in the recipe. Mix all ingredients well. Place into a container and freeze. After the cranberry ice has been in the freezer for two hours, remove and stir well. Place back into the freezer until frozen. Because this is an ice it will require a scraper, fork, or sharp blade to scrape the ice out for serving.

Watermelon Ice

¼ or ⅛ of a watermelon
Optional:
Sugar or other sweetener
Seed watermelon and cut into chunks. Process the watermelon in either a food processor or a blender until mushy. Sugar is not required or necessary; however you can all a small amount of sugar if desired. Place the liquid watermelon into a freezer container and freeze. Use the tines of a fork or other sharp blade to scrape out servings of the watermelon ice.

Raspberry Sorbet

Back in the day, many commercially made sorbets contained milk. This was my solution for that so that my kids could have what other children were having...

¾ cup water
¾ cup sugar
2 cups raspberries (fresh or frozen)

Mix water and sugar in a saucepan. Heat to make a simple syrup as above and cool. Strain the seeds from the raspberries by mashing them through a fine mesh strainer. Mix the raspberries and simple syrup and place in ice cream maker. You can vary the strength of the taste by the quantity of simple syrup you use and the quantity of fruit.

Strawberry Sorbet

¾ cup water
¾ cup sugar
2 cups strawberries (fresh or frozen)

Mix water and sugar in a saucepan. Heat to make a simple syrup as above and cool. Strain the seeds from the strawberries. Mix the strawberries and simple syrup and place in ice cream maker. You can vary the strength of the taste by the quantity of simple syrup you use and the quantity of fruit.

BEVERAGES AND SMOOTHIES

Sparkling Lemonade

This is a recipe that my son Luke came up with to use up leftover club soda! Yes, you never let anything go to waste! With a bit of tinkering, this is a refreshing, no calorie treat that most people will enjoy!

1 cup club soda or 2/3 of a can
¼ teaspoon Stevia powder
1-1/2 teaspoon lime juice
1-1/2 teaspoon lemon juice

Mix lemon and lime juice and stevia powder in a glass. Add club soda and stir. Makes 1 cup.

Strawberry Lemonade

I got the idea for this recipe when I was out to lunch with some friends. I cringed to see the food dye-laden beverage consumed at the table! I promptly came home to concoct one that was without high fructose corn syrup and red food dye. Stevia makes it more suitable for those individuals watching their sugar or avoiding sugar.

2 cups water
1 cup frozen strawberries
2 tablespoons lemon juice
1 teaspoon stevia or other sweetener to taste

Place all ingredients in a blender and puree until smooth. This makes 2 cups.

Fresh Squeezed Lemonade

I never thought about making fresh squeezed or homemade lemonade until Sister Helen Sharkey from Saint Elizabeth's parish in Whitehall, Pennsylvania taught me. This has come in helpful when you have a child who cannot tolerate preservatives and additives. I've listed sugar as an ingredient, however you can use any other sweetening agent if you cannot tolerate cane sugar or if you are doing a rotation diet and use a different sweetener on your lemon day. Besides using fresh squeezed lemon juice, you may also use bottled organic lemon juice. You can use more or less sugar depending upon your tolerance for tartness.

Ingredient	Single Serving	One Quart	Half Gallon
pure water	¾ cup	3¼ cups	6½ cups
lemon juice	2 tablespoons	½ cup	1 cup
sugar	2 tablespoons	½ cup	1 cup

As a reference, 1 large lemon equals about 3 tablespoons of lemon juice.

Noah's Fright Night Punch

Noah came up with this as a punch to serve guests for a spooky Halloween party. Double or triple the quantity for your party size.

½ cup organic grape juice
½ cup pure drinking water
1 cup organic cranberry juice
2 Tablespoons sugar or to taste

Mix all ingredients well until sugar is dissolved. This recipe makes about 2 cups.

Apple Smoothie

Who needs a recipe for a smoothie? Well, after making a really bad one - I do!

1 cup pure drinking water
Greens of your choice – spinach, dandelion, etc.
2 medium or large apples, cored and seeds removed, cut in chunks

Place water, greens and apple chunks into a blender. Blend for a few seconds. Remove blender top and mash the ingredients down. Return blender top and blend again for a few seconds. Repeat this process until the blender contents are smooth and creamy. It will be a bright green color. Makes approximately 2-1/2 to 2-2/3 cups.

Orange Banana Smoothie

This is a great way to use up over-ripe bananas and excess greens from our CSA share!

> **2 Tablespoons orange juice concentrate**
> **1 banana, peeled**
> **3-4 large leaves of greens (not bitter)**
> **½ cup water or orange juice**

Place water, greens, banana and orange juice concentrate into a blender. Blend for a few seconds. Remove blender top and mash the ingredients down. Return blender top and blend again for a few seconds. Repeat this process until the blender contents are smooth and creamy. It will be a bright green color unless you use the purple colored kale. Makes approximately 2-1/2 to 2-2/3 cups.

Noah's Fruiti-Tutti Smoothie

This is a fruit smoothie that Noah invented at probably age 9. It is quite tasty.

> **2 cups orange juice**
> **½ cup raspberries (fresh or frozen)**
> **½ cup strawberries (fresh or frozen)**
> **2 bananas**

Place all ingredients in a blender and blend until smooth and creamy. Best served cold. Makes about 3 2/3 cups.

Hawaiian Breeze Smoothie

Noah came up with this recipe to use pineapple and to get use out of the same old smoothie rut!

2 cups diced pineapple
1 cup orange juice
½ cup fresh or frozen blueberries

Place all ingredients in a blender and puree. Makes almost 3 cups.

Blue Banana Smoothie

This was another smoothie that Noah invented to keep us from getting stagnant! Pretty good for a 10-year old!

¾ cup fresh or frozen blueberries
¾ cup orange juice
2 bananas

Place all ingredients into a blender and puree until smooth. Makes about 3 cups.

Apple Berry Smoothie

2 cups fresh or frozen berries (strawberry, raspberry, blackberry)
2 large apples, peeled, cored, seed removed and cut into pieces
2 cups pure water

Place all ingredients into a blender and puree. If you use frozen berries, you will get a frozen smoothie beverage, which is reminiscent of those mall drinks. This makes about 4-1/2 cups of smoothie.

Purple Berry Blast

Noah came up with this delicious smoothie as a ten year old! Yum!

½ cup raspberries
½ cup strawberries
¼ cup cherries (make sure these have the pits removed)
¼ cup blueberries
2 bananas
1 ¾ cup orange juice

Blend all ingredients in a blender. If some of the fruit is frozen, it will give the smoothie a nice frozen drink consistency. This makes 4 cups.

Passion Peach Pleasure

This is one of my favorites. We don't always have kiwi's or plums, so we don't make it all the time. We use strawberries and peaches from the freezer if we don't have fresh when we make this.

3 kiwi's, peeled and sliced
4 small peaches, peeled, sliced and pitted
8 strawberries, hulled
2 plums, peeled and pitted
1 cup orange juice
2 cups pure water

Place all ingredients in a blender and puree. This makes about 4 cups. We love this particular beverage that packs a power punch of nutrition!

Old Fashioned Hot Chocolate

This is how we made hot chocolate when I was growing up as a kid!
We did not purchase the hot cocoa mixes, but made this fast and easy
recipe every time we made hot chocolate. Be forewarned – this is
very, very rich! You may want to cut the recipe in half to make it less
rich as we do at times.

 2 tablespoons acceptable cocoa powder
 2 tablespoons cane or other sugar
 Dash of salt
 Dash of vanilla
 1 cup of acceptable non-dairy milk

Place dry ingredients in a mug and stir well. Heat non-dairy milk to
acceptable temperature and then add about 2 tablespoons of hot milk
to mug with the cocoa powder. Stir well to make a chocolate syrup.
Add remaining milk and stir. Makes one serving of hot cocoa.

Vitamin Water

My son Noah saw "vitamin water" in the health food store and
wanted to make some at home! I thought this was a fabulous idea.
Noah went right to work and created this recipe. We saved some
empty 12-ounce glass bottles that had organic lemon juice in them
and they made the perfect vitamin water bottles.

 ½ cup pure cranberry juice (or other juice)
 ½ cup pure drinking water
 4 teaspoons sugar or other sweetener
 Vitamins and minerals of your choice

Mix all ingredients well. Makes 1 cup. I can say with certainty that
this is one great way to get vitamins and minerals into your children.
You can use any other kind of juice with water. The sugar or other
sweetener is only necessary if you use pure cranberry juice because it
will be too tart otherwise.

Heavenly Kahlúa

This is a recipe that was given to me by my friend Barb some years ago. This is an excellent recipe that fooled even some astute bartenders in my hometown. This is for adults only!

2 cups vodka (80 proof)
2 cups pure drinking water
1¼ cups sugar
1½ tablespoons vanilla extract
1½ tablespoons instant coffee

Place the water and sugar in a saucepan and bring to a boil. Boil for about 5 minutes and then remove from heat and add vanilla extract and instant coffee. Allow to cool and then add the vodka. Serve on the rocks and share with a friend!

SPICE MIXES

Taco Seasoning Mix

This recipe is from my first allergy and gluten free cookbook and it is one of my favorites! It is easy to make and free of the preservatives found in many commercial taco seasoning mixes. I usually make a double batch.

6 teaspoons chili powder
4½ teaspoons cumin
5 teaspoons paprika
3 teaspoons onion powder
2½ teaspoons garlic powder
⅛ teaspoon cayenne pepper

Mix ingredients together and store in an airtight container. This is twice as strong as the store-bought packets and has none of the preservatives, so use one-half the amount or sparingly. This makes about 2 ounces (7 Tablespoons) or 3/8 cup.

Note: We've found this to be a great item to mix and have on hand for when we are making quesadillas or tacos, etc.

Everything Spice Mix

This is the recipe I made up for everything bagels. It is a versatile recipe that can be used on top of dinner rolls and other baked goods.

2 tablespoons sesame seeds
3 tablespoons ground sunflower seeds (not whole)
2 tablespoons dried minced onion
2 tablespoons poppy seeds
1-2 cloves of garlic, minced

Mix and apply to bagels, rolls or other baked good. You can mix this up without the minced garlic and store it adding the minced garlic when you are using it.

Special Seasoning Salt

This an old recipe I developed early on, which is used in a few recipes in this book.

> 1 tablespoon salt
> ½ teaspoon white pepper
> 1 teaspoon garlic powder
> ½ teaspoon sweet basil
> 1 teaspoon onion salt
> ½ teaspoon crushed rosemary
> ½ teaspoon thyme
> 1 tablespoon chopped dried onion
> ½ teaspoon dried mustard
> ½ teaspoon oregano
> 1 tablespoon parsley
> 1 tablespoon sugar
> Dash of turmeric
> Dash of paprika

Optional:
> Dash of cayenne pepper
> To taste: fresh ground pepper

Mix all together and store in a airtight container. This can be used on French fries, mashed or sliced potatoes, on meats, or vegetables. It is an ingredient in the dry soup base in this cookbook.

Gourmet Meat Rub

This is an easy to make meat rub without additives or preservatives!

1 tablespoon paprika
2 tablespoons sea salt
1 tablespoon ground black pepper
1 teaspoon onion powder
1 teaspoon garlic
2 teaspoon dried basil
4 whole cloves of garlic, peeled and cut lengthwise

Make small cuts into the end grain of the roast and bury the clove quarters. Mix the dry spices together. Rub the spices on all sides of the roast. Roast meat in the oven.

JAM, JELLY & PICKLES

Pear-Cranberry Jam

I received some lovely organic pears from my brother and after thinking about what to do with them, I decided to make some jam. This jam was a huge hit with the kids and I. I used a form of pectin that allows you to reduce the amount of sugar used in jams and jellies.

> 5 cups of peeled and diced pears
> 1 pound of washed, rinsed and picked over cranberries
> 4 teaspoons of calcium water (in the box of reduced sugar
>   pectin)
> 1-1/2 cups sugar
> ¼ cup organic lemon juice
> 3 teaspoons pectin

If you are canning this jam, wash and rinse your canning jars and then boil the jars and lids and rings. Turn off the water after it has boiled and let the jars, lids and rings stand in the hot water. Place the cranberries and pears into a large stockpot and add the calcium water and lemon juice. Stir well. In a separate bowl, place the sugar and add the pectin powder and stir well. Bring the cranberries and pears to a boil over medium high heat. Add the pectin/sugar mixture and stir constantly to dissolve the sugar and pectin. Keep stirring while the jam comes to a full boil again. Remove from heat. Makes about 5 (1/2 pint jars). For hot water bath canning – fill jars to ¼ inches from the top, wiping the rims clean and screwing on the two-piece lids. Placed filled jelly jars into boiling water and boil for 10 minutes. Remove from boiling water and allow to cool. If your jam does not seal properly from the canning process then do not store at room temperature. See canning directions with your canner for additional directions.

Hot Pepper Jam

A great recipe if you happen to have sweet peppers on hand! Great on crackers or toast! This recipe uses the low sugar pectin available to reduce the amount of sugar required in the recipe.

6 cups assorted sweet bell peppers, washed and cut into pieces
1 hot pepper
1-1/2 cups organic apple cider vinegar
2 cups sugar
1-1/2 teaspoon low sugar pectin
2 teaspoons calcium water

Chop or process the peppers in a food processor until finely chopped or pureed. Place the pureed or very finely chopped peppers in a large stockpot with the vinegar and bring to a boil. Reduce the heat and simmer for 5 minutes. Add 1-1/2 cups of the sugar (reserving ½ cup for later) and stir until dissolved. Mix the reserved sugar with the low sugar pectin and follow the manufacturer's directions for adding the calcium water and pectin mixture with the sugar. Follow the directions for canning based on the method you choose.

Bread and Butter Pickles

My Paternal Grandmother, Nan Lundy, taught me how to make bread and butter pickles when I was roughly 12 years old. She had a very large old-fashioned crock to make her bread and butter pickles because she made a gigantic batch. We really love this recipe.

Combine in a glass bowl (not metal) and cover with a heavy plate for 6-8 hours:

15 cups sliced cucumbers
3 sliced onions
¼ cup coarse salt
4 cups ice
Filtered water to cover the cucumbers

2-1/2 cups organic cider vinegar
2-1/2 cups sugar
¾ teaspoon turmeric
½ teaspoon celergy ceed
1 tablespoon mustard seeds
You can use your own mix of pickling spices if you prefer

It is very important that you use a glass bowl and not metal for this recipe. After the cucumbers and onions have sat in the ice water and salt bath for 6-8 hours, drain and rinse with fresh water. Place the vinegar, sugar and spices in a large nonreactive* - meaning stainless steel, glass, enamelware - stockpot and bring to a boil. Once all of the sugar is dissolved then add the cucumbers and onions and bring the mixture back to a rolling boil. Once the mixture has reached a boil then use a slotted spoon to pack your pre-prepared canning jars (washed, rinsed and sterilized sitting in hot water) with the cucumbers and onions. Once you have packed your canning jars full of the cucumbers and onions leaving about one inch of headspace in the jars, pour the sugar/vinegar syrup over the cucumbers and onions being sure to leave about ½ inch of headspace. Wipe the rims of the jars clean and close with rims and lids. Boil in hot water for 15 minutes or more (more for higher altitudes) and remove to cool. Your jars should make a popping noise as they seal. Improperly sealed jars should be stored in your refrigerator.

*Reactive pots and pans include those that contain aluminum, copper, brass and iron. Using a metal pan that contains these components will cause the metals to leach out of the pans and into your pickles.

Bread and Butter Pickles – Larger Batch

We were so happy with the original bread and butter pickle recipe that I decided that it would be more efficient to make a larger batch. This makes 7 pints.

Combine in a large glass mixing bowl (not metal) and cover with a heavy plate for 6-8 hours:

4 pounds of cucumbers OR about 4-six inch cucumbers, sliced

2 pounds of onions sliced

½ cup coarse salt

4-6 cups of ice

Filtered water to cover

Place in a large nonreactive* stockpot and set aside:

2 cups sugar

2-1/4 cups organic cider vinegar

2 tablespoons mustard seed

2 teaspoons turmeric

2 teaspoons celery seed

Nonreactive pots include glass, stainless steel and enamelware. *Reactive pots and pans include those that contain aluminum, copper, brass and iron. Using a metal pan that contains these components will cause the metals to leach out of the pans and into your pickles.

Follow directions for the previous bread and butter pickle recipe as the process and directions are the same.

MISCELLANEOUS

Tick and Bug Repellant

After moving to the country, a natural and non-toxic bug and tick repellant became a must! This recipe is flexible. After experimenting with various bases, I ended up using rubbing alcohol. You can use Witch Hazel. You can add other essential oils.

3 ounces of rubbing alcohol
20 drops of Citronella Essential Oil
20 drops of Lemongrass Essential Oil
10 drops of Eucalyptus Essential Oil
10 drops of Lemon Essential Oil

Mix ingredients in a small measuring cup or bowl and place in a spray bottle. You can purchase spray bottles at craft stores, health food stores or online. From my research, it is said that the brown bottles are better for storing this type of item. There are many, many other essential oils that could be used in this mixture.

Hand Sanitizer

I researched how to make a World Health Organization compliant hand sanitizer once we were in the pandemic. To be WHO compliant a 91% rubbing alcohol needs to be used in conjunction with other ingredients as it is the ratio of the alcohol and other ingredients that makes a sanitizer compliant. While water can be used and still be WHO complaint, I did not do the calculations for that recipe.

12 ounces 91% rubbing alcohol
1 tablespoon hydrogen peroxide
2 teaspoons glycerin (or glycerol)
15 drops organic lemon essential oil
10 drops organic orange essential oil
10 drops organic tea tree essential oil

For external use only! Mix all ingredients and put in a spray bottle. This makes about 12 ounces.

Allergy-Free Baking Powder

If you are really restricted because of your allergies, you may need to make your own baking powder. At least we did for a few years. This recipe is one that you make in small quantities as it does not store well.

½ teaspoon cream of tartar
¼ teaspoon baking soda
¼ teaspoon potato starch or tapioca flour

This will equal one teaspoon of regular baking powder. You can use cornstarch for the potato starch or tapioca, but the recipe above is corn-free for those restricted in their corn use.

Laundry Soap

If you have trouble with allergies, it may be wise to consider some hypoallergenic laundry supplies. We have found the following works very well for regular laundry loads. Baking soda and vinegar can be purchased in large quantities in discount warehouse-type stores rather inexpensively. This mixture would not be cost effective if you are not purchasing the baking soda and vinegar at a warehouse supply store.

For an Extra Large Load:
½ cup baking soda
1 cup white vinegar

Start your laundry on hot water and add the baking soda right away so it begins to dissolve. The reason for this is that baking soda dissolves better in hot water than in any other temperature we have found. You can swish the water around to speed up the process. Add ⅓ of the vinegar to the washtub, ⅓ to the bleach cup, and ⅓ to the fabric softener cup or dispenser. Then turn your wash load to the temperature that you plan on using like warm or cold, and add your laundry. For smaller loads, use less.

For Extra Dirty Loads or Bleaching Effect:
Use the same ingredients above, and add:
¼ cup Borax
¼ cup Arm & Hammer Washing Soda

Dissolve these ingredients in the washer tub, add you laundry and wash as usual. We find that these two products work well to brighten white loads or to add extra washing power to dirty loads.

ARTS AND CRAFTS

Gluten-Free Play Dough

This is our family play dough recipe converted to be gluten-free.

    1½ cups gluten-free flour
    ¾ cup salt
    3 teaspoons cream of tartar
    1½ cups cool water
    1½ tablespoons oil
    Natural Food coloring

Mix dry ingredients together in a large pot. Add all of the liquids and mix well. Cook over a medium heat, stirring constantly. Remove from heat when the dough pulls away from the sides of the pot and can be pinched without sticking. Turn onto a board or counter and knead until smooth. Professional decorating pastes (used in frostings) can be used to color the dough instead of food coloring. Of course, natural food colorings are ideal. This recipe makes about 3 cans of play dough. You can double this recipe. It does work best to have the coloring added during cooking instead of trying to add it after the dough is made.

Baking Soda Play Clay

This is an easy recipe which children will enjoy. This play clay can be allowed to air dry if your children make items that they want preserved.

2 cups baking soda
1 cup cornstarch
1¼ cups water
Optional:
Natural food coloring or non-toxic paints

Place the baking soda, cornstarch and water in a medium saucepan and mix well. Over low heat, cook mixture, stirring continuously until the dough becomes a consistency of mashed potatoes. This will take up to 15 or so minutes. Remove from heat and separate into 3 or 4 bowls if you are adding food coloring. Add a different food coloring to each and enjoy! If you don't want to use natural food coloring, you can use candy coloring add or the cake frosting coloring to the play clay. This will air dry in about 12 hours. The play clay pieces can also be painted with non-toxic or acrylic paints. As with all play dough or play clays, you can use cookie cutters, a garlic press, and other kitchen tools to style and shape your clay figures. This makes about 3 cups of play clay.

Finger Paints

This is an old recipe for homemade finger paints. The finished product is not nearly as nice as store-bought finger paints. However, for children who react to some ingredients in commercially made finger paints, this at least provides an alternative.

4 tablespoons sugar
½ cup cornstarch
2 cups cold water
Natural Food coloring

In a medium saucepan, mix the sugar and cornstarch together. Add the cold water and then cook over medium heat until the mixture thickens. This will thicken a bit more once it is cooled. Divide the mixture into three or four bowls or containers and add a different food coloring to each. Naturally made food colorings can be found at some health food stores or on-line. These naturally made food colorings are made from colorful foods like beets, turmeric, and blueberries and I strongly recommend them.

Homemade Stickers

Can you believe it? Stickers made at home. And wait until you see how easy they are to make! Start with this small batch. A little bit goes a long way! This is the perfect way to recycle old gift wrap. This is a great activity to do with children and adults.

Small Batch Size: **(Enough for 3 or 4 children to use)**
   2 tablespoons white, washable, non-toxic glue
   2 tablespoons white vinegar

Large Batch Size: **(Enough for a large group)**
   ¼ cup white, washable, non-toxic glue
   ¼ cup white vinegar

The following are needed for all batch sizes:

   **Collection decorative papers or scraps of old recycled gift
      wrap or cut out pictures from magazines.**
   1 paint brush for each child or adult
   Several cookie sheets (for sticker paper to air dry on)

Mix equal parts of glue and vinegar in a small mixing bowl. Using a paint brush, quickly paint the white liquid on the back of decorative papers, scraps of old gift wrap, and/or pictures from magazines. Allow to air dry. We found it best to work on a surface of scrap paper and to then move the wet papers to a cookie sheet to dry.

Once the papers are dry, apply a second coat of the white glue mixture to the back of the papers and allow to air dry again. The sticker paper is now ready to use. You can use decorative paper punches to punch out shapes, or you can cut out your own shapes. To moisten the sticker for use, wet a paper towel or sponge and dab the back of the sticker.

APPENDIX

Internal USDA Cooking Temperatures

I am including this because this chart is one that we live by and it is just that important!

Minimum Internal Cooking Temperatures as Recommended by the USDA

IMPORTANT! These are the minimum INTERNAL temperatures that food must reach to be considered safe to eat no matter how you prepare them. The following temperatures are recommended but personal tastes may be different. Note: *The USDA does NOT recommend RARE 140° as a safe eating temperature.

Fresh ground beef, veal, pork . . . . 160°F/72°C
Beef, Veal, Lamb – roast, steaks, chops
    *Rare . . . . 140°F/60°C
    Medium Rare . . . . 145°F/63°C
    Medium . . . . 160°F/72°C
    Well Done . . . . 170°F/77°C
Fresh Pork – roasts, steaks, chops
    Medium . . . . 160°F/72°C
    Well Done . . . . 170°F/77°C
Ham
    Fresh (raw) . . . . 160°F/72°C
    Precooked (to reheat). . . . . 140°F/60°C
Poultry
    Ground Chicken, Turkey . . . . 165°F/74°C
    Whole Chicken, Turkey. . . . . 180°F/83°C
    Breasts, Roasts. . . . . 170°F/77°C
    Things and Wings . . . . 180°F/83°C
Fish *cook until opaque and flakes with a fork* . . . . 145°F/63°C
Stuffing . . . . 165°F/74°C
Egg Dishes. . . . . 160°F/72°C
Leftovers, Casseroles . . . . 165°F/74°C

INDEX

CPSIA information can be obtained
at www.ICGtesting.com
Printed in the USA
BVHW080948050421
604209BV00011B/892